P9-EGD-061

African American Males in School and Society

PRACTICES AND POLICIES FOR EFFECTIVE EDUCATION

African American Males in School and Society

PRACTICES AND POLICIES FOR EFFECTIVE EDUCATION

EDITED BY

Vernon C. Polite and James Earl Davis

FOREWORD BY **Edmund W. Gordon**

Teachers College, Columbia University
New York and London

Published by Teachers College Press, 1234 Amsterdam Avenue, New York, NY 10027

Copyright © 1999 by Teachers College, Columbia University

All rights reserved. No part of this publication may be reproduced or transmitted in any form or by any means, electronic or mechanical, including photocopy, or any information storage and retrieval system, without permission from the publisher.

Library of Congress Cataloging-in-Publication Data

African American males in school and society : practices and policies
    for effective education / edited by Vernon C. Polite and James Earl
    Davis ; foreword by Edmund W. Gordon.
        p.   cm.
    Includes bibliographical references (p.   ) and index.
    ISBN 0-8077-3871-9 (alk. paper). — ISBN 0-8077-3870-0 (pbk. :
alk. paper)
        1. Afro-American young men—Education—Social aspects.
    2. Academic achievement—United States.   I. Polite, Vernon C.
    II. Davis, James Earl, 1960–   .
    LC2731.A34   1999
    371.829'96073—dc21   99-32817

ISBN 0-8077-3870-0 (paper)
ISBN 0-8077-3871-9 (cloth)

Printed on acid-free paper

Manufactured in the United States of America

06 05 04 03 02 01   8 7 6 5 4 3 2

This work is dedicated to Barry Anderson, Sundra K. Henderson Banks, Roderick Blair, Karl R. Boykin, Nancy Gaulman, Beverly Rock, Neil S. Rodgers, and Gail Ann Washington. Thanks for the years filled with love, support, and smiles.

Vernon C. Polite

The work is also dedicated to Larry D. Davis and Darrell L. Tiller, two wonderful examples of African American manhood, and to my mother, Minnie B. Davis.

James Earl Davis

Contents

Foreword

The Experiences of African American Males in School and Society

A REVIEW OF THE accumulated popular and scholarly literature concerning African American males provides a troublesome picture of these men and boys. They are depicted as a homogeneous, dysfunctional, alienated, and threatening subpopulation, which some have dubbed a threatened species (Gibbs, 1988). The stereotype reflected in this literature is that of an undereducated, unemployed, antisocial, oversexed, drugged, and incarcerated population of misfits whom some see as rejecting the hegemonic standards of the European American culture, and whom others see as biologically inferior and thus incapable of adapting to that culture. Thus the picture of Black males that dominates popular media as well as the conceptualization that is generally advanced in the scholarly press is a picture of pathology bordering on hopelessness—sometimes found even among those whose motivations appear to be humane and sympathetic.

In general this literature is severely limited in its conceptualization of the issues and in its coverage of the range of adaptations, behaviors, characteristics, and conditions that are manifested in the lives of African American males. It is primarily a literature of Black male failures and dysfunctional behaviors, and is most charitably described as responses to oppression and disadvantagement (Kardiner & Ovesey, 1951; Lewis, 1965). It is a literature of life in depressed inner cities where African Americans are overrepresented. Since this picture appropriately applies to a minority of the Black males in the United States, these foci suggest that the majority of members of the targeted group are being overlooked (Gordon, 1997). These foci also mean that such issues as age, class, gender, and geographic differences are neglected. The fact that the full range of adaptive and maladaptive behaviors and conditions is largely undocumented and has not been subjected to analysis is of even greater significance. Given the remarkable achievements of this group, just a century removed from enslavement and continuing to experience racism, this truncated picture provides a distorted popular view and an inadequate knowledge base for both public policy and the continued production of knowledge. Gordon (1996) has referred to the "African American male problematique" to reflect the view that this generalized distortion of the conditions and status of Black males in the United States is an artificial or at best a manufactured problem. Some African American males are in trouble, but the African American male condition is not one of universal failure.

The research literature specifically concerning African American males is a product of the latter half of the 20th century. This emerging literature tends to focus on questions having to do with dysfunctional males and their contribution to what was considered to be the problems with Black families, the legacies of slavery, and their impact on Black males. Examples include the killing off of the most assertive and smartest and the disruption of family relations in enslaved peoples, the distortion of cultural traditions, and the continuing deprivation of opportunities for Black males to exercise responsibility for themselves and their families. Toward the mid-20th century, attention turned to studies of urbanization, poverty, and single-parent families. Since the early 1980s the focus of much of this work has been on political/economic and social/psychological issues. Much of the emphasis has shifted to unemployment, lack of opportunity for meaningful participation in the political economy of the nation, institutionalized racism, and the impacts of these structural phenomena on the attitudes and behavior of African American males.

Upon review of the literature on African Americans males, we note that a shift in focus occurred in the late 1980s and early 1990s with regard to the issues surrounding Black males and Black people in general. During the 1940s, 1950s, 1960s, and early 1970s, the emphasis in this literature was primarily on the problems and ills of African Americans and the impact of the legacy of slavery and contemporary poverty. The major thrust of this debate was whether Black families had a history of being two-parent and intact, with some middle-classness, or whether these families were predominantly matriarchal and increasingly poor and dysfunctional. In the past 15 years, the debate has shifted to economic and psychosocial issues. Much more emphasis is currently placed on unemployment, lack of educational and economic opportunity, the weight of institutional racism, and the impacts of these forces on the behavior and psyches of African Americans—African American men in particular.

Special attention has been given to Black males' ability to survive and succeed in U.S. society. Many studies examine how Black men handle the trappings of urban life: drugs, crime, homicide, prison, discrimination, school drop-out, and so on. More and more studies address issues related to culture, from what it means to how it differs for different populations, how Black males move between cultures, how they adjust to a society whose dominant culture is often alien and disrespectful of their own, how they are affected by the stereotypes of Black men, and how they cope with discrimination, both overt and covert. Four major issues or areas of concern are addressed in the research literature on African American males. Included among these are demographic and status analyses, investigations of psychosocial context and developmental issues, analyses of economic factors and status, and examinations of issues related to educational opportunity and achievement.

With respect to the status and demographic analyses, the research in this category highlights the plight of African American males in terms of their high rates of dysfunctional and pathological behaviors and conditions. This has led some writers to suggest that Black males are an "endangered species," for on just about every social indicator, African American males are reported to be in trouble or marginally related to the mainstream of contemporary society. Notably absent is any extensive treatment of the segment of the African American male population that is functioning well. Although much of the literature emphasizes these negative indicators, questions remain concerning the accuracy and, more important, the interpretation, of the data and statistics used to support these negative conclusions. These questions, however, receive far less attention. The causes of the negative demographics for African Americans still have not been adequately analyzed and remain hotly debated. Much less analysis focuses on what the statistics mean or how to make and understand the fine distinctions between absolute and relative numbers. Due to the confounding of ethnic and class factors, these decontextualized quantitative treatments of the status of Black males are limited in their explanatory power.

The general causes of the crisis for African American males addressed in the literature are often incorrectly addressed as separate issues in the psychosocial, economic, and educational domains. In the psychosocial literature, emphasis is given to how African American males behave and react to societal conditions, particularly to discrimination, poverty, and marginalization. Some attention has been given to Black male coping strategies or the lack thereof. Several studies address African American males' relationships with their families, with underground economies, and with alternative lifestyles. A growing number of studies provide cultural analyses as well as psychological assessments. Indeed, among the strongest recent developments in this literature is the emergence of ethnographic analyses of African American males' life experiences and the recognition of subcultural norms that are unique to segments of this population.

The emphases in the economic studies on Black males are on economic status, employment/unemployment, the relationship of skill of mastery to employability, the expanding Black underclass, and the disproportionate suffering of African American males from economic downturns and structural inequalities in U.S. society. Unemployment and economic marginality are considered to be major issues and causes of much of African American poor performance. Although the system itself, and especially its discriminatory behavior, is seen as the main culprit or cause of the problem, some of this literature places the cause of Black economic insufficiency squarely on the dysfunctional behaviors of Black males. Missing in this literature is any systematic treatment of the political economy of the African American male experience, which is marked by the absence of any meaningful control of the wealth and power to influence the life chances of Black people.

It is perhaps the literature on the conditions of the education, miseducation, and undereducation of African Americans, males included, that has received the greatest attention. This literature is replete with studies that document

1. African Americans' unequal access to and facilities for formal education;
2. the poor quality of schooling available to large numbers of African American students;
3. the cultural differences between most of these students and their teachers;
4. the inadequate home and family support they receive for academic learning;
5. their poor academic socialization;
6. the high African American school drop-out rates and declining college and graduate school attendance;
7. the disparities in rewards for educational achievement between Blacks and other groups; and
8. the low expectations of academic productivity held for African American students, particularly males.

Much of this literature is descriptive of possible interventions, some of which have been hailed as highly promising, but they lack sufficient data to support their claims. In recent years, the educational literature on Black males has included attention to the claims for Afrocentric emphases in curriculum and a return to race- and gender-specific settings for learning. Unfortunately, this literature is considerably richer in its descriptions of the fact that problems exist than it is in the provision of solutions to these problems.

It is toward the suggestion of solutions to issues involved in the development and rehabilitation of African American males that the chapters in this volume are directed. Interventions advanced by these authors are heavily focused on education and pedagogy. This is in part a reflection of the professional backgrounds from which many of the writers come. However, this concentration is also a reflection of the fact that the case can be made for education and the political economy as the two most critical domains of intervention in support of Black male development. Other nonpedagogically grounded chapters deal with issues related to technology, identity, fatherhood, and community violence.

Like much of the research literature, the nonpedagogical contributions made available through this collection give greater attention to the problems than to the solutions. Given the nature of the larger society that is the context for our thinking and for our work, it may well be that educational intervention is the most viable possibility. The times may simply not be right for a serious engagement of alternatives that are to be found in the political economy of "the African American male problematique." The real problems may suggest alternatives that are too radical to receive serious attention by a conservative-to-reactionary social order. Manipulating the experiences of African American males in schools may be the treatment of choice. The essays that follow move us in that direction.

Edmund W. Gordon

Introduction

Vernon C. Polite and James Earl Davis

And herein lies the tragedy of the age: not that men are poor,—all men know something of poverty; not that men are wicked,—who is good? not that men are ignorant,—what is Truth? Nay, but that men know so little of men.
—W. E. B. Du Bois, *The Souls of Black Folk*

RESEARCH FOCUSED ON BLACK MALES

Although considerable research emphasis is placed on gender differences in educational achievement, most of this research—with the exception of a few studies on African American girls in school—does not provide separate, in-depth exploration of the intersection of race and gender. In particular, the exclusive study of African American males' experiences in school and related achievement and social outcomes has a very limited place in the academic literature. This is a critical omission given the disproportionate rates of school failure, special education assignment, suspensions, and expulsions for African American males. Consequently, very few researchers attempt to link the social meanings of gender with schooling and social outcomes. In this book, we sought not only to understand the determinants of success in school for African American male students, but also to document their academic and social lives.

To be an African American male in school and society places one at risk for a variety of negative consequences. Negative school and societal experiences are viewed in varying degrees as products of structural factors,

African American Males in School and Society: Practices and Policies for Effective Education. Copyright © 1999 by Teachers College, Columbia University. All rights reserved. ISBN 0-8077-3870-0 (pbk), ISBN 0-8077-3871-9 (cloth). Prior to photocopying items for classroom use, please contact the Copyright Clearance Center, Customer Service, 222 Rosewood Dr., Danvers, MA 01923, USA, tel. (508) 750-8400.

results of cultural adaptations to systemic pressures, and maladaptive definitions of masculinity (Hunter & Davis, 1992; Majors & Billson, 1991). Unfortunately, what has emerged from this focus on the educational "crisis" of African American males is a myopic lens given to view behavioral problems, while scant emphasis is being placed on structural and economic marginality.

The years following the civil rights movement of the 1960s were an era of increased white-collar jobs for people of all races. Many African Americans, in particular, secured opportunities for placement in jobs and educational programs that previously had been unavailable to them. However, the gap between African American and White men's earnings continues to widen. For example, with regard to the number of hours worked per week in 1997, African American men between the ages of 25–64 worked far fewer hours per week than did their White counterparts. The men in this age group worked 7 hours fewer per week than did White men of the same age grouping. The year 2000 will find the average African American man earning 58% of the average White man's salary if the trend continues (National Research Council [NRC], 1989). Not only are working African American men earning less than their White counterparts, the unemployment rates have remained nearly twice as high for African American as compared to White men. The precarious employment status of a large percentage of African American men adversely affects their families, communities, and society in general.

Economic Factors and Their Impact on Black Males

How does the economic conditions of the average African American man affect his relations with his family? Social researchers attribute much of the instability in certain African American families to the ineffectiveness of African American men to provide a steady economic foundation from which the African American family could prosper. Their meager earning power negatively impacts their relationship with their family, contributing in part to the very common incidence of female-headed households. Too many of single, African American mothers reported that they received no financial support from their children's fathers, and a large percentage of African American children are reared in destitution (NRC, 1989).

Historically, African American men played an integral part in their families and community life. This position is contrary to the widely held contemporary notion that a viable and adaptive presence of African American men failed to develop and flourish in African American communities. We argue that at the core of African American males' experience in school and society is persistence and triumph—one that has been overshadowed by the literature and discourse that focus primarily on the social pathology of African American men (Duneier, 1994; Hunter & Davis, 1994). This core conception, we suggest, is based on the common experiences of ordinary African American males in schools and families, leading ordinary lives in stable families and communities. Education is no exception. Although many African American males are achieving at commendable levels and are navigating the academic and social currents of their lives, their experiences have often gone unnoticed. Although, as a group, African American males may be at risk for numerous social, economic, and educational ills, within that context of risk many have survived and progressed successfully.

We believe that education has been and will continue to be a solid rock in an ever shifting quicksand of economic downturn, recycling of unfounded racist theories of genetic inferiority, and right-wing posturing that results in political retrenchment for African Americans. The American Council on Education (ACE) (1994) articulated the need for a special effort to increase the number of African American men earning college degrees. The council listed numerous factors that accounted for the scarcity of African American men on the college and university campuses of this country, namely, chronic health problems and lower life expectancy, high unemployment rates, low teacher expectation, disproportionate discipline and expulsion incidents, and disproportionate time spent in special education classes. Even with increased educational opportunities, there was no guarantee of economic parity with White men. Among college-educated men with degrees, 1 in 9 was unemployed for African American men as compared with 1 in 29 for White men (National Urban League, 1998).

Schooling and Education

One reason commonly mentioned for the alienation and poor academic performance of some African American males is that they perceive most educational experiences as irrelevant to their masculine identity and development. Furthermore, it is also argued that schools and teachers impose a feminine culture on males that inadvertently induces oppositional behavior (Holland, 1989). Given these alienating school contexts and consequences, particularly those focusing on gender expectations, many African American males become both victims and participants in their own educational marginalization. In AFRICAN AMERICAN MALES IN SCHOOL AND SOCIETY, we focus primarily on disentangling the effects of student's background, school context, and ecological issues of students' success and experiences in an out of school. In identifying important factors associated with student performance and exploring innovative theoretical and methodological approaches, we aim to better understand and improve academic and social outcomes for African American males. We have a particular interest in exploring how African American males negotiate schooling and how their experiences frame broader educational and social outcomes, such as post-secondary school attendance, employment, and fatherhood.

Issues in Higher Education

Higher education poses a true hardship for many African American men. The National Council on Education (1997) and the National Urban League (1998) maintains that getting a larger number of qualified African American men involved in higher education is the key to reversing the economic trends. The 18-to-24-year-old population is considered the traditional college-going age group (ACE, 1994). The use of this age group as a standard provides an understanding of the number of persons who were actually enrolled in college by race and gender. Although up to recent times in history, African American men maintained a higher in-college rate than their female counterparts, that began to wane during the Reagan-Bush era. By 1992 the percentage of African American males enrolled in college had dropped to 29.7%, down from 34.3% in 1991. This decline in African American male college enrollment is in contrast to the gains of other students of color. For instance, the proportion of African American females who enrolled in college was at an all-time high of 37.5% in 1992, up from 30.9% in 1991.

A report from the National Center for Education Statistics (1993) indicated that by the year 2000 there would be a 50% turnover in faculty members in the nations' colleges and universities. There will be few African American men prepared to fill those vacancies unless there is a concerted effort to encourage more African Americans men to enter the education pipeline. African Americans received 4.5% of the doctorates awarded in 1977 and the number declined to 3.8% earned in 1987 (NRC, 1993). During that period (1977–1989) there was a marked increase in the number of African American women recipients and a decline in the number of African American men recipients; a contributing factor for these statistics is the ability to finance the education at the doctoral level. Fewer African American men were financially able to support the expense of advanced education. Some argue that African American women, however, were more likely to receive scholarships due to pressure put on graduate programs to accommodate multiple-minority categories. When it comes to access to education, there should not be competition between African American women and men, because their children need strong modeling from both mother and father.

Violence and Crime

The social pathological issues of violence, crime, and imprisonment are constructed and reported widely in the media. Does the history of African American men in this country provide any explanations for these present day conditions? We argue yes! Although a portion of African American males have made it into the mainstream of society and contribute significantly to the national labor force, we can not deny the residual effects of 200 years of enslavement and another 100 years of legal discrimination. These historical facts continue to negatively impact the African American community, particularly African American men. These conditions are all too familiar to those of us who live in the African American communities of this nation. We find particularly distressing the multiplicity of problems facing adolescent males in urban America, such as gangs, negative peer pressure, antischooling attitudes, and drug trafficking. Although personal-behavior issues, such as maladaptive conceptions of masculinity and their ramifications, are important, they tend to be presented in ways that implicitly are universal and unidimensional. Hence, these discussions often obscure the diversity and complexity of African American males' experiences in school and society. We view broader political, sociological, and economic forces as undermining both the development and appropriate expressions of many African American males in school, particularly among the urban poor.

SCOPE OF BOOK

As we approach the close of the century, we find the words of W. E. B. Du Bois to ring true—men know so little of men. Our overarching goal in preparing this work was to showcase those experiences that are most critical to the betterment of African American men as they approach the new millennium. Our goals were to construct an insightful overview of the critical issues affecting African American males in school and to link those issues to educational attainment, job procurement, quality of life, and responsible fatherhood. This volume provides not merely a problem-identification focus, but solution and policy foci as well. Each chapter includes concrete recommendations to parents, school administrators, and policy makers who concern themselves with the well-being of African American boys and men. By expanding the traditional discourse of "black males as victims," this volume attempts to provide a richer sense of African American males' experiences in school and society. Our contributors bring their own set of interests to bear on their reflections and analysis of black male's issues. In total, however, these chapters challenge theoretical and methodological perspectives on the intersection between race and gender. In Chapter 1, Foster and Peele explore issues related to teaching African American males. They present data from expert teachers about their experiences and lessons learned—both successes and failures—in teaching Black males. In Chapter 2, Carver challenges established thinking about Black males' role in a technologically advanced society. Despite grim indicators of African American males at-risk status for educational and occupational failure, Carver posits that technology and specifically computers can be used productively to reach and teach them. In Chapter 3, Harry and Anderson tackle the devastating problem of the frequent placement of Black males in special education programs. They offer an unforgiving analysis of how the social construction of disabilities mediates the disproportionate placement of African American males. Implications are clearly outlined, followed by concrete strategies to ameliorate this problem in order to increase the educational success of Black males in U.S. schools. In Chapter 4, Ford, Grantham, and Bailey make a convincing argument for more inclusive and appropriate methods for identifying giftedness among African American males. Corbin and Pruitt turn to an examination of African American male identity in Chapter 5. They explore critical developmental contexts, such as family and school, and analyze how these contexts influence and are changed by identity development. In Chapter 6, Murrell examines responsive teaching styles for African American males in middle school. Chapter 7 takes up the interesting and important theme of educating African American males in suburbia. Polite presents a scathing picture of educational neglect in mathematics instruction and achievement within a suburban school context. His findings suggest that suburban education also provides many challenges for Black males.

Hawkins raises the question of the missing contribution of the "talented tenth" among African American men in Chapter 8. By exploring the educational outcomes of Black boys in one of the wealthiest school districts in the nation, Hawkins causes us to pause to question the dichotomy between schooling and education. In Chapter 9, Brown provides a critique of current policy activity and legal issues that threaten the future and success of African American males in higher education. Brown concludes by providing implications for educational policy and practice joined with an insightful policy perspective for assuring equal opportunity in higher education. Davis, in Chapter 10, argues for a more focused discussion on both race and gender in examining the experiences of African American men on college campuses. His findings suggest the need to reexamine the social support of Black males in college, perhaps including more expansive meanings of social support for different college contexts.

Mason, in Chapter 11, challenges dominate economic perspectives on individualism and meritocracy that inform the socioeconomic status of African American men. He presents data that suggest that general increases in inequality and average wage rate cannot be solely attributed to market forces, but are also linked to material incentives for the exclusion of Black men. Gadsden and Bowman focus on critical issues of practice, policy, and research on African American fathers in Chapter 12. They present data from responsive fathers programs serving young fathers. They highlight important issues about responsible fatherhood and provide conclusions that expand the discourse on African American fathers and family support. In the final chapter, Polite offers reflections and personal history as a heuristic device to construct meaning about the confluence of race, class, and gender. Through its description of struggle, tragedy, and loss, this autobiographical record shows another African American male's triumph over adversity—his beating the odds by having purchase of personal resiliency nurtured by the power of Black women and family.

CONCLUSION

We believe that the chapters that follow provide rich insights into the issues affecting African American males in schools and society. We trust that the works presented in this volume will engender a greater interest in the education of African Americans males. Our nation is not so rich in resources, talents, and skills that it can afford to ignore the potential contribution of African American males to the workforce, family life, and community.

1   Teaching Black Males: Lessons from the Experts

Michele Foster and Tryphenia B. Peele

WHAT KNOWLEDGE, SKILLS, AND dispositions are required to successfully teach African American males? What are the characteristics of teachers who are effective with African American males? Can the knowledge, skills, and dispositions of teachers who are successful with African American males be learned by prospective teachers? This chapter addresses these issues. After a brief review of the literature on teaching, we describe the philosophy and practice of successful teachers of African American males. Next, we compare these findings to what African American males have to say about the characteristics of teachers that they viewed as highly effective. Our primary purpose in this chapter is to initiate a dialogue with researchers, practitioners, and policy makers about the kind of teachers best suited to teach African American males.

RELATED RESEARCH ON TEACHING

The research literature on teaching is voluminous. Although some of this research has attended to dimensions other than pedagogical ones—the ethical and moral aspects (Noddings, 1995)—most often the research on teaching emphasizes the cognitive, pedagogical, and managerial dimensions such as subject matter knowledge, pedagogical content knowledge, instructional approaches, and student assessment. In some instances, the moral and pedagogical dimensions have been yoked in the analysis (Ball & Wilson, 1996), but even in these cases the moral is subordinated to the pedagogical.

African American Males in School and Society: Practices and Policies for Effective Education. Copyright © 1999 by Teachers College, Columbia University. All rights reserved. ISBN 0-8077-3870-0 (pbk), ISBN 0-8077-3871-9 (cloth). Prior to photocopying items for classroom use, please contact the Copyright Clearance Center, Customer Service, 222 Rosewood Dr., Danvers, MA 01923, USA, tel. (508) 750-8400.

The focus on the pedagogical dimensions over the nonpedagogical ones is evident in the standards developed by the National Board of Professional Teaching Standards (the Board), a certification board similar to national boards for lawyers and physicians, charged with establishing advanced standards for experienced teachers and determining who meets them. Concerned with developing an assessment system that corresponds more closely to what teachers do in their day-to-day practice, the Board has developed a set of core propositions and created performance-based assessments grounded in them. Working collaboratively with parents, being knowledgeable about students' community and culture, and other nonpedagogical dimensions are components of the core propositions. To date, however, the creation of activities that pertain to the cognitive dimensions of teaching and learning have proceeded more effortlessly than others, such as, for example, those intended to gauge how well teachers work collaboratively with parents or those that address issues of culture in their teaching practice. Consequently, despite their inclusion, the nonpedagogical components are not adequately tested and are consequently subsumed to the pedagogical. Indeed most of the work approaches teaching at the technical level, as methodologies the teachers employ in classroom.

When considering standards for teaching, it is essential to determine whether the attitudes, behaviors, and skills required to teach predominately White middle-class students are those needed to teach predominately African American students, especially if those classrooms are composed primarily of urban pupils who live in poverty. Several researchers have addressed this issue. Irvine (1990) argues that lack of cultural synchronization—the tendency of teachers to misunderstand and fail to appreciate the cultural backgrounds, language(s), values, home environments, or learning styles of African American students—is the cause of students' academic failure.

Other scholars who have examined teachers achieving success with African American students from poor urban and rural communities have identified the characteristics of their practice. Based on a review of the literature as well as on her own empirical work, Foster (1993, 1994) has specified five elements that characterize the practice of effective Black teachers, most of whom teach predominantly Black students. From her empirical study of effective teachers of African American students, Ladson-Billings (1994) has developed sets of postulates that mark culturally relevant as opposed to assimilationist teaching. These postulates are concerned with teachers' conceptions of self and others, of knowledge and of social relations. Finally, in a longitudinal research of successful urban teachers, Haberman (1995) has identified the attributes of "star" teachers, individuals who are successful with poor, urban students.

Haberman argues that the primary issue for teachers who work in poor urban communities is not the ability to teach a particular subject. It is the ability to teach that subject to a group of children who attend a particular school, in a particular community given the institutional constraints and the children's out-of-school lives (Haberman, 1992). He insists that merely knowing subject matter or being skilled in various teaching strategies will not equip teachers to work with poor, urban students (Haberman, 1992). There is no doubt that pedagogical considerations are important. There is some evidence, however, that in the case of African American males, pedagogical skills only will not make for successful teaching. Siddle-Walker (1992) argues that a singular emphasis on teaching methodology obscures the affective domain and that "the subjective relationship between pupils and teachers is influenced by, but not limited to methods of instruction" (p. 322).

PERSONAL CHARACTERISTICS

Many teachers give up when confronted with students who are indifferent, resistant, have behavior problems, or are achieving below grade level. Other teachers are overwhelmed by the problems that confront their students, especially if those students, come from communities plagued by violence, drugs, and death. Effective teachers of African American males possess the emotional stamina, persistence, and resilience that enable them to negotiate the school bureaucracy, solve difficult problems, and help their students cope with day-to-day setbacks and misfortunes as well as more serious hardships (Foster, 1997; Haberman, 1992, 1995; Ladson-Billings, 1994). Expert teachers of African American males take responsibility for teaching and engaging all of their students in learning, whether they are indifferent, resistant, or achieving significantly below grade level. Convinced that even seemingly recalcitrant students enjoy learning, expert teachers believe that they can teach even those whom others find impossible to teach. In fact, expert teachers take pride in their ability to reach students whom other teachers have given up on. A veteran high school teacher with more than 30 years of experience observed:

> "Teaching anywhere today is hard work. It's especially hard in the cities because there are so many forces out there fighting against you. Teachers take the kids' resistance as not wanting to learn. But as soon as the teachers stop pushing, the students say that teachers didn't care because they would have kept on pushing them. The kids see it as a contest. Every day when I went into the classroom, I knew I had to be up to the challenge. I never understood, but I never gave up because I'm not a quitter." (in Foster, 1997, p. 49)

An elementary school teacher noted:

> "Instead of taking time to correct Black children or discipline them, the teachers send them home or else they suspend them. I don't send children home. I work with the children and their parents until their behavior changes. You've got to care and you've got to be positive and determined. Teaching urban children effectively requires more than good teaching techniques. It requires the ability to solve problems; it requires commitment, psychological strength, and determination." (in Foster, 1997, p. 31)

Relationships with Students

Expert teachers of African American males develop productive relationships with their students. Sometimes, these relationships are expressed in the teachers' use of kinshiplike terms or in the use of metaphors with which teachers express a particular kind of alliance between themselves and their students (Casey, 1990; Foster, 1991). The following quote illustrates the metaphorical reference to these connections:

> "Black people have to convince Blacks of how important it (education) is. And how they are all part of that Black *umbilical cord* because a lot of (Black) teachers, they don't do it consciously, but we are forgetting about our roots, about how we're *connected to this cord*, and about everyone we've left behind. We have it now, and we don't have time for the so-called underclass. But we have to educate ourselves as a group because otherwise what's going to happen to us all? You see what I mean. If I can't see that kid out there in the biggest project, if I can't see how he and I or she and I are of the same umbilical cord and (if I) do not strive to make us more connected, with a common destiny, then we're lost." (in Foster, 1997, p. 52; emphasis added)

Even if these terms and metaphors are unarticulated, expert teachers respect their students and are able to develop productive relationships with them. Expert teachers of African American males sometimes adopt an authoritative style but if so, it is one that integrates respect, acceptance, and involvement with firm control and psychological autonomy. A high school social studies teacher described his approach to students:

> "I am part disciplinarian and part cheerleader. My demeanor is relaxed and my personality is very outgoing, I smile a lot; the kids used to call me "Smiley." I tend to be upbeat and to let the kids get to know me as a human being. ... When the kids get to know me as not just their teacher, they are less likely to act up in class and more likely to cooperate with me. Developing these personal relationships prevents a lot of problems and makes it easier for me to get something accomplished in the classroom. I treat my students with

respect. No matter who the student is, I believe we can always reach a common ground and common point where we can get along and work together. My students respect me. You can't do anything without respect and discipline." (in Foster, 1997, p. 54)

An elementary school teacher echoes this same view:

"You've got to demand respect in a respectful way. You have to be tender but firm and positive. It's only after you've established some affection that you can talk about discipline. As far as I am concerned, right-wing, left-wing, no-wing, everybody needs discipline. You can't accomplish anything without discipline." (in Foster, 1997, p. 52)

This style of teaching closely resembles an authoritative parenting style, which integrates acceptance and involvement, firm control, and psychological autonomy (Dornbusch, Ritter, Liederman, Roberts, & Fraleigh, 1987; Lanborn & Mounts, 1990; Steinberg et al., 1990). Quoting a Black woman, Casey (1990) provides an example of what she calls a teacher's "sensitive and benevolent assertion of her authority," which illustrates how an authoritative style, one that integrates acceptance and involvement, firm control, and psychological autonomy, is enacted in a teacher-pupil relationship:

"There were times when I said, 'If you skip my class, I'm coming down to the mall to get you.' So sometimes, I would go down to the mall, and it would be a big scene because the class would be waiting there, anticipating my coming back with these six feet, you know, men. And I would go down to the mall, and I would say, 'Hi John!' 'Uh, Hi!' You know. They were always really surprised. I said, 'Well, we come to get you.' And they looked, 'We?' Those kind of confrontations could really get to be sticky, because you had to measure how you were going to approach that, and you had to know who you were talking to and what kind of child this was, and how they gonna react to you. The students, of course, thought that I was just walking into it, and not thinking each step of the way as to how I was going to do it. Some of these students were very, very belligerent about coming to class, and some of the classes they didn't go to. And it was just kind of, they'd like pass the word, 'Don't skip ———'s class, I mean, she'll come and get you and that's embarrassing you know.'

      "We would start up the stairs together, and then I would notice that they were walking ahead of me. And that was my signal, to not go in the door at the same time with them, because that would be really embarrassing, and the objective was not to embarrass somebody once you get them to class." (in Casey, 1990, p. 76)

It is through developing alliances and personal relationships with their pupils that these teachers help students develop attachments to learning that they otherwise might not have. In their dealings with students, expert teachers express concern and have respect for their pupils, command respect in return, and expect their students to meet high behavioral and academic standards.

Attitudes Toward Learning

Effective teachers of African American males believe that their students are capable of learning the school curriculum. They believe that academic achievement results from concerted and consistent effort, not from ability. Consequently, successful teachers of African American males accept responsibility for motivating students. Constantly searching for ways of engaging students, they continuously search for ideas that will interest their students. Often this means linking classroom content to students' out-of-school interests. A high school math teacher comments on how he accomplished this with his pupils:

"I remember being assigned to teach a course for students who were difficult: Black students who weren't supposed to be good at academics. I developed a course I called applied mathematics. What I did was make everything in the course apply to the real world. I asked how many kids in the class were interested in brick masonry and there were about six. All the work they were assigned in this class was based on brick masonry: how to calculate money, how to calculate the cost of material, even how to figure out your income tax. For those who were interested in carpentry, everything in the course was connected with carpentry in some way. They learned how to measure off a room, how to read a blueprint, and other practical things. There were four categories, some in auto mechanics and the rest in computers. The course was algebra, but all the algebra was linked to students' interests. The students in that class didn't cause any trouble. On any given day, you could walk by that room and almost hear a pin drop, because all the students were interested in what they were doing." (in Foster, 1997, p. 9)

A fifth-grade teacher describes how she tries to make her science curriculum relevant to the lives of her students and their families:

"Our science curriculum deals with the human body—the various systems of the human body. Students learn how to take blood pressure readings and interpret them. They use thermometers and to take their temperatures and learn how to read them when we learn about basal temperatures. We learn about various diseases, both the accepted medical terms and the terms that are widely used in their communities. It isn't unusual to hear the expression 'yellow jaundice' used by Black adults. Older Black people will say, 'I have sugar.' We talk about why people might use that term instead of the medical term." (in Foster, 1997, p. 62)

Linking classroom content to students' experiences characterizes the practice of effective teachers of African American males. In the classrooms of these teachers, students are helped to see the relationship between what they are learning in school and their out-of-school lives (Foster, 1987, 1989; Henry, 1990; Ladson-Billings, 1991a, 1991b; Ladson-Billings & Henry, 1990). Effective teachers believe that using real-life experiences, folk knowledge, and stories support meaningful learning for their students. Consequently, they deliberately structure classroom activities to make such linkages possible (Foster, 1987, 1989; Hollins, 1982).

SOCIAL AND CULTURAL LEARNING EVENTS

Most of what occurs in traditional classrooms encourages competitive behavior and individual achievement. Yet some research has shown that tremendous gains have been achieved in schools and classrooms for Black students where learning is organized as a social event, not as a competitive or individual endeavor.

Effective teachers of African American males embrace patterns of collectivity, incorporating them into classroom activities. Students are encouraged to support each other, work together, and study collaboratively (Foster, 1997, 1989; Ladson-Billings, 1991a, 1991b). Ladson-Billings (1991a, 1991b) reports that the teachers she interviewed continually stressed the need to build "a community or family" and that both they and their students were more at ease working in cooperative, collaborative classrooms. A high school biology teacher describes the collaborative approach she uses in her classroom:

> "Students are required to do a lot of group work in my classes. That's to build responsibility and group cohesiveness. During the lab work, they assume various roles. One role is that of technical advisor. Another student assumes the role of secretary. Another, who is responsible for gathering all of the materials, another is the coordinator. Each student has to assume the responsibility of the role. Together they work on the various experiments." (in Foster, 1997, p. 53)

THE WHOLE STUDENT

Successful teachers of African American males concern themselves with the development of their pupils, not just with their cognitive growth. Teachers who are effective with African American males conceive their role more broadly than that assigned them by the narrow, utilitarian purposes of schooling. Thus, although they accept the institutional goal of promoting cognitive growth, their personal definition of the teachers' role is not merely confined to developing academic skills but includes the social and emotional growth of students. Haberman (1992) contends that successful teachers of urban students make use of their teaching; indeed they believe that the purpose of teaching is "to develop good people—people with character" (p. 125). Speaking about her goals for her students, an elementary school teacher remarks:

> "A teacher has to be concerned with much more than academics. As a Black teacher teaching Black children, I am just as interested in the kind of people that my students become as with what they are learning." (in Foster, 1997, p. 143)

The practice of teachers who are effective with African American males reflects this fact. These teachers accept responsibility for nurturing in their students the prerequisite skills and knowledge needed for success in school. They explicitly teach and model personal values—patience, persistence, responsibility to self and others—that can serve as a foundation to current as well as future learning; they foster the development of student attitudes, interests, and motivation—aspiration, self-confidence, and leadership skills. Sometimes these teachers employ rituals and routines that reinforce the values they seek to impart, but even in the absence of rituals teachers are self-consciously aware of how their day-to-day practice reinforces their ideals and goals. These teachers are also aware of the structural inequalities in society and their practice evidences a "hidden curriculum" designed to help students cope with the exigencies of living in a society that perpetuates institutional racism while professing a rhetoric of equal opportunity (Foster, 1997; Haberman, 1992; Hollins, 1982; King, 1991; Ladson-Billings & Henry, 1990). Despite the dissimilarities among Catholic, African-centered, and segregated pre-*Brown* schools, reports and research about these schools have uncovered the role that a shared set of common values can have on motivating and committing African American pupils to higher levels of achievement (Irvine & Foster, 1996; Kifano, 1996; Lee, 1992a; Siddle-Walker, 1996).

THE VOICES OF AFRICAN AMERICAN MALE STUDENTS

Several unrelated studies have examined what adolescent African American males say about the qualities of teachers they prefer and are responsive to. Their comments confirm the findings above. Collectively, these studies argue that African American males prefer teachers who are strict and caring—personally supportive, but insistent that their students perform academically (Delpit, 1988; Foster, 1987, 1989, 1994; Hollins & Spencer, 1990; Noguera, 1996; Polite, 1993a, 1993b; Siddle-Walker, 1992).

Consider the images of the teachers described by several of the students in Polite's longitudinal study of a cohort of 115 African American male students who attended Metropolitan High School, a predominantly African American suburban high school in the Midwest. Asked about their high school teachers, one young African American male responded:

> "I don't really feel the teachers were pushing and encouraging us to succeed. I don't really don't. I had the greatest interest in my computer and English classes. I had Mrs. Jackson [An African American teacher] a few times. She was great and Mr. Rubenstein was good too. He challenged us in a way; not to the extreme, but he did give us a little challenge. Mrs. Jackson was always on us. She [Mrs. Jackson] pushed me to do better. The majority of the other teachers did next to nothing." (in Polite, 1993a, p. 38)

Another young man replied:

> "I wished the teachers would have cared more. For example, I went through like my senior year carrying a 3.4 [on a 4.0 scale]. I never brought books home and everything was just easy. You know no teachers cared." (in Polite, 1993a, p. 38)

A third young man described a teacher, who despite not including material about African American in his classes was effective nonetheless:

> "D. Bloom was challenging, real challenging. It was hard to get a 'B' in his class. He had us reading every day, but he spent half the course teaching us about the Holocaust and World War II, interesting stuff, but he never taught us about Black things. I don't think that was right, but he was a good teacher. . . . To me, they (teachers in general) could have been a little more pushy. If they were better and pushed us back then, you know, half of the people that didn't graduate might have graduated. . . . I guess it was the way Mrs. Jackson ran her class, and I guess the control she had over the class. She was one of these [teachers] that was hard. Her class was hard and it was difficult. . . . We did a lot of work, and it was challenging and that was very seldom at Metro-

politan High. . . . Once you get past the teacher relationship, that's the biggest thing to me." (in Foster, 1997, p. 38)

Caring teachers who make demands of African American male students while simultaneously encouraging them is a recurring theme in the comments of African American male students enrolled in a San Francisco Bay Area continuation school. When students were questioned about what made a good teacher, the qualities most often cited were firmness, compassion, and an engaging style of teaching. Students depicted some of their best teachers as being like relatives—mothers, aunts, or big sisters. The students also mentioned that their best teachers respected them, inspired them to work hard, and made learning interesting and relevant. The African American male students indicated they preferred strict teachers because, as one noted, "if a teacher is scared of me, they can't teach me. I can tell if they are scared, and if they is usually you can do whatever you want in their class I can respect a teacher that's strict and really tries to get the students to learn something" (Noguera, 1996). However, like the African American male students interviewed by other researchers (Foster, 1987, 1989, 1994; Siddle-Walker, 1992), these students noted that strictness was only effective when combined with caring and an interesting style of teaching (Noguera, 1996).

In the following excerpt from research conducted by Polite a student describes what teachers do to demonstrate that they care:

> "If they (teachers) tell me to be in class, do my work or tell me I can pass their class . . . that I can be somebody . . . words of encouragement . . . telling me things like that—that's 'caring.' But somebody that don't care only says you do this or you do that, saying that I've done well when they know I got the majority of answers wrong. There are some teachers who just can't cope with the class. A good teacher can get their class in order and get the students to respect them too. Mr. Adelstein is a good teacher. I had him last year. He always told us to do our work and his class was under control. . . . He gave us homework and class work and we had to do it too! He gave us chances, but we couldn't push him. He wasn't one of those sorry teachers that says, 'oh you pass,' without doing some work. With Mr. Adelstein, you had to do your work." (in Polite, 1993a, p. 39)

CONCLUSION

In this chapter we suggest that there are several factors that characterize the practice of expert teachers of African American males. Generally speaking, these teachers are effective, persistent, and able and willing to solve complex problems centered on their role as a teacher of African American males. They strive to develop productive relationships with their students; they are capable of engaging students in active learning and critical thinking. They embrace cooperative and supportive classroom environments that require African American males to work collaboratively.

It is important, also, that teacher-preparation programs recognize the diversity of backgrounds, cultures, and learning styles of the students living in the urban enclaves of America. We suggest the following, based upon the lessons learned from the experts with respect to teaching the African American male student:

1. As a rule of thumb, treat every Black male as you would treat your own son.
2. Set a tone for learning each day and remain consistent from day to day. Do not expect to accomplish anything without structure and discipline.
3. Learn to manage your classroom. Instead of taking time to correct inappropriate behaviors among Black males, too often teachers, Black and White, will move for suspension and expulsion.
4. Know that it becomes impossible to discipline or teach the Black male unless the boy believes that you care.
5. Understand that African American males, from as early as second grade, are haunted by and have to overcome the negative portrayals of who they are.
6. Believe that African American males are perfectly capable of performing at high academic levels. The one thing that the Black male student does not need is teachers who accept the statement "I can't do this."
7. Learn as much as possible about the community in which the Black male lives. To the extent possible, attempt to relate course content to the real world of Black males, but also assist them in their efforts to understand global issues.
8. Seek out ongoing career planning and in-service training with a clear focus on encouraging students to set career goals.
9. Aid Black males in sorting through career options and help them to understand the importance of setting career objectives, specific achievement strategies, and a plan of action for fulfilling the course requirements needed to realize those goals. Students should review and adjust their goals and strategies annually under the direction of teachers and counselors.
10. Participate in a continuing education program. This program should provide the teacher with skills in multicultural learning, communica-

tion, culture, and social and learning styles, with an emphasis on African Americans.

11. Do not assume that every Black male is a troublemaker.
12. Expect, regardless of your race, social class, background, or teacher preparation to struggle to find ways to establish meaningful relationship with African American male students. Your experiences influence how you see the world and cannot be dismissed, devalued, or ignored. Establishing a meaningful relationship does not mean an interpersonal "friendship" between you and the student. Rather, successful teachers let African American males know that they care.

2

The Information Rage: Computers and Young African American Males

Bernard A. Carver

NO ONE CAN REASONABLY ARGUE that the computer has not assumed great importance in society today. Navigation of the information superhighway on the Internet is an excellent example of the type of informational exchanges that occur for those who have access to the technology and understand its use. Computers and their usage cut across diverse aspects of modern culture. A principal factor that has spawned rapid computer usage is the invention and mass production of the microcomputer. Its low cost, power, speed, and ease of use has helped to spark widespread acceptance of computer technology. Thus the microcomputer can be viewed as a gateway technology that allows its users access to the plethora of information available electronically.

Dizard (1982) and Toffler (1990) describe our current condition as the "Information Age" or the "Third Wave" of societal development, respectively. Both descriptions characterize a new era of human development in which information will be increasingly viewed as a commodity, and one that is directly linked to economic and social mobility. More recently, Burgess called it the "Digital Divide." McLuhan (1989) claims that this phenomenon is global and that, as it spreads, separate and discrete societies will be transformed and restructured into "global villages."

The success our nation enjoys with technology adoption is in part attributable to aggressive pursuits of societal objectives established by visionary leaders in business, education, and government. In this movement, a technological infrastructure is being built to foster greater school-to-work transitions. These forces agree that the starting point for technology adop-

African American Males in School and Society: Practices and Policies for Effective Education. Copyright © 1999 by Teachers College, Columbia University. All rights reserved. ISBN 0-8077-3870-0 (pbk), ISBN 0-8077-3871-9 (cloth). Prior to photocopying items for classroom use, please contact the Copyright Clearance Center, Customer Service, 222 Rosewood Dr., Danvers, MA 01923, USA, tel. (508) 750-8400.

tion and usage begins with our youth. Our national priorities, for technology adoption, are even reflected in the U.S. Department of Education's Goals 2000 project, designed to fund creative technology plans for schools.

On the downside of this technological challenge is the reality that as we move more toward the year 2000 and more fully into this Information Age, economic and societal woes will prevent many from being productively involved. Almost 30 years ago, Toffler (1971) warned of the emergence of a dichotomy of the "information-rich"–"information-poor" in the United States. It appears that due to the general lack of economic, educational, and other societal opportunities available to them, African Americans and other minorities will constitute a large segment of the information-poor category. Thus, these populations would be at risk of failure in the Information Age.

Although a lack of resources and opportunities will prohibit many African Americans from large-scale involvement in the Information Age, it is young African American males who will be most significantly affected. Gibbs (1988) has already suggested that African American males are quickly becoming an "endangered species." As she and others (e.g., Johnson & Watson, 1990; Yeakey & Bennett, 1990) report, a growing and alarming number of African American males are either becoming victims of negative circumstances (e.g., dropping out of school at an early age, being sent to penal institutions, or succumbing to urban violence) or becoming participants in activities that are counterproductive to their development (e.g., involving drugs and gangs). Despite the grim indicators of a diminished quality of life for African American males, there are many who believe that technology, and more specifically computers, can be used productively to reach African American men and boys before they become at risk for educational and occupational failure. Whether this can be accomplished is the central focus of this chapter.

In this chapter I report on a research investigation undertaken to describe the context of early computer learning for African American males attending two large urban elementary schools.

PREPARATION OF STUDENTS FOR THE INFORMATION AGE

To determine whether schools are fostering meaningful school-to-work exchanges that reflect our national priorities of having a globally competitive workforce in the Information Age, it becomes important to examine exactly what they are doing in terms of preparation and actual practice in the following areas: the availability of computers to students, actual computer-usage patterns of students, and curriculum- and instruction-development efforts of educators. These areas taken together allow for a glimpse at student computer preparation occuring in our nation's schools. Additionally, this type of specific assessment of schools' role in the promulgation of the efforts to prepare our youth for this ever increasing reality will also allow us to examine the impact that these plans have on African American males.

Access to Computers

Access to computers is a vital link in the process of preparing students for the Information Age. If, as previously mentioned, a principal goal is to involve young students in promoting effective school-to-work exchanges, then their ability to engage in computer instruction is enhanced by access to them. We have come a long way in this area in a relatively short period of time. In 1994, it was reported that 98% of all U.S. public schools had computers available in some form for students (McAdoo, 1994). This statistic includes schools located in both the large urban areas and remote rural settings. Further credence was given to this trend in 1995, when it was reported that the student/computer ratio in schools was 12:1, which is a significant decrease from the 1988–89 figure of 22:1. Those involved in orchestrating the Info Age realize that making the technology available ensures success in implementing their goals. Over the years, a number of programs have occurred to highlight our education-technology priorities. The latest, and most noted, is the presidential involvement through the establishment of NetDay '97. This particular project demonstrates the importance placed on access to students in the nation's schools. NetDay was essentially a national set of activities that had as its goal the wiring of all schools to the Internet. The results of these efforts have culminated in significant increase in student access to the Internet. According to a recent survey conducted by the National Center for Education Statistics (NCES), 65% of U.S. public schools had access to the Internet in fall 1996. This represented a gain of 15 percentage points in each of the past two consecutive years. Whereas 61% of all public elementary schools had Internet access, about three fourths (77%) of secondary schools had this available access.

Student Usage of Computers

Although access is an important step in the student-computer learning process, students' actual usage of the technology is a more adequate guage of computer preparation. Overall, what we know about student usage of computers is that the percentage of students reported using them is up dramatically over previous periods. From a national perspective, the National Center for Education Statistics (1995) reported that in 1993, 68.1%

of all American schoolchildren reported using a computer at school or at home. This figure is nearly double the rate reported in 1984. In 1993, the majority of students reported using a computer at school (59%) with a marginally lower percentage (27.8%) reporting at-home use. An interesting comparison between early-grades usage (Grades 1–6) and that in the upper grades (7–12) reveals striking parallels with our national priorities. A slightly higher percentage of elementary-grade students (69.7%) reported using a computer compared to students in junior high or high school (61.2%). What these data reveal is that computer usage is growing in schools and is directed toward achieving national priorities.

SCHOOL CURRICULUM INTEGRATION OF COMPUTERS

Besides the growing number of students who have access to computers and use them in schools, the way in which educators use them becomes another important link in the overall process. To a great extent, usage of computers by students is directed by teachers. Educators provide the direction and motivational impetus for learning via computers. Provided with the proper computer instruction, students can be motivated to learn and achieve (Becker, 1994). A decade ago, the most pervasive use of computers in schools was as a method of improving students basic skills in math or language (Becker, 1991). Computer-assisted instruction (CAI) became the primary mode of delivering instruction. CAI consisted, loosely, of software programs that aided the instructional process. Most of the CAI software was of the drill-and-practice type. Educators liked the CAI software because it could easily fit into their instructional programs and it took a minimal amount of time for them to learn how to work it. At the secondary level, in addition to CAI, a primary form of instruction consisted of computer programming. As computer usage increased in schools, educators began to reevaluate that usage and ultimately placed computers into at least four roles for schools: (a) as tools of automation (Naron & Estes, 1986); (b) as sources of entertainment (Reed, 1986); (c) as a medium for instruction (Reed, 1986); and (d) as tools of information storage and retrieval (Hannah, 1986). These perspectives on how computers could be used in school settings eventually became practice in how they were actually utilized. Basically today the application of computers in instruction still centers around the third and fourth roles as previously outlined. Most educators who use computers use them primarily as an instructional medium employing CAI software. The big change in this usage is that more instructional software is available for educators to select from and use in their instructional endeavors. With the availability of the Internet and introduction of the World Wide Web, the computer has become a tremendous tool for information storage and retrieval. Progressive educators are using the computer to teach writing skills through word processing and analytical skills through spreadsheets and database programs. With the Internet and World Wide Web, educators are also teaching students valuable search and retrieval skills, web page design and construction, E-mailing and discussion-group etiquette. Essentially, the visions of the Information Age are being realized through effective computer instruction in the schools.

YOUNG AFRICAN AMERICAN MALES AND COMPUTERS

Despite the dismal prognosis for young African American males in society, many believe that computer technology can be utilized to reach them and aid them in becoming productive and contributing members of the new society (Bialo & Sivin, 1989a, 1989b; Casey, 1992; Haile, 1990; Lee, 1986; Merrell, 1991; Pogrow, 1990; Ross, Morrison, Smith, & Cleveland, 1990; Wepner, 1991). Unfortunately, few empirical studies have been conducted on the effectiveness of computers for reaching at-promise African American males. What is known about this issue can be gleaned from the discussion of the educational imperative for using computer technology to reach at-promise learners originally set forth by the National Commission on Excellence in Education (1983). In its landmark report, *A Nation at Risk*, the commission condemned the public system of education for its failure to educate the at-promise student population (of which a large number are African American males). The commission also recommended that computer competence, that is, knowledge and skills in using the computer, should be added to the public school curricula after reading, writing, and arithmetic as the fourth basic skill needed by U.S. students for global competitiveness.

After the issuance of this important report, the first national assessment of computer competence was conducted (Martinez & Mead, 1988). The most striking finding reported was that computer competency appeared significantly related to students' use of and access to computers and to the types and amounts of in-school computer instruction received. These data also demonstrated very striking differences in computer competency based on race and school location (urban, suburban, or rural). Essentially, the findings suggested that African American students were generally less computer competent than Whites.

The differences in computer competency between African American and White American students can be attributed in a large measure to issues of inequity existing in our nation's public school systems. Inequity in students' access to and usage of computers in U.S. schools has been reported by a number of researchers (e.g., Becker, 1991, 1992; Becker & Sterling, 1987; Neuman, 1991). All of these assessments indicate that significant differences exist in in-school computer access and usage based on race. As Becker and Sterling noted in 1987, African American students were less likely to attend schools that had and used computers for instruction, and whose teachers used computers, than were their White student counterparts. Nearly 10 years later, the findings are basically the same (U.S. Department of Education, 1996c) and what is even more alarming is that the inequity exists even in Internet access and usage.

As has been previously stated, roughly 98% of all U.S. public schools have computers; however, this figure is very misleading, especially when we look at computer access for African American school students. For example, it says nothing about how many computers are available in the schools, nor does it describe the types of computer equipment installed. In the case of the large urban schools, which a majority of African American students are likely to attend, the case is that there are far fewer computers per student and the types of computers they have access to are much older and less powerful machines than what is availiable to their White suburban school counterparts. Additionally in the area of computer usage, the NCES document of 1995 reports that student use of computers is on the rise, and it is. However, when we compare African American school students with White students, African American students lag behind White students in computer usage. For example, in elementary schools it is 21 percentage points below that of Whites. Further, in Grades 7–12, African American usage of computers is nearly 17 percentage points below that of Whites. An examination of at-home usage of computers reveals even more disparate patterns. African American elementary school student usage of computers at home is around 9% nationally, yet their usage is nearly 22 percentage points below that of Whites. A similar pattern exists for African American students in grades 7–12 in at-home usage of computers; whereas 11% use them at home, nationally, this figure is still 26 percentage points below that of Whites.

The use and nature of computer interactions experienced by African American students is still vastly different from that of their White peers in outlying urban and suburban schools (McAdoo, 1994). McAdoo suggests that although most African American students have access to computers, they generally receive computer instruction for either isolated skill development and remedial work or for drill-and-practice programs aimed at enhancing basic skills. The disparity between African American and White American students in computer usage and access continues. Key indicators (e.g., home-computer ownership and World Wide Web usage) further demonstrate the difference. In a recent study by Hoffman and Novak, these authors report that whereas 73% of White students own a computer at home only 32% of Black students own a computer. When we examine World Wide Web usage, these data indicate that White students' usage is substantially higher than that of Blacks (66% and 49%, respectively). Thus, despite their having more access to computers today, primarily at school, the picture of computer usage and instruction for African Americans remains bleak, with no substantial changes on the horizon. African American school students face a technological disadvantage in the Information Age, and, based on previously mentioned indicators, young African American males stand to lose out most.

A DESCRIPTIVE STUDY OF COMPUTERS AND YOUNG AFRICAN AMERICAN MALES

As stated earlier, very little research exists on computers and African Americans, especially on the young males. From the literature on computing, three prominent factors have been identified as having a demonstrated effect on learning using computers: (a) the degree of social interaction, or cooperative learning, occurring within a school (DeVillar, 1989; Male, 1993; Vygotsky, 1978; Watson, 1991; Weir, 1992; J. Wilson, 1992); (b) the instructional preparedness of the school curriculum for computer learning (Bruder, 1989a, 1989b; Bullough & Beatty, 1991; Scott, Cole, & Engel, 1990); and (c) the school's computer status (Scott et al., 1990). For the purposes of the present study, these variables together comprise what can be labeled the context of early computer learning. This investigation examines the self-reported responses of a group of African American male urban public school students to questions during structured interviews involving the variables of the study. The study was guided by two major questions:

1. What is the context of early computer learning for African American males in the two schools measured?
2. Does the context of early computer learning for African American males differ by the type of school attended?

Although most of the existent information on this topic is anecdotal, this study provides a rich empirical description of computer usage among this group as well as information on how this usage differs from that of the general population. More important, this study provides insights into the potential viability of African American male involvement in and preparation for the technological innovations of the 21st-century workforce. Finally, the findings of this investigation yield sound educational advice for school officials on which computer practices to maintain or abandon to better enhance African American males' life chances in the Information Age.

The Sample Group

The sample was composed of 16 young African American males who attended two separate elementary schools located in a large, urban, mid-Atlantic-region public school district. Each school's sample consisted of 4 fifth graders and 4 sixth graders. Students were selected to participate in the study by teachers within each school, who were asked by me to choose students whom they felt were typical of African American male students in the district and in their respective classrooms. To select the specific schools for analysis, the researcher relied on school records, visitations to the schools, and school officials' reports of computer activity in the schools. The two schools recruited for this analysis (school A, which shall be referred to as the Midtown School, and school B, the Uptown School) were deemed representative of the range of schools within the district based on available computer resources and activities. The schools also had a range of students who were involved in computer activities.

Hardware in the Schools

At the time of the study, Midtown School housed two computer laboratories. One of these labs held from 10 to 12 IBM PC Junior computers; the other contained from 6 to 8 identical computers, which were exclusively devoted to running Reading-to-Write software for kindergarten and first-grade students. Uptown School, on the other hand, housed three computer labs: one with 12 to 18 IBM XT computers, another with 10 to 15 Macintosh computers, and a third with a mixture of about 10 Apple and Commodore computers. Thus, Midtown School represents the typical school with very limited computer resources, whereas Uptown serves as a good example of schools with more than ample computer resources.

Social Interaction and Computer Usage

For this study, thirteen items were developed to measure some aspect of the social interaction of students while using computers. Items that were included measured the nature and level of social interaction students engaged in. The data clearly indicated that teachers were the most influential persons in these African American males' computer learning experiences. Learning to operate a computer was, for the African American male students in this sample, primarily a teacher-directed experience. This suggests that classroom teachers can serve as catalysts for Black boys' early involvement in the Information Age. However, whereas teachers provided the initial instruction through which the students first came into contact with computer technology, responsibility for following through on computer instruction was later shifted to computer coordinators, who may or may not have been grounded in educational theory and practice. A potential factor that may contribute to a shifting of instructional control from teachers to computer coordinators is the level of knowledge and experience teachers have in the technology.

From a national perspective, the preservice instruction of teachers does not promote familiarity or instructional development with computers (U.S. Department of Education, 1996c; Valde, 1996). Additionally, in-service training programs for teachers in computer use is either scant or nonexistent (Becker, 1992; Hirumi & Grau, 1996). As a result, more teacher training in the use of computer technology is obviously needed. This training should instruct teachers how to incorporate computers into the classroom curriculum and objectives more effectively.

The finding that learning about computers from family members was more common for these students than learning about computers from peers suggests that stronger partnerships should be forged between teachers and the families of their African American male students. Involving a child's family in the learning process can serve as an impetus for learning. More communication between the child's teachers and significant family members will lead to more substantive interactions in the family, thereby reinforcing learning in the home. This notwithstanding, the respondents reported engaging in a reasonable amount of social interaction during those occasions when they had to work cooperatively with their peers on the computer. The high degree of shared computer usage among these students can be partly attributed to the limited resources and access to computers that typically occurs in large urban schools. Despite their schools' lack of computer resources and the respondents' lack of access to those resources, the students in the present study reported positive feelings about the various kinds of social interactions they engaged in while using computers. Their recollections of and appreciation for the computer activities and experiences they shared with others implies that social interaction is a powerful positive factor. This supports the notion that computer technology could be very successful in aiding these students to learn.

Instructional Preparedness and Computer Usage

Seventeen items were developed and used to measure the construct of instructional preparedness. They were developed to capture students' perspectives on how computers are used in the curricular efforts of their schools. They addressed the following aspects:

1. How were computers used in instruction?
2. Who were the primary providers of computer instruction?
3. What knowledge of computers did school personnel have?
4. How did the level of instructional use of computers compare to the level of noninstructional use?
5. How much access to computers did students have after classroom/school use?

Computer instruction was limited in both of the schools involved in this study. Most of the instructional use of computers, which, according to student's reports, occurred on average "about once a week," involved drill-and-practice mathematics instruction. This indicates that teachers or administrators did not routinely consider using the computer as an instructional tool in other subjects, and that more coordination is needed to match the classroom curriculum with meaningful computer experiences for these students. It also signifies, as Wepner (1991) notes, that teachers apparently view the drill-and-practice format as an effective means of instruction for these students. Admittedly, mathematics drill-and-practice software has been found effective in the teaching of basic competencies (Small, 1989). However, using the computer predominantly in this way (that is the general case for African American students in large urban school systems) is not the most productive use of the technology. Indeed, it could actually be a disservice in that it inadequately prepares students for the Information Age. Using the computer as a productivity tool and for problem solving are novel ways in which computers are being used in settings outside the one studied. Different types of software programs, those that engage students from a cognitive perspective and foster more skill development, are desperately needed for African American students, particularly males, who are more often "turned off" to education earlier than are females.

The School's Computer Status

Eight items were developed to get at the students' assessment of their school's computer status. The items pertained to the classroom availability of computers, the existence of computer-based resources in the schools, and students' overall assessment of the schools' computer learning environment. An absence of computers in the classrooms at both schools was apparent. This lack of technology, coupled with a lack of instructional coordination, made spending time on the computer an isolating experience for these students. Emphasizing computing as an out-of-classroom activity with very little relationship to classroom instruction sends the wrong message about the technology to young learners. No real differences were found in the students' assessment of their school's computer programs. Although the students at the more "computer-advantaged" Uptown School had more computers available to them, their assessment of the school's status in this regard basically mirrored those of the students at the less advantaged Midtown School. This finding could be attributed to the comparably poor levels of access to computers and the limited types of software available for students in both schools.

Despite the students' access to computers being quite limited, their considerable knowledge of their schools' computer resources is indicative of high levels of interest in computing. The students were able to provide both reasonably sound assessments of the status of their schools' computer resources and tangible suggestions for improving those resources. The desire for more computers and software and for greater opportunity for access to computers were recurring themes among these students. The finding that a number of the respondents believed that their schools were disadvantaged in these areas when compared with other schools in the district further strengthens the notion that these students were keenly interested in computers. In these students' eyes, neither school was ideal in terms of its readiness for computing. One can only wonder what would happen if their school-based computer environments were enhanced to match their curiosity.

It is widely recognized that dynamic teacher involvement, liberal access to computers, and exposure to challenging software can considerably improve the computer experiences of African American boys who attend schools in large urban areas (Becker, 1991, 1992; Lee, 1986). The implementation of plans that operationalize all of these elements is crucial. In the absence of such efforts, these students will truly be left behind and in danger of failure as the nation moves into the 21st century and the burgeoning Information Age.

Differences Between Schools

Student scores within the three major research constructs (social interaction, instructional preparedness, and the school's computer status) were summed and compared. Data from a means comparison suggest that, on average, students from Uptown School (the high-computer-activity school) reported slightly higher levels of social interaction and instructional preparedness at their school than did students from Midtown School. Regarding the school computer status variable, however, the pattern was reversed: On average, students from Midtown believed that their school was more prepared for computing than did their Uptown counterparts. A key to understanding the differences in scores for this latter variable can be found by examining the variation in student scores within the schools. The mean and variation within scores of Midtown's students were significantly higher and varied a lot more than the mean value for the Uptown students.

Despite the higher response levels of the Uptown students on the social interaction and instructional preparedness variables and of the Midtown students on the school computer status variable, a series of Kruskal-Wallis one-way analyses of variance were employed to determine if any statistical significant existed in these data. Data from this analysis suggest that no real differences exist among the African American males in the two schools with regard to the levels of social interactions that occurred and the students' impressions of how computers were used in instruction at the two schools. However, a significant difference was found between the students' responses to the school computer status construct. The scores for students at the Midtown and Uptown schools were significantly different. In essence, the findings imply that even though more resources were available to them, the African American male students at Uptown School did not believe that their school was living up to its full computing potential. Indeed, they believed that much more needed to be done to alleviate their situation.

IMPLICATIONS AND RECOMMENDATIONS

Obviously, in an information age, those who know what information is available and how to use it will reap tremendous benefits. The technology base of this era, computer technology, is transforming the lives of us all. Technologically competent and computer-literate individuals stand to become the productive citizens of the future. Demographic shifts in the United States will necessitate the nation's greater reliance on minorities to constitute the workforce of the coming century. Census data suggest that by the year 2000, one third of the nation and 29% of the new entrants into the workforce will be members of a group presently called "minority" (Johnston & Packer, 1987; U.S. Department of Labor, 1996). Although these demographics should point to expanding opportunities for minorities, the disappointing reality is that significant numbers of them, particularly large numbers of African American males, will not be able to participate substantially in this employment explosion.

On all fronts, opportunities are dwindling for young African American males as they are systematically being placed at risk for failure in the Information Age. Without adequate support systems, including but not limited to parental involvement in schooling efforts, more equitable expenditures for schools serving African American students, and new and expanding curriculum endeavors aimed at enhancing these students' computer competencies—this age may see the total disappearance of African American males from the technology-driven workforce. Parents, educators, and other concerned persons will have to work increasingly hard to ensure a technology-rich future for African American males. More thought and coordinated, dedicated effort must be given to transforming the home and school environments of young African American males into environments that provide them with a wealth of knowledge about computers and the role and importance of computers in society.

FOR TEACHERS AND PARENTS

1. Formalize teaching and learning strategies that take advantage of the powerful social interaction triad that exists between teachers, family members, and peers.
2. Explore ways to use computer games as instructional aids to direct student learning and coordinate successful interactions with peers and family members. Apparently, computer games spark some of the initial social interaction engaged in by African American male students. This is not surprising, given that computer gaming is considered a male-dominated activity.
3. Expose African American male students to experiences with computer-based technology that is more meaningful than that offered by drill-and-practice mathematics instruction. Though this form of computer-assisted instruction can be useful in some instances, the use of computers as productivity and problem-solving tools with applications across the school curriculum should be investigated.
4. Communicate more deeply with African American male students to get feedback on their likes, dislikes, and ideas for improvement regarding computer activities. Reaching African American males at the middle school/junior high school ages and grade levels, when most are still impressionable and eager to learn and use the technology, is crucial.

FOR SCHOOL ADMINISTRATORS

1. Provide teachers with additional and ongoing in-service training in the use of computers so that they can better direct and maintain African American male students' interest in and learning of computers. This training should promote effective ways for teachers to engage these students in computer use from a cognitive perspective and help them use computers as productivity and problem-solving tools. Provide additional training on how to integrate classroom instruction and the computer-lab experience.
2. Empower teachers to become computer literate by strategically placing computers in their classrooms.
3. Develop a reasonable and ever evolving knowledge of computers and their uses in education computer technology.
4. Conduct formative evaluations of teacher-based plans and actions for computer instruction to ensure that positive, relevant computer activity is occurring.
5. To continually spark African American male students' motivation and learning, ensure that school computer resources keep up with changes in the technology and that opportunities for access to computers keep up with students' needs.

3

The Social Construction of High-Incidence Disabilities: The Effect on African American Males

Beth Harry and Mary G. Anderson

WE WILL BEGIN THIS CHAPTER with an anecdote experienced by the first author. Early in my career as an assistant professor of special education, I had the occasion to engage in a heated discussion with two colleagues regarding the impact of racial stereotypes on teachers' perceptions of African American males' behavior. The debate was sparked by one colleague's report of a teacher who had been offended by a young African American boy's walking into the classroom in what she described as a "pimp roll." It appears that the teacher interpreted the student's rhythmic swaggering as an affront to her—an attempt, perhaps, to intimidate her or to challenge her authority. The student was in elementary school.

The discussion that ensued focused on whether the teacher would have been similarly offended by a student who entered the classroom turning cartwheels, or by a pair of young sweethearts who entered the room with their arms around each other. We concluded that it would be likely that the teacher would, indeed, find these behaviors inappropriate for the classroom, and might indicate to the students that they should reserve them for the playground or other social situations. I argued that a teacher who objected to a swaggering walk in the classroom would be entitled to advise the student in a similar vein, but ought not to find the behavior personally offensive. Further, I argued that this teacher's reaction reflected underlying racist attitudes towards African American males, in particular, stereotypi-

African American Males in School and Society: Practices and Policies for Effective Education. Copyright © 1999 by Teachers College, Columbia University. All rights reserved. ISBN 0-8077-3870-0 (pbk), ISBN 0-8077-3871-9 (cloth). Prior to photocopying items for classroom use, please contact the Copyright Clearance Center, Customer Service, 222 Rosewood Dr., Danvers, MA 01923, USA, tel. (508) 750-8400.

cal fears of White America regarding Black male sexuality. The word "racist" was met with vociferous objection, and I found myself having to defend what seemed to me to be a perfectly obvious explanation.

The foregoing anecdote points to the issue of individual teacher judgment in the interpretation of students' behaviors. This chapter is concerned with applying this principle to a nationwide phenomenon—the disproportionately high placement of African American males in special education programs. Because the large body of literature addressing this topic has tended to focus mostly on the assessment process, in this chapter we will take a somewhat different approach. We will pursue two main concerns: First, an understanding of how the process of social construction of the high-incidence disabilities works against African American males; and, second, a consideration of ways in which instruction in regular education programs can build on the strengths of African American males, rather than an interpretation of cultural and learning differences as deficits. Before we turn to our larger concerns, however, the meaning and extent of disproportionate placement must be made clear.

THE MEANING AND EXTENT OF DISPROPORTIONATE PLACEMENT

Disproportionate placement of a group of students in any educational program means that those students are represented in the program in a significantly greater percentage than their percentage in the school population as a whole. For more than 2 decades, the U.S. Department of Education, through its Office for Civil Rights, conducted biannual surveys of the relative percentages of White versus minority students in a variety of categories and programs, including special education programs, programs for gifted and talented students, and students suspended, expelled, and given corporal punishment. To assess whether disproportion should be considered significant, Chinn and Hughes (1987) have suggested that we offer a leeway of plus or minus 10% of the percentage that would be expected. Thus, if African Americans account for 16% of the school-age population, we would expect them to account for 16%, plus or minus 1.6%, of special education programs (i.e., a range from 14.4% to 17.6% would be acceptable). In the case of African American students, disproportionate placement in most disability categories is way beyond those parameters. In 1986, 1990, and 1992, African American students were placed in programs for those named Educable Mentally Retarded (EMR) at a rate at least twice that which would be expected, and in programs for students labeled Trainable Mentally Retarded (TMR) and Seriously Emotionally Disturbed (SED) at roughly one and a half times the expected rate. Only the Speech Impairment (SI) and Specific Learning Disability (SLD) categories show reasonably proportionate placement.

When gender is taken into account, it becomes clear that the pattern of disproportionate placement is more extreme for African American males than the aggregate percentages indicate. Additionally, corporal punishment is applied to African American males almost three and a half times as frequently as would be expected and suspension almost three times as frequently.

These patterns are by no means new. Historically, it was the EMR category that was identified as the problematic category for disproportionality (Artiles & Trent, 1994). There is a history of litigation that points to the use of this category as a means of effecting racial segregation after the *Brown* decision in 1954 (see *Prasse & Reschly*, 1986; *Johnson v. San Francisco Unified School District*, 1974). The effects of psychological testing on inappropriate placement was brought to nationwide attention in the case of *Larry P. et al., v. Riles*, and resulted in the 1979 Supreme Court decision that the testing process reflected an "unlawful segregative intent" (Dent, Mendocal, Pierce, & West, 1991). The judge in the case banned the further use of IQ tests for the placement of African American students in special education programs, and ordered the reevaluation of students already placed in special education programs.

In 1982, a National Academy of Sciences panel (Heller, Holtzman, & Messick, 1982) was charged with a detailed study of the phenomenon of overrepresentation in the EMR category. The findings indicated three important trends:

1. African American students were overrepresented in EMR programs nationwide. Overrepresentation of other minorities varied significantly by state, and was more likely to occur as the percentage of the group in a school population increased.
2. The larger the size of the EMR program in a district, the more disproportionate was the placement of minority groups in that program.
3. Districts with larger numbers of students from low socioeconomic levels displayed greater disproportion.

Further, the panel premised its report on a discussion of the essential question of this phenomenon: Is disproportionate placement of a minority group in special education programs a problem and if so, why? This question must be addressed directly, since there are many who would assume that such placement is not a problem because the students have special needs that are being met by these programs.

IS DISPROPORTIONATE PLACEMENT A PROBLEM? IF SO, WHY?

The National Academy of Sciences panel (Heller et al., 1982) identified this as the central question in the debate on disproportionate placement. The panel concluded that the phenomenon must be seen as problematic if the circumstances under which it occurs are unfair to students. They offered a formula for analysis that, in effect, implicated the entire educational process, as follows:

> Two key issues are at the heart of the debate about disproportion. First, disproportion is a problem when children are invalidly assessed for placement in programs for educable mentally retarded children. Second, disproportion is a problem when children receive low-quality instruction. This problem may arise in the regular classroom, where opportunities for academic success may be restricted, or in the special education classroom, where a child's educational progress may falter due to lowered or inappropriate expectations and goals. (p. xi)

This approach allows us to see that special education placement is not only a matter of biased assessment, which, in the wake of the *Larry P.* (1979) decision, formed the centerpiece of the debate surrounding disproportion. The point that Heller et al. (1982) made is that a child whose educational needs are not met in regular education is at increased risk of being referred to special education. If the assessment tools are biased in terms of cultural or linguistic content, the child is at a further disadvantage; and finally, if the child is placed in a special education program where the instruction is inadequate to meet his or her needs, the cycle of discriminatory practice is complete.

In addition to the foregoing concerns, there is the critical question of the validity of the disability categories upon which the placement process is based. If the categories themselves are not valid, then the entire process must be suspect. In the remainder of the chapter we will examine, first, the ways in which high-incidence "disabilities" are constructed, and then the question of how the deficit model that leads to "disability" can be relinquished.

THE SOCIAL CONSTRUCTION OF DISABILITY AND ITS IMPLICATIONS FOR AFRICAN AMERICAN MALES

The debate over the validity of disability categories is not new. More than 2 decades ago, Mercer (1973) distinguished between disabilities that have a physiological basis and are, therefore, "culture blind," and those that are determined by the developmental and behavioral norms of a given society. Mercer referred to the former as the pathological model of disability, and to the latter as the "statistical" model, whereby abnormality is defined "according to the extent to which the individual varies from the average of the population on a particular trait" (p. 4). Thus, the controversy over disproportionate placement is mainly concerned with students designated as having disabilities in what are commonly referred to as the "judgment" categories. The most controversial and persistent of these has been Educable Mental Retardation (EMR). Serious Emotional Disturbance (SED) has also shown consistently high rates of placement for African Americans, and it is only the Severe Learning Disability (SLD) and Speech Impairment (SI) categories that do not show this trend in nationwide figures. We will now turn to the implications of the notion of social construction for the EMR and SED categories in particular.

Educable Mental Retardation and Specific Learning Disability

The fact that the high-incidence categories of disability are socially constructed is made indisputably clear by the history of definitional changes to the construct of mental retardation. Until 1973, the American Association on Mental Retardation (AAMR, or the then American Association on Mental Deficiency, AAMD) identified an IQ score of 85 as the cutoff point for mental retardation. In 1973, the AAMD's change of the criterion to an IQ score of 70 immediately declassified thousands of individuals and returned them to the "normal" population.

Another clear illustration of the arbitrary nature of these disabilities is the well-documented "categorical drift" (Ysseldyke, Algozzine, & Thurlow, 1992) away from usage of the EMR classification and toward greater reliance on the SLD category. The U.S. Department of Education's (US-DOE) *Fifteenth Annual Report to Congress* (1993) reported that between 1992 and 1997 the number of students classified as EMR was reduced by approximately half, while the number in the SLD category doubled. This pattern requires close examination in order to see how it relates to African American males.

Although we are not aware of any summary figures revealing the extent to which the categorical drift from EMR to SLD differs among ethnic groups, an examination of the OCR figures for 1986 and 1994 suggests that the drift applies more to White and, possibly, Hispanic students than to African American and Native American students. (The figures on Hispanic students are difficult to interpret because of the existence of competing programs such as bilingual education, which can absorb many students who might otherwise be designated as needing special education services.)

This is reminiscent of Sleeter's (1986) observation that in the first 10 years of the SLD category's existence, the population so designated was "overwhelmingly white and middle class" (p. 50). Why should this be?

First, it is well acknowledged that the EMR category represents the more stigmatized "disability," since it suggests an overall and pervasive developmental deficit. Learning Disability, or LD, by contrast, refers to deficits in specific areas that do not necessarily affect an individual's overall functioning. White, middle-class parents are more likely to have the social influence needed for an effective lobby in favor of the more acceptable category.

There are two other very important explanations, however, both of which have to do with the way SLD is defined (Collins & Camblin, 1983). One aspect is the discrepancy criterion—that students should score in the normal range on IQ tests, but show a significant discrepancy between measures of IQ and measures of academic achievement. That is, the student's academic achievement must be significantly lower than would be expected by an average score on an IQ test. This reduces the likelihood of African American students being considered eligible, since this group is known to score considerably lower on IQ tests than do White children (Samuda & Kong, 1989). Another discriminatory aspect of the definition of SLD is the exclusionary clause, which requires that students' difficulties should not be explainable by environmental disadvantage. This means that students are likely to be excluded from SLD eligibility if their home environments are thought to be detrimental to school achievement. The reasoning underlying this formulation is the presumption that SLD represents a deficit of cognitive processing that is intrinsic to the individual, not created by detrimental circumstances. So students whose learning difficulties are thought to be caused by circumstances do not qualify to be considered as having a disability. The ironic aspect of this is that although it would be seen as preferable not to have a disability, for many students exclusion from the SLD category means exclusion from specialized services or may mean classification in the more stigmatized mental retardation category.

The Speech Impairment (SI) category has not received much attention in the controversy over disproportionality since African American students are underrepresented in this category. However, it seems likely that the mild stigmatization attached to this "disability" might also account for its greater assignment to White students.

Serious Emotional Disturbance

Despite the ongoing controversy over EMR, the socially constructed nature of the judgment categories is nowhere so dangerous as in the SED category. Once more, this charge is not new. In the case of *Lora v. Board of Education of New York* (1975), the court ruled in favor of plaintiffs who charged that African American and Hispanic students were being inappropriately placed in segregated facilities for students with emotional disturbance. After more than 2 decades, this situation is readily evident in numerous school districts around the country and is reflected in the OCR figures. We will discuss six reasons why the SED category is dangerous.

The Interpretation of Observable Behaviors

First, any student can be identified as SED. The SED disability classification, like constructs of IQ, normalcy, and disability, are the result of social invention. Socially sanctioned authorities determine the social conditions by which they decide when observable student behaviors are important and problematic. Within the situational constraints of "regular" classroom interactions, students who act or talk in ways that violate adult expectations for behaving are often judged disabled and unable to benefit from general classroom instruction. The fact that there are no standardized measures for determining the presence of emotional disturbance means that an inherently subjective process is left entirely up to individual teacher judgment (Anderson, 1994; Kauffman & Hallahan, 1981).

The low expectations held for African American children is evidenced by the fact that regular educators increasingly identify African American children at the elementary level as difficult to teach (USDOE, 1992). African American learners comprise 16% of the total student population, but 27% of the total SED population, with more than three fourths (76.4%) of them male (USDOE, Office of Civil Rights (OCR), 1993). Research reveals that there has been more than a 48% increase in SED placements since 1977, with a recent increase of more than 9,000 students (2.6%) between 1990–1991 and 1991–1992 alone (USDOE, 1993a). Unfortunately, a common professional assumption is that a disability label, such as SED, "carries with it an expectation of misbehavior and lower academic performance" (Kauffman, 1994, p. 239). According to the USDOE's (1992) *Fourteenth Annual Report to Congress*, "School professionals are more likely to refer and place minority and poor children in special education because of lower expectations regarding the educability of these children" (p. 15).

It is critical to recognize that the SED or Behavior Disordered (BD) terminology describes adult interpretations or impressions of observable student behaviors, "rather than presumed underlying mental pathologies" (Kauffman & Hallahan, 1981, p. 165). The SED classification itself depends significantly upon the moods of those who perceive the behavior as disordered (Rothwell, 1982), rather than upon professional concerns related to cognitive deficits, academic failure, superior ability, or sensory or physical differences (Anderson, 1994; Ditton, 1979; Kauffman, 1994).

Consequently, the federal categorical definition of SED is not clear or comprehensive enough to "determine appropriate eligibility in this category" (Forness & Knitzer, 1990, p. 4). Nevertheless, student behavioral violations are presumed to evidence inherent child deficits or disability. To date, by the time children reach the third grade, the expectations and judgments of regular education teachers frequently result in disproportionate numbers of African American male children being identified SED (USDOE, 1990, 1992, 1994, 1996a). Anderson (1992) has argued that, in large measure, without professional identifications of students and their behaviors as problematic, and therefore deficient, there would be no disability.

Educational Placement of Students Labeled SED

Second, once students are classified as SED, their educational placement is most frequently separate and restrictive. Under Part B, Subchapter II of the Individuals With Disabilities Education Act (IDEA), teaching personnel who serve children and youth with identified disabilities must be prepared to meet the goal of full educational opportunity for them by maximizing the extent to which "educationally disabled students" are educated with students who are not disabled, assuring the right to a free and appropriate public education in the least restrictive environment. However, according to the USDOE's (1996a) *Eighteenth Annual Report to Congress*, 67% of the students labeled SED and living in inner-city districts and 42% of those living in non-inner-city districts are removed from students in regular classes and placed in full-time, separate, and restrictive special education schools and classes. To a large degree, their disproportionate numbers suggest a national perception that separate and restrictive learning environments are "appropriate" educational placements for many Black boys. Despite the numerous descriptions of a continuum of specialized services available to labeled students to enable them to benefit from special education, few students labeled SED ever "qualify" for educational experiences with their nonlabeled peers. Currently, the segregation of these students under the guise of compliance with the mandate of "appropriate placement" continues to result in less than a 10% rate of declassification or return to mainstream or inclusive settings, and in extensive school failure and high drop-out rates (National Mental Health Association 1993; USDOE, 1996a; Wald, 1996; Walker, Singer, Palfrey, Orza, Wenger, & Butler, 1988).

Curricula for Students Labeled SED

Third, "appropriate" educational intervention for students labeled SED primarily comprises social-skills training curricula that are commonly added on to teacher-controlled, behavior management programs (Anderson, 1992; Hollinger, 1987; Johnson, 1990). These interventions are designed to "treat" identified surface-communication behaviors by directly teaching prosocial behaviors. Students are either rewarded for demonstrating these behaviors or punished for noncompliance (Anderson & Webb-Johnson, 1995; Newman, 1981; Safran & Safran, 1985). They are deliberately geared to give direct control of decision making and role definition to the teacher in face-to-face communication interactions (Elias, 1989; Robinson, 1972). Students labeled SED find that they are not able to order their social relationships or build academic or vocational competencies in their own ways. They are not able to operate from positions that reflect themselves as authentic sources of their own control. Students, then, are not exposed to normative patterns of personal interaction and learning opportunities that exist in regular education and society as a whole. As a result, student-determined negotiations and collaborations during the learning process are often forbidden (Johnson & O'Neil, 1984; Rath, Wassermann, Jonas, & Rothstein, 1986).

The point made here is that schools need to recognize that Black males, like their peers from other groups, already have a repertoire of "prosocial" behaviors; the fact that these interactions may look different from mainstream, middle-class social skills does not mean that they should be rejected. Rather, teachers need to acknowledge and value the authentic cultural style already mastered by Black youth, building on it rather than trying to replace it.

Nationally, although the effectiveness of these behaviorally driven, externally controlled programs, as compared to more inclusive regular-class placements, has not been demonstrated (Epstein, Foley, & Cullinan, 1992; Knitzer, Steinberg, & Fleish, 1990), SED instruction continues to overemphasize behavior-control strategies at the expense of academic enrichment. Ironically, the lack of attention to academic enrichment is in compliance with the 1982 U.S. Supreme Court decision on *Rowley v. Board of Education of Hendrick Hudson Central School District*. The Court found that appropriate education in special education programs does not require the maximizing of educational potential. This ruling sanctions the lack of special educator responsibility to provide opportunities for academic enrichment or to maximize achievement.

Discipline of SED Students as a Preparation for Punitive Environments

Fourth, students in such programs are being well prepared to be on the receiving end of a punitive justice system. In schools, the main procedural response for controlling and changing "inappropriate" or unwanted behavior is discipline (Baron, 1992; U.S. Department of Justice, 1995). Discipline is primarily understood to mean punishment, which is intentionally used to decrease the probability of occurrence of unwanted behaviors in order to maintain social or situational controls. Communication behaviors such as name-calling, teasing, verbalizing anger (including using threatening words, talking back, or displaying threatening postures) are punishable offenses (Brantlinger, 1991; Rosell, 1986; Rubenstein & Rezmierski, 1983). Further, talking without permission (Costenbader & Reading-Brown, 1995), truancy, tardiness, skipping class, smoking, or fighting—ranging from a slight push to an incident involving a weapon (Brantlinger, 1991)—are also punishable as school-rule infractions.

In large measure, schools' responses to behavioral infractions overwhelmingly result in the excessive punishment of Black males, regardless of labels (Anderson, 1997). To date, African American males are at greater risk of receiving suspension and corporal punishment than any other student population (USDOE, Office for Civil Rights, 1987, 1993). This pattern was illustrated by a study of nine schools in a south Florida school district (McFadden, Marsh, Price, & Hwang, 1992), which found that African American students received a disproportionately high rate of these disciplinary actions and a lower rate of in-school suspension than did their White counterparts. The schools' records did not indicate a pattern of more severe infractions of rules or of criminal-type behavior on the part of the African American students so disciplined.

According to the Commission for Positive Change in the Oakland Public Schools (1992), in 1990–1991, African Americans were suspended three times as frequently as all other students combined. African American males accounted for only 28% of the total student enrollment, but 53% of all suspended students. Males were 2.5 times more likely to be suspended than females. Nationally, African American males comprise 31% of all corporal punishment cases (Quality Education for Minorities Project, 1990). Among confined juveniles in punitive social institutions, the greatest increase between 1987 and 1991 in "minority" populations was among Blacks, rising from 37% to 44% incarceration (Office of Juvenile Justice and Delinquency Prevention, 1994).

The social and academic consequences of school punishment continue to be characterized by high rates of absenteeism, peer and adult rejection, poor academic performance, and increased administrative punitive actions (Kortering, Haring, & Klockars, 1992; Steinberg, Mounts, Lanborn, & Dornbusch, 1990; USDOE, 1992). Students often report that the school-related punishments they received (i.e., classroom penalties, office interventions, suspensions, expulsions, court actions) significantly contributed to their inability to get along with teachers and to their decisions to leave school beginning in the 10th grade (Brantlinger, 1991; Kortering, Haring, & Klockars, 1992). Drop-out rates among students identified as SED exceed that of students in the EMR or SLD categories (37.2%, 21.6%, and 22.2%, respectively).

Additionally, Anderson (1997) proposes that fundamental and synonymous relationships exist between school discipline and prison punishment. She points out that many of the behaviors punishable in schools are congruent with punishable offenses in America's prisons. She further states that the control of student behavior through involuntary separation, confinement, and physical force (including time out, in-school suspension, physical restraints, and corporal punishment), are synonymous with the intentions, actions, and effects of imposed prison punishment controls. The placement of students in SED classrooms is characterized by a number of calculated limitations and restrictions that students cannot evaluate, examine, or reject (Robinson, 1980). Students labeled SED are given little control over with whom they interact during the school day and can neither initiate contact nor escape undesired ones. Such restrictions of social-role control are disconcerting, particularly since they mimic specific prison controls such as loss of privacy, loss of power and prestige, and restrictions of movement" (Lightfoot, 1973, p. 226).

Anderson identifies the synonymous relationships between school discipline, SED placements, and prison punishment, and their impact on the quality of life experienced by disproportionate numbers of Black boys and men, as the result of a socially sanctioned, traditional perception that those punished are, like slaves, "subjugated for their own benefit" (Harris, 1992, p. 194), as well as being for the benefit of the desired social order. Her argument is that educational disciplinary actions teach fundamental prison messages of learned powerlessness—commonly named compliance and often misnamed self-control. Teaching students to take individually determined responsibility for their own thinking and behaving is counter to the disciplinary purposes and actions that give authorities external control over observable student conduct. Even in school settings, Anderson concludes, where educators are proponents of popular theories of child centered education, the message of discipline is one of powerlessness and external control.

The Impact of Unqualified Instructional Personnel

Fifth, there is the fact that teacher shortages have resulted in the widespread use of unqualified personnel, substitute teachers, and paraprofessionals. Data from a number of sources evidence a national shortage of teachers qualified to work with students labeled SED (e.g., National Mental Health Association, 1993; USDOE, 1992, 1993b). National special education vacancy rates that reflect an 8.25% increase for all students identified as disabled but a 12.91% increase for students labeled SED continue to exacerbate the teacher shortage (USDOE, 1992). Data from the *Seventeenth Annual Report to Congress* (USDOE, 1994) indicate that approximately 25,829 special education professionals were needed to fill the positions currently held by uncertified individuals.

Further, even though many practicing teachers are untrained and uncertified, they remain legally mandated to participate in the referral, assessment, classification, and treatment components of due process. Unfortunately, inadequately prepared special and regular educators are "more susceptible to problems related to behavior than those associated with other child characteristics" (Ysseldyke & Algozzine, 1981, p. 434). Nevertheless, when untrained teachers make written references regarding a student's communication behaviors, and identify those behaviors as problematic, their references have the same powerful influence on the nature and outcome of the classification decision as do those of trained professionals (Harber, 1981; Myles & Simpson, 1989; Wolman, Thurow, & Bruininks, 1989; Ysseldyke & Algozzine, 1981). Additionally, after classification decisions are made, few if any interpersonal-communication goals are ever written into the Individual Education Plans (IEPs) (Smith & Simpson, 1989), or integrated into subject-area content considerations (McLaughlin, M. W., & Talbert, 1990).

Thus, the effects of knowledge and skill deficiencies among even a small number of inadequately trained teachers is severe. African American learners labeled SED, as well as their nonlabeled peers identified as presenting problematic behaviors in school, are in danger of having unqualified teachers, inappropriate curricula and teaching methodologies, and ineffective or alienating communication interactions. The overall quality of instruction received is undoubtedly inferior.

The Student-Teacher Ethnic Disparity

Finally, the foregoing patterns are exacerbated by the tremendous disparity between the ethnicity of the majority of students labeled SED and the school personnel who interact with them. Stevens (1981) found that referral, assessment, and placement decisions of teachers and school psychologists were influenced by both the perceived ethnicity and socioeconomic status of the students. McIntyre and Pernell (1985) reported that "teachers tend to recommend students for special education placement who are racially dissimilar from themselves" (p. 112). These authors also proposed that the overrepresentation of Black males in special education classes is primarily due to the fact that most of the teachers in public schools are White, and "White teachers referred students five times more often than did minority teachers from other racial groups" (pp. 112–113). Data compiled by the National Center for Educational Statistics (NCES) (Choy, Henke, Alt, Medrich, & Bobbitt, 1993), regarding the 1990–1991 ethnic distribution of teachers to students in all U.S. educational environments, indicated that "13.5% of the U.S. teaching force was composed of people of color, whereas 31.4% of all students represented diverse populations" (p. 1). The disparity between the ethnic representation of educators and that of students reflects a critical-need area of teaching supply and demand, especially in view of the projection that by the turn of the century, the teaching workforce will be overwhelmingly White and female (Hawkins, 1994). The ethnic demographic characteristics of special education teaching professionals are similar to those of general education teaching professionals. According to Cook and Boe (1995), 86% of special education teachers and 87% of general education teachers are White.

THE RESURRECTION OF THE "CULTURAL DEFICIT" ARGUMENT

In the foregoing sections we argue that cultural biases, biased assessment procedures, and ambiguous or biased criteria for eligibility all play a central role in the designation of students as "disabled." One crucial premise of these arguments is that cultural difference must not be interpreted as cultural deficit—as has been the case in historical interpretations of African American cultural traditions. This distinction between difference and deficit is now well known, yet we are alarmed at the way in which this notion can be distorted to reinforce negative stereotypes about specific cultural groups.

We refer specifically to the recent introduction of the McIntyre Assessment of Cultures (MAC) behavior checklist, which offers a 1990's mechanism for identifying the cultural/ethnic bases of negative school behaviors (Anderson & Webb-Johnson, 1995). McIntyre (1995) uses the literature on cultural traditions as a base for listing 103 discrete student behaviors purported to be typical of certain ethnic groups. McIntyre argues that many of the behaviors commonly understood to evidence educational disability, particularly SED, can now be attributed to the learned values and expectations of the "nondominant" cultural traditions that children bring to school with them. He asserts that the MAC should be used as a "resource" for assisting "school-based teams" in distinguishing between school behaviors that are culturally based from those evidencing educational disability.

To give a few examples: The MAC specifies that "cheating on tests" is a behavior commonly found among Hispanic and American Indian children. McIntyre argues that this pattern results from those groups' traditions of sharing and group identity, and implies that, since the children cannot distinguish between the two behaviors, cheating should be interpreted as a culturally normative activity for such children. An example given for African American students is that they are often "disrespectful or rude towards the teacher," a trait that McIntyre explains by the historically induced oppositional feelings of Black students and their not wanting to "act White." Meanwhile, McIntyre also identifies this item as characteristic of White students, but in this case attributes it to Whites' child-rearing practices, which encourage a sense of being "equal to all and inferior to none," "informality in interaction," and "an autonomous, independent, individualistic, questioning, personality" and which teaches children to "resolve problems and issues by themselves and believe that teachers are fallible" (p. 31). McIntyre's repeated explanation that the negatives in Black students' behavior relate to "past societal abuses" in no way mitigates the overall negative effect of this cataloging of supposedly cultural behaviors. Indeed, it is easy to see that when rudeness and disrespect are attributable to autonomy and high self-esteem, they do not seem so disrespectful, but when they are attributable to oppositional angry feelings, they remain threatening.

The effects of this systematic itemization of discrete behaviors is more than evident to any casual reader. First, it is a prime example of stereotypical thinking, which encourages school personnel to turn to a cookbook of ethnic indicators rather than try to understand the dynamics of particular social circumstances that lead students to behave in certain ways and that lead teachers to interpret those behaviors according to their own preconceptions. Indeed, this approach simply offers another set of preconceptions on which to base one's judgments. Most insidious are the many items in the checklist that are based on research that, when taken out of context and presented in this stereotypical way, damns the very groups for which that literature was advocating. Most overtly objectionable are those items that have no basis whatever in fact or research, such as the statement that African American students typically have difficulties in mathematics because "the structure of Black English Dialect may interfere with the acquisition of mathematics concepts" (p. 45). The most superficial understanding of linguistics would lead to rejection of such a notion.

Second, the instrument vastly oversimplifies the complexity of concepts such as "group identity" or "traditions of sharing" and, as in the case of "cheating," underestimates children's ability to differentiate between requirements for working together and working individually. Further, since behaviors such as cheating are still unacceptable according to school values, to assume that a preference for sharing knowledge will lead to cheating is almost certain to encourage a devaluing of the sharing tradition in the mind of the person who judges that the child is cheating. Using a model such as this, it is hard to escape the implication that certain cultural traditions result in negative behaviors. In essence, this kind of instrument simply replaces the idea of individual pathology with one of cultural/ethnic group pathology.

Finally, McIntyre's ethnic pathology perspective, like the legally mandated individual pathology perspective, neglects to attend to the deficiencies of school cultures, including the contributions of teacher interactions to perceptions of unwanted student behaviors. Our overriding concern with the MAC itself is its failure to address the real-life cultures of schools, the significant influence and effect that people cocreating classroom cultures have on one another, and the magnitude of effort involved in changing what actually happens to children in schools so that children can benefit from and contribute to their own successful educational outcomes. We assert that the MAC has the potential to be a formidable barrier to authentic and effective school reform and to student success.

We conclude this section with a comment about assessment in general: Although the IDEA and Section 504 of the Rehabilitation Act both acknowledge the discriminatory effects of assessment instruments and practices, they require the use of tests to "test" children before making decisions about disability placement and services. Indeed, this pairing of the federal acknowledgment of bias with the legal mandate to use tests presents one of the central paradoxes of the law. Both the acknowledgment and the mandate are treated as if "the contradictions between them don't exist" (Anderson, 1994, p. 97).

We do not deny that a distressingly large proportion of African American males are experiencing serious difficulties in schools. We do, however, reject the notion that the explanation for this lies in learning, behavioral, or developmental deficits intrinsic to the majority of these students. We reject also the notion that treating these students as if they were disabled represents a solution. As have many others, we argue that the key to making school a successful experience for African American males is in identifying and building on their strengths. If schools would place as much emphasis on identifying the cultural competencies and strengths of African American males as they do on identifying their deficits, a totally different picture would emerge.

The Goals 2000 Act states that all children will be "ready to learn." This statement belies the real issue—that children mostly are ready to learn, and that the challenge is for teachers to figure out what it is that the children are ready for and to begin there, rather than comparing children to models of expected school readiness that may be nonexistent for many students. Without such understanding, students' behavioral and learning differences are all too readily seen as deficits to be remediated, rather than as strengths to be built on. The cycle that ends in inappropriate assessment and special education placement begins early. In this section we are concerned with the question, What needs to be done differently in regular education to diminish the likelihood of failure and eventual special education referral?

CONCLUSION

In sum, the continuing overrepresentation of African American students offers yet another example of the long-lasting effects of centuries of oppression and racism. To believe that African American males are disproportionately more "disabled" than the rest of the population is counterintuitive and is too easily refuted by competing explanations. To attempt to "solve" the problem by labeling, segregation, and punishment is simply to perpetuate it.

Differentiation from the norm is the reality, not a problem. Because learners are different and perform differently, professionals must integrate these differences into the design of educational process and evaluation if they seek to avoid reproducing the biases and inaccuracies inherent in traditional teaching-learning understandings and approaches. If a beneficial connection is to exist between educational purpose, process, and outcomes for African American learners, then professionals must make a commitment to understanding the meaning of the entire context of the educational experiences of these children. Pointing to individual pathology, or to culturally based features that present as "deficits" in school, represents efforts to deal with the challenge by pigeonholing and stereotyping. Direct and explicit professional efforts toward providing greater opportunities for success among African American learners, paired with an emphasis on self-determined consensus, rather than traditional dictates of social compliance, are a necessity.

Our concluding recommendations are simple and reflect the main points that we have argued in this chapter:

1. Assessment of students should be criterion referenced rather than standardized, using individual student baseline data.
2. School systems should develop means of monitoring teachers' motives

and feelings toward and perceptions of African American males so that biased teacher perceptions are not allowed to be the main criterion for decisions about students' behavior.

3. Curriculum and instruction should explicitly build on students' verbal and behavioral repertoires instead of this instruction being an attempt to replace them. Students should be shown how their adaptations can help them to be more productive academically.

4. Choice and self-determination should be central aspects of behavior-oriented programs.

5. Teachers who are considering referring African American males for special education evaluation should ensure that their own assessment of the students include observations in a wide variety of settings and situations and that these observations be included in the formal evaluation.

6. Teachers should work on building relationships with parents and other family members long before children get to the point of being considered for special education referral.

7. Parents and other influential family members should be included in the prereferral and assessment process as fully as possible.

Finally, the time has come to dismantle the separate structures of regular and special education, which succeed only in reifying the deficit perspective through which African American males are viewed. Students should not have to "qualify" as disabled in order to gain appropriate services. Appropriate services for all students must become the norm in our educational system.

Identifying Giftedness Among African American Males: Recommendations for Effective Recruitment and Retention

Donna Y. Ford, Tarek C. Grantham, and Deryl F. Bailey

NUMEROUS ARTICLES AND STUDIES of gifted education have focused on issues of gender. Fewer than a handful have focused on gifted males, and even fewer have focused on gifted African American[1] males. The result is a large gap in our knowledge base regarding how best to identify and serve males, particularly Black males, in gifted programs. In this chapter, the authors seek to close this gap by discussing both barriers and recommendations to the recruitment and retention of Black males in gifted programs and services.

Several premises guide this chapter. The first is that gifted Black males face issues unique to being Black and male in this society; namely, discrimination and racism take their toll on the motivation and achievement of Black males. A second premise is that Black males have academic, social, and emotional needs that differ from those of other students. In the process of identifying gifted Black males, these differential needs cannot be ignored or minimized. The third premise is that researchers and educators cannot sufficiently describe the issues facing students without focusing on the impact of race and gender in their analyses. Studies and discussions in education must reflect the heterogeneity of students. The following questions guide this chapter:

African American Males in School and Society: Practices and Policies for Effective Education. Copyright © 1999 by Teachers College, Columbia University. All rights reserved. ISBN 0-8077-3870-0 (pbk), ISBN 0-8077-3871-9 (cloth). Prior to photocopying items for classroom use, please contact the Copyright Clearance Center, Customer Service, 222 Rosewood Dr., Danvers, MA 01923, USA, tel. (508) 750-8400.

1. What barriers contribute to the underrepresentation of Black males in gifted programs?
2. How relevant and informative are the literature and research on gender issues in education to gifted Black males?
3. What are some of the specific concerns of gifted Black males and how can educators more effectively address their needs?
4. How can educators better recruit and retain Black males in gifted programs?

RECRUITMENT—IDENTIFICATION AND ASSESSMENT ISSUES

It is common knowledge that Black students are underrepresented in gifted education programs nationally. Although Black students represent 16% of the school population, they comprise only 8.4% of students identified as gifted (U.S. Department of Education [USDOE], 1993b). To date, no national study has addressed the underrepresentation of gifted students by race *and* gender. Thus, we do not know whether this underrepresentation is most evident among Black males or Black females. However, upon reading the literature on the educational and social status of Black males, it seems reasonable to conclude that this group may be more underrepresented than Black females in gifted education programs.

Many urban scholars have written about the "endangered Black male" (e.g., Wright, 1992). Reports in general, gifted, and special education have all focused on the educational plight of Black males. Two of the most comprehensive and disturbing reports appeared a decade ago. Specifically, the *Carnegie Quarterly* (1984) and the College Board (1985) described the poor educational status of Black students. These reports and more recent data (USDOE, 1996b) indicate that Black males are less likely to be placed in gifted programs than other students. Several decades ago, Jenkins (1936) conducted one of the most extensive studies on gifted Black students. The sample consisted of Black students (primarily females) referred by teachers for identification. He reported that Black females were twice as likely to be identified as gifted than Black males. He did not find differences, however, between the IQ scores of Black males and females. Given that significant differences were not found, one can attribute part of this imbalance to teacher perceptions; namely, teachers may be more willing to accept Black females as gifted. That is, teachers may hold more negative stereotypes about Black males, perceiving them as aggressive, violent, disruptive, uncooperative, and unmotivated. Albeit dated, Jenkins's findings continue to be relevant today.

Irvine (1990) found that Black males at all educational levels are more likely to receive qualified praise and controlling statements than are White students and Black females. That is, Black males are most likely to (a) be labeled deviant and described negatively by teachers; (b) have their abilities judged inaccurately by teachers; (c) receive nonverbal criticism from teachers; and (d) be reprimanded, sent to the principal's office, and suspended. Conversely, Black males are least likely to receive positive teacher feedback and to interact with teachers within and outside the classroom. These perceptions and stereotypes have grave, negative consequences for Black males; indeed, they place Black males of all ability levels at risk for poor educational and social outcomes.

In 1993, Hebert (1993) conducted one of a few studies that specifically focused on gifted Black and Hispanic males. His ethnographic study examined the reasons that 12 males from similar family and educational situations took alternative paths to achievement and success. Underachieving males often became filled with despair and confusion, eventually losing sight of their goals. They also reported negative curricular and counseling experiences. According to Hebert (1993), the minority males *learned* to dislike school and teachers who ignored their strengths, potential, and individual learning styles.

Ford (1993) examined gender differences in underachievement among gifted Black males and females in Grades 5 and 6. Results indicated that Black males were more likely than Black females to underachieve, they exerted considerably less effort in school, and they held more negative attitudes about school than did females. Black males found school less relevant and personally meaningful than did their female counterparts. Further, they were more pessimistic about social factors than were Black females. For example, several of the Black males spoke with anger and disappointment about the injustices with which Blacks must wrestle. Although they believed that hard work, effort, and persistence are part of the success equation, they also believed that the American dream benefited Whites more than it did Blacks. The findings suggested that the Black males needed and desired (a) more information on their racial heritage, (b) more exposure to male and Black role models, (c) increased affective educational experiences to feel connected to teachers, (d) an increased sense of ownership of their schooling, and (e) counseling experiences to cope more effectively with their anger and disappointment regarding social injustices.

In a similar study, Ford (1995) examined gender differences between Black male and female underachievers in Grades 6 through 9. Half of the Blacks males in the sample ($n = 27$) and 37% of females ($n = 35$) were underachieving. The male students were also less optimistic than females; a finding that is consistent with Ford (1993). In essence, data indicate the disappointing reality that some Black males are well represented among students experiencing poor educational outcomes and apathy.

In an embedded multiple-case study, Grantham (1997) explored the perceptions of two groups of high school gifted Black males by focusing on variables that influenced their motivation to participate or not to participate in gifted and advanced-level classes. For the group of Black males who chose not to participate in gifted and advanced level classes ($n = 2$), their choice was based on (a) negative participation competence expectancy (i.e., "I don't think that I have the ability to be successful in gifted and advanced-level classes"), (b) negative outcome attainment expectancy (i.e., "I can't put forth enough effort to meet the demands of gifted and advanced-level classes and reach desirable outcomes"), and (c) negative valence of gifted program outcomes (i.e., "The benefits of taking gifted and advanced level classes aren't important and don't outweigh the consequences"). Grantham's findings indicate that the problem of underrepresentation may be intensified when gifted Black males hold negative perceptions of gifted and advanced-level classes and, as a result, choose not to participate.

Many efforts are under way to increase the representation of Black and other minority students in gifted programs. Recommendations primarily emphasize finding alternative ways to identify gifted Black males. In the following subsections we present specific barriers to the recruitment of Black males in gifted programs, including problems associated with instrumentation and gifted program procedures. Following this discussion, we offer recommendations to reverse underrepresentation among Black males in gifted programs.

Instrumentation Barriers

The overwhelming majority of articles on the underrepresentation of Black students in gifted education focus on Black students' poor test performance. Although this is certainly a valid concern, it places a heavy burden on Black students to perform well on traditional standardized tests. In effect, little attention is given to problems associated with the test itself. As described below, many problems are associated with testing Black students, including traditional definitions and theories of giftedness, invalid and unreliable instruments, inadequate consideration of noncognitive factors, and an emphasis on current test scores.

Traditional Definitions and Theories of Giftedness

Traditional conceptualizations of giftedness are confined to a psychometric orientation. Thus, most schools rely heavily or exclusively on tests of intelligence and achievement to decide who is or is not gifted. Little attention is given to those abilities that are difficult to measure by standardized instruments, such as creativity, leadership, practical intelligence, and social competence. Just as important, traditional definitions and theories emphasize values associated with a dominant or mainstream culture and fail to consider manifestations of giftedness valued in different cultures (Gardner, 1983). They ignore the reality that what is valued as gifted in one culture is not necessarily viewed this way in another (Sternberg & Davidson, 1986). Hence, traditional definitions and theories are limited in their ability to capture the promise of Black males and other ethnically and culturally diverse students. They are inadequate measures of giftedness for some, perhaps many, students.

Invalid and Unreliable Instruments

Arguments against using standardized tests with Black students have a long history. These arguments have proliferated in recent years on the grounds that ethnically and culturally diverse students are assessed by tests that do not effectively measure their intelligence and achievement. Specifically, because the life experiences and educational opportunities of minority and White students vary considerably, the reliability of traditional standardized tests may be questionable for Black and other minority students. When considering gender and race, the different experiences and opportunities between Black and White males makes the reliability even more questionable. The result is that traditional tests, too often, are biased against Black students (see Hilliard, 1992, for details).

Noncognitive Factors Overlooked

Many factors affect students' performance in evaluative situations. Most test manuals caution test administrators to seriously consider such noncognitive variables as health, self-perception, familiarity with testing, quality of educational experiences and opportunities, level and type of academic motivation, and learning style in the testing, interpretation, and decision-making process. All of these variables affect test performance and can obscure students' abilities. For instance, when there is an incompatibility between Black males' learning styles and the instructional preferences of schools—which generally favor field-independent, abstract, and analytical styles of learning—academic failure and poor test performance may result (Saracho & Gerstl, 1992).

Research suggests that the learning styles of gifted, White, and achieving students are different from those of Black and underachieving students (e.g., Saracho & Gerstl, 1992). In general, gifted, White, and academically successful students prefer formal-learning classroom designs, less structure in learning materials, and auditory modes of presentation, and they are reflective, tactile, kinesthetic, and field-independent learners; they are responsible for their own learning, persistent, motivated, and task oriented. Although some Black students' learning style preferences may be similar, many others are likely to be field-dependent, holistic, relational, and visual learners; they learn best in cooperative settings and are socially oriented. Underachievers also tend to be impulsive, low task-oriented, nonconforming, creative, and visual learners.

In essence, the learning style preferences of gifted White and achieving students appear oppositional to that of Black students and underachievers. This must certainly pose a dilemma for gifted Black students by hindering their school performance. Black students who are gifted do not fail in school because of learning style differences, but because schools fail to accommodate these differences.

Emphasis on Current Test Scores

Placement in gifted programs is often based on most recent test and school performance. This is problematic for middle and high school–aged Black males who are overlooked in elementary school. Although data indicate that early test scores are generally less reliable than are later scores, an examination of early scores for minority students is important because their test scores tend to *decrease* the longer they are in school. Hence, if Black males are not identified early, they may be overlooked completely. When their abilities are not recognized and nurtured, they are likely to underachieve, act out in school, stay off task, and otherwise demonstrate boredom and frustration.

Procedural Barriers

In addition to instrumentation barriers, procedural barriers must be examined if we are to better identify and serve gifted Black males. Cox, Daniel, and Boston (1985) reported that teacher nominations were most often used for identification (91%), followed closely by achievement tests (90%) and IQ tests (82%). More recently, Archambault, Westberg, Brown, Hallmark, Emmons, and Zhang (1993) surveyed more than 3,000 third- and fourth-grade teachers regarding identification practices. Results indicated that most of the public school teachers used achievement tests (79%), followed closely by IQ tests (72%) and teacher nominations (70%). Whereas the percentages and rankings of screening and identification sources appear to have changed over the years, the three primary identification sources remain the same. Like tests, teachers can serve as gatekeepers who block Black males' entrance into gifted programs.

Heavy Reliance on Teacher Referral

The practice of using teachers as primary identifiers of gifted learners carries numerous implications for the recruitment and retention of minority students, particularly as many teachers are not sufficiently prepared in either gifted or multicultural education. This lack of preparation and experience decreases the probability that Black males will be identified for and served in gifted programs. Teachers who lack familiarity with gifted students may hold biased notions of gifted students as neat, fluent in speaking standard English, cooperative, well behaved, motivated and persistent, high achieving, good at test taking, and having good study habits and skills. Those gifted students who do not demonstrate these ideals may go unrecognized.

Similarly, when students are culturally different from school personnel, it can be difficult to recognize their strengths (it is easy, however, to recognize their weaknesses!). Teachers who lack familiarity with and understanding of cultural manifestations of giftedness in Black students are likely to ignore their potential and fail to refer them for screening. We will use three examples to illustrate this point. First, a Black male who asks many questions may be perceived as "talkative," whereas a White male may be considered "inquisitive and curious." A Black male who questions social injustices such as discrimination and racism may be considered "too sensitive," whereas a White male may be considered "compassionate and caring." Finally, a Black male who asserts himself, who expresses himself openly, may be considered "hostile and aggressive," whereas a White male may be considered "assertive and independent." Thus, a Black and White student may show similar characteristics of giftedness—curiosity, concern about injustices, and independence—but educators may interpret these characteristics differently for the two groups. Such differential interpretations of behaviors and characteristics contribute to the poor referral of Black students for screening (Hall & Udall, 1983).

Selection Committee Demographics

Selection committees for the gifted program often include a teacher, counselor, psychologist, gifted program coordinator, and the school principal. Some committees may also include a parent representative. Beyond knowing their professional titles, we know little about the demographics of selection committees relative to race, gender, and socioeconomic status (SES). The demographics of committee members can impact their perceptions and decisions. Analogous to the literature on variables affecting teacher expectation of minority students and Black males, these variables can influence the decisions of individual committee members. For instance, are White members most likely to place White students in the gifted program? Are Black males biased in favor of White males when making their decisions? Are higher SES members less supportive of poor students?

In sum, numerous variables affect the recruitment of Black males in gifted programs. Although tests play a major role in the identification process, teacher referrals and selection committee demographics can also influence Black male representation in gifted programs. In some districts, the major barrier may lie in the instruments used; in another district, the major barrier may be lack of teacher referral; in a third district, the primary barrier may lie in the definition of giftedness adopted. Certainly, a combination of barriers may exist. Comprehensive evaluations of the nature and extent of Black male underrepresentation in gifted programs must be conducted.

REVERSING BLACK MALE REPRESENTATION IN GIFTED PROGRAMS

In this section, we attempt to describe effective ways in which to increase Black male representation in gifted programs. We contend that proactive efforts must focus on effective recruitment strategies, placement considerations, and retention strategies.

Recruitment Strategies

Adopt Contemporary Theories and Definitions of Giftedness.   In recent years, two theories of intelligence have been developed that hold much promise for being culturally sensitive. Gardner's (1983) and Sternberg's (1985) theories hold that intelligence cannot be adequately measured by traditional, narrowly defined means. They also support the notion that gifted students must be assessed within a contextual framework that includes consideration of the students' cultural and ethnic background and the quality and quantity of their learning opportunities. Likewise, in 1993, the U.S. Department of Education adopted its most culturally sensitive definition of giftedness to date:

> Children and youth with outstanding talent perform or show the potential for performing at remarkably high levels of accomplishment when compared with others of their age, experience, or environment. These children and youth ex-

hibit high performance capacity in intellectual, creative, and/or artistic areas, and unusual leadership capacity, or excel in specific academic fields. They require services or activities not ordinarily provided by the schools. *Outstanding talents are present in children and youth from all cultural groups, across all economic strata, and in all areas of human endeavor.* (USDOE, 1993a, p. 26; emphasis added)

Adopting contextually and culturally sensitive definitions and theories will increase the likelihood of inclusive rather than exclusive recruitment practices.

Adopt a Philosophy of Assessment. Assessment provides more specific information—diagnostic and prescriptive information—regarding how the student is gifted, as well as his or her strengths and needs. With assessment, comprehensive information is gathered from parents, teachers, and students themselves, and *all* information is deemed useful in the decision-making process. With Black students, it is important that information be gathered from family and community members, particularly because parents, grandparents, aunts, uncles, and close friends are more likely than teachers to understand and be familiar with the Black students in their homes and communities. Thus, family and community members are able to serve as cultural advocates and liaisons for gifted Black males.

Use Appropriate Instruments. Valid and reliable instruments must be developed and used in the gifted program recruitment process. School personnel must take into consideration the purpose of the instrument, the target population, the norming sample, and the limitations of the instrument itself. In essence, the least biased or most culturally sensitive instruments should be adopted (e.g., Ravens Matrices Analogies Test, Naglieri Matrix Analogies Test). Just as important, nomination forms and checklists for parents must be valid and reliable, as well as sensitive to all reading and educational levels. These instruments must include characteristics of minority students and examples and descriptors of these characteristics. Teachers and parents should complete the same checklists so that the selection committee or decision makers can explore consistencies or discrepancies in the responses.

Use Contextual Definitions of Underachievement. Educators must use quantitative and qualitative indices to effectively identify and better understand underachievement. For instance, underachievement should be analyzed relative to locus of control, fears and anxieties, self-concept, self-esteem, and motivation and effort. One should consider the influence of peer pressure on achievement and effort (e.g., Fordham, 1988; Lindstrom & Van Sant, 1986). Finally, exploring underachievement in the context of external factors is warranted, including (a) the influence of discrimination, (b) low teacher expectations and limited counseling support, and (c) cultural barriers to achievement such as home and community values that differ from school values.

Focus on Potential.   Potentially gifted students include underachievers, minority students, low SES students, learning and behavioral disordered students, and physically challenged students. The emphasis on potential represents a progressive, future-oriented definition by denoting students' capacity to become critically acclaimed performers or exemplary producers of ideas in spheres of activity that enhance the moral, physical, emotional, social, intellectual, or aesthetic life of humanity (Tannenbaum, 1983, p. 86).

The 1993 federal definition of giftedness, presented earlier, offers much promise for equitably identifying gifted Black males. The definition recognizes a broad range of ability and, for the first time, specifically mentions that no racial, ethnic, or SES group has a monopoly on giftedness. Renzulli and VanTassel-Baska's theory of giftedness is also useful for tapping potential in minority students. Renzulli's talent-pool approach broadens the notion of ability and recognizes that some students face barriers to talent development. Renzulli has continuously advocated for inclusive rather than exclusive definitions of giftedness. Talent pools acknowledge that lower test scores do not automatically equal lower intelligence or ability, and that many talents are resistant to formal testing. The notion of talent development is a contemporary view of giftedness that is dynamic and relative, rather than static and absolute (Borland, 1996; Callahan, 1996; Treffinger & Feldhusen, 1996).

Consider Past Records.   By examining early and current school records, teachers can develop profiles of students' achievement. When Black males are underachieving, teachers can better understand whether underachievement is, for instance, subject specific versus global, situational versus general, chronic versus temporary, and teacher related or peer related. Teachers can also explore records for potential indicators of giftedness; the comments of parents and former teachers, inconsistent test scores and grades, discrepancies between subtest scores, and discrepancies between tests, for example, may represent important indicators of potential.

Consider Noncognitive Factors.   Attention to motivation, school attitudes, test anxiety, self-perceptions, learning styles, and health promise to further our understanding of (a) the reasons gifted Black males underachieve, (b) their poor test scores, and (c) the difficulties of identifying Black students.

If the tests used are inappropriate and testing conditions are not optimal, school personnel must interpret the results with caution, and decisions based on the results must be made carefully. To repeat, the more information gathered on students, and the more sources (e.g., parents, community members) used to gather data, the more effective the identification and assessment process for Black males.

Recognize Cultural Manifestations of Giftedness. Our collective experiences suggest that gifted Black males share many of the strengths of gifted students in general—they retain and recall information well, enjoy complex problems, can tolerate ambiguity, are creative, are extremely curious, perceptive, evaluative, and judgmental, and are interested in adult and social problems. We must not let biases, fears, and stereotypes blind us to the promise of children of color. To better understand and appreciate the strengths of minority students, educators must get to know them both as cultural beings and individuals and use their strengths for diagnostic and prescriptive educational purposes.

Prepare Teachers in Gifted Education. Teacher expectations are influenced by their values and beliefs, which significantly influence referrals. Teachers who hold stereotypes about gifted students as conforming, well behaved, motivated, and academically successful are unlikely to refer students for gifted programs who do not fit these stereotypes. Training in gifted education can increase teachers' levels of awareness, understanding, and competence in recognizing gifted behaviors among *all* students, regardless of gender, race, and other demographic variables.

Provide Multicultural Training for Teachers. To be successful in school and life, gifted minority students have been required to be bicultural, bicognitive, bilingual, and bidialectic. These skills are not choices; they are prerequisites to school success. Unlike Black or minority students, non-Black or nonminority teachers are seldom required to take on this arduous task. Multicultural preparation that focuses on individual differences attributable to race, gender, SES, and geographic locale must be infused throughout preservice and graduate curriculum in gifted education. Comprehensive preparation should reeducate teachers (and all school personnel) so that cultural-deficit models do not hinder Black males' self-perception, racial pride, motivation, and achievement.

Diversify Gifted Program Selection Committees. When the selection committee is diverse, including both gender groups, White and minority members, and members from all SES levels, we can increase the probability that gifted Black males will be selected at higher rates. Just as important, at least one member must be familiar with the student being considered for placement; that individual must be able to serve as an advocate who can communicate the student's strengths and need for gifted education services.

Placement Considerations

It can be a difficult decision for some Black males to enter gifted programs that are predominantly White, female, and middle class. Black males may have to make significant personal, family, and social adjustments. Many Black students may come from schools and communities in which they were in a numerical majority; in gifted programs, they often represent a numerical minority. The negative concerns that Black males may have about entering gifted programs necessitates that we examine the services offered and the implications of our placement decisions.

The services offered to gifted students are quite broad. For Black males and minority students in general, it is important to examine the type and location of program or services (e.g., acceleration, enrichment, resource room, etc.). Some of these students may feel uncomfortable with pullout programs where they are transported to a different school. In many cases, this type of program can contribute to or exacerbate negative pressures from peers; that is, peers may be envious about what they perceive as "special" attention for their gifted Black classmates.

The demographics of the gifted program—students' and teachers' ethnicity, gender, and SES level—are also important considerations. The more diverse the program, the more likely Black males will feel a sense of belonging, membership, and ownership. Black males who feel isolated and alienated may not want to remain in the gifted program. Interviews with students and their families about such concerns and other potential problems would be helpful when making placement decisions.

Finally, when making placement decisions, school personnel must gather as much information as possible on Black students' shortcomings in basic skills and learning style preferences. Gifted Black males who lack basic skills will continuously play "catch up" and "keep up" with other students; along with underachievers, they may have high rates of attrition from the gifted program. Ideally, all efforts must be made to place gifted Black males with teachers who can accommodate diverse learning styles and skill levels in the classroom—teachers who are effective at differentiating the curriculum and otherwise meeting individual student needs.

Retention Strategies

Once Black males have been identified as gifted and placed, we must ensure that they are retained in gifted programs. Retention efforts should focus on

(a) providing multicultural educational programs, (b) recruiting minority teachers, (c) seeking meaningful and substantive family involvement, and (d) developing resilience. These efforts can support gifted Black males at the classroom and school level by ensuring a healthy and nurturing learning environment.

Provide an Education That Is Multicultural. The infusion of multicultural education into the content is empowering for gifted Black males. For instance, a Black History Month each February is too brief to instill Black males with pride in their racial and cultural heritage. Essentially, an important component of multicultural education promotes both social and cultural awareness and understanding. Questions such as the following must be given serious and ongoing attention:

1. Does my class assist students with knowing the multicultural history of this society?
2. Does my class expand students' knowledge of major perspectives, views, and frames of reference contributed by diverse groups?
3. Do my students know the contributions of people of color, women, and other groups to the development of this nation?
4. Do my students know about the major societal issues shaping the experiences of minority groups?
5. How does curriculum and instruction in my class affect students' self-image and self-understanding?

Recruit Minority Teachers into Gifted Programs. A significant problem in both general and gifted education is the scarcity of minority teachers (Ford, Grantham, & Harris, 1997). Although minority students represent a large percentage of the school population (about 41%), less than 15% of the teaching profession is African American, Hispanic/Latino, Asian American/Pacific Islander, and Native American combined. More specifically, the Hispanic/Latino teacher representation is 3.1%, the Asian–Pacific Islander representation is 1%, the Black teacher representation is 9.2%, and the Native American and Native Alaskan teacher representation is 0.7% (American Association of Colleges for Teacher Education, 1994). The percentage of minority teachers is expected to decline from 12% to 5%. As such, demographic projections indicate an inverse relationship between the number of minority students and minority teachers; specifically, just as the number of minority students is increasing, the number of minority teachers is decreasing. There is a strong possibility that gifted minority students will go through their entire formal schooling without a minority teacher. This shortage of minority teachers in gifted education translates into fewer role models and mentors for gifted minority and White students.

Seek Meaningful and Substantive Family Involvement. Substantive family involvement results in increased achievement for all students (Clark, 1983; Comer, 1988). Parents play a crucial role in developing giftedness in children. When parents are substantively involved, the likelihood of both recruiting and retaining Black males in gifted programs also increases. School personnel must also involve other family members in the educational process. Research indicates that Black students are more likely than other students to live in extended family situations; grandmothers, other relatives, caregivers in the community can contribute to students' education and achievement. Thus, more contemporary and cultural definitions of parent involvement are needed; these definitions must be inclusive of other family members. This broader definition is that of "family" involvement.

Provide a Supportive Learning Environment. Schools have an obligation to provide a healthy organizational climate that is conducive to optimal personal-social and academic learning. Students should be offered environments that provide individuals with a feeling of significance, a sense of competence, and a belief that they have some control over important aspects of their surroundings. The lack of these elements in public school is a predominant cause of student failure (Childers & Fairman, 1986). Educators must place students at the center of learning. School personnel must recognize that (a) Black males have their own set of psychological and socioemotional needs, (b) they can help Black males to identify and seek ways to satisfy their psychological and socioemotional needs, and (c) students gain more from an academic curriculum when these needs are concurrently met (Boy & Pine, 1988). When Black males have empathetic, accepting, understanding, and genuine teachers who foster a "curriculum of caring," their academic achievement, self-perception, motivation, attendance and class participation, and feelings of belonging increase.

Develop Student Resilience. "Resilience" refers to a student's level of persistence in the face of challenges. Black males in gifted programs must have a high level of resilience to overcome the odds for success. School personnel can help gifted Black males develop resilience by setting clear and realistic expectations, enhancing their school competence, establishing mentoring groups, and providing counseling and guidance services:

1. *Set clear and realistic expectations for students.* When expectations are clear and realistic, Black males are more likely to persist and succeed in gifted programs, and less likely to feel overburdened and discouraged.

2. *Enhance students' school competencies.* Self-understanding and self-awareness are important for school success. Teachers and counselors should help gifted Black males to gain a better understanding of their learning styles, area(s) of giftedness, and strengths and shortcomings. Relatedly, educators must take active and early actions to prevent or reverse underachievement.

3. *Establish mentoring groups.* These groups include students assigned to a mentor during and after school. Mentors provide mutual emotional and social support, as well as create a sense of responsibility for the success of others.

4. *Provide comprehensive counseling and guidance services.* Educators are encouraged to empower gifted Black males to feel that destiny is on their side, and that they represent the future. Providing students with comprehensive services is empowering for the students. *Career and vocational guidance* can provide gifted Black males with practical experiences that enhance or sustain their vision of the future. Internships, in particular, provide opportunities for gifted Black males to see success in action. *Personal guidance and counseling* are also needed to help those students experiencing personal and interpersonal difficulties (e.g., in peer relationships, self-concept, or racial identity or test anxiety, stress, etc.). Family, individual, and group counseling can be utilized to address their personal and interpersonal needs. *Academic guidance and counseling* related to improving students' academic competencies is also needed, particularly tutoring, study skills, organizational skills, thinking skills, and other basic and enrichment academic training.

SUMMARY AND RECOMMENDATIONS

In 1991, a special issue of the *Roeper Review* focused on the social, emotional, and academic needs of gifted males. The issue was both timely and long overdue in education. The authors noted that gifted males contend with issues about bonding, emotionality, and maintaining a macho image (Alvino, 1991; Hebert, 1991; Kline & Short, 1991; Wolfle, 1991), oftentimes by channeling their efforts into sports rather than academics. The authors also noted that gifted males are more likely than females to be labeled hyperactive, and they are less likely to be recommended for acceleration, early school entrance, and grade skipping. More recently, Colangelo, Kerr, Christensen, and Maxey (1993) found that 90% of the underachievers in their national study were White males. Findings by race were not reported due to the small percentage of Black students in the study. One shortcoming of the special issue of *Roeper* (and many other articles on gender issues in gifted education) is that "gifted males" were addressed as if they are a monolithic group; little attention was devoted to issues confronting gifted Black males.

As discussed in this chapter, Black males have unique needs and concerns that cannot be ignored or minimized. These needs differ from those of Black females, other minority groups, and White students. Too many Black males experience educational disengagement because their abilities and potential have not been adequately recognized and assessed. Stereotypes, misperceptions, and fears hinder the ability of school personnel to meet the academic and socioemotional needs of gifted Black males. Equally delimiting is the use of traditional measures of intelligence and achievement, and a heavy reliance on teacher recommendation and referral.

To increase the representation of Black males in gifted programs, school personnel must focus on factors that contribute to effective recruitment, placement, and retention. Proactive efforts must be guided by the development of appropriate interventions. We suggest the following measures:

1. Culturally sensitive definitions and theories must be adopted by school districts.
2. Instruments must be chosen with care. Those deemed valid, reliable, and culturally sensitive should be adopted.
3. Interventions must address underachievement and other factors that hide students' abilities.
4. School personnel must receive substantive and ongoing training in both gifted and multicultural education.
5. Gifted programs must be more representative of the diverse student population.
6. Efforts must be made to increase minority teacher representation in gifted programs.
7. Family and community members must be involved throughout the recruitment and retention process.
8. Gifted Black males need to have a supportive learning environment.
9. Schools must help to develop resilience among Black males for them to participate successfully in gifted programs.

The poor participation of Black males in gifted education must be addressed. Each school district must evaluate its particular set of circumstances regarding Black male underrepresentation and tailor prevention and intervention accordingly. Efforts must be ongoing and proactive. There is no defensible reason or rationale for the persistent underrepresentation of Black males, or other minority students, in gifted education. As long as gifted Black males remain undiscovered, they will continue to be placed at risk for failure in our schools.

NOTE

1. The terms "Black" and "African American" are used interchangeably in this chapter, as are the terms "minority" and "ethnically and culturally diverse."

5   Who Am I? The Development of the African American Male Identity

Saladin K. Corbin and Robert L. Pruitt, II

THE DEVELOPMENT OF IDENTITY is a complex process that involves a multitude of psychosocial factors. Ultimately, identity achievement includes defining who one is and hopes to be within a social context. The individual explores different social roles while experimenting with various attitudes, emotions, and behaviors. Feedback from others validates or invalidates which of these roles will be assimilated. The achievement of this identity has long been considered to be central to adolescent development. Adolescents are faced with finding out who they are, what they are all about, and where they are going in life. Having lost their former childhood status but not yet having acquired adult status, these youth find themselves in a transitional period. Failure to achieve an identity can lead to confusion and discouragement (Erikson, 1968). Typically, confused adolescents withdraw, isolating themselves from peers and family, or immerse themselves in their world of peers and deindividuate, losing their identity in the crowd (Simons, Kalichman, & Santrock, 1994). James Marcia (1980) suggests that Erikson's theory of identity development involves four possible outcomes or "statuses" of identity that are ways of resolving the identity crisis: diffusion, foreclosure, moratorium, and achievement. While attempting to achieve an identity, Marcia says, adolescents undergo a crisis, that is, an exploratory period during which individuals choose among meaningful alternatives. Individuals also attempt to commit themselves to, or show an investment in, what they have decided to be. "Diffusion" refers to persons who have not explored meaningful alternatives or made any commitments. "Foreclosure" describes persons who have not explored meaningful alter-

African American Males in School and Society: Practices and Policies for Effective Education. Copyright © 1999 by Teachers College, Columbia University. All rights reserved. ISBN 0-8077-3870-0 (pbk), ISBN 0-8077-3871-9 (cloth). Prior to photocopying items for classroom use, please contact the Copyright Clearance Center, Customer Service, 222 Rosewood Dr., Danvers, MA 01923, USA, tel. (508) 750-8400.

natives yet make a commitment. The foreclosure commitment is usually one that is passed down from parent to child in such a way that exploration is inhibited or unnecessary. "Moratorium" is used to describe individuals who are in the midst of exploration and have not actively committed themselves to anything. Finally, achievement occurs when adolescents have explored their alternatives and made a commitment.

When attempting to describe the development of the African American identity, the aforementioned theories are somewhat limited, particularly in their application to young Black males. In fact, Watson and Protinsky (1991) found that among Black adolescents, in general, females were less diffused than males and were in higher identity statuses. These youth are faced with sociocultural, academic, and economic dilemmas that generate experiences and identity conflicts that are specific to African American males. Failure to address these conflicts can thwart identity development if left unresolved. Our purpose in this chapter is to discuss some of the key issues that affect identity development in this population. The key issues that stand out as affecting African American male identity development is their ethnic identity, role model identification, and peer acceptance issues (Harris, 1995; Hudson, 1991; White & Parkham, 1990). These issues will be explored individually, along with the impact that social violence has on the African American male's identity development, followed by recommendations for educators.

ETHNIC INFLUENCE ON IDENTITY DEVELOPMENT

As African American children develop, they become aware of the inequalities that exist within American society. Some citizens are treated well, whereas others suffer from limited opportunities. The development of this awareness begins in childhood and gradually intensifies through adulthood. The media, newspapers, and even our classroom textbooks project images of Eurocentric power, dominance, and beauty (White & Parkham, 1990). The child hears that America is the land of equal opportunity and justice for all, yet his or her experiences suggest otherwise. For example, African American males are disproportionately placed in remedial and special education courses, have lower grades, and have a greater number of expulsions and suspensions than do their female counterparts (Irvine, 1990). Given the absence of positive feedback from the academic environment and the media, and the frequent encounters with violence, police harassment, and incarceration, African American males develop a sense of pessimism toward the future (Harris, 1995).

Phinney, Lochner, and Murphy (1990) suggest that African Americans need to resolve two primary issues or conflicts that stem from their status as members of a minority group in society. First, they must resolve prejudicial attitudes from society, and second, they must resolve an adoption of two differing sets of values, one from the majority culture and the other from their own minority one. African Americans may actively explore resolution to these issues that results in an achieved ethnic identity, or they may ignore them, resulting in identity diffusion. Prejudicial stereotypes will affect their identity development (i.e., self-concept) only if they are accepted and believed. In fact, African Americans may reject these stereotypes and redefine themselves and their group in more positive terms (Tajfel, 1978).

The second issue appears to be more difficult to resolve. That is, young African Americans feel both included and excluded from American society. This conflict is a core issue of the identity struggle and promotes feelings of anger and indignation (White, 1984). Furthermore, they must struggle with adopting two different value systems, African American and Euro-American. Total rejection of either reality can restrict their choices, personal growth, social interactions, and economic opportunities (White & Parkham, 1990). If the individual identifies solely with the Eurocentric values of individualism, competitiveness, emotional suppression, power, and dominance, he or she may achieve success at the cost of being isolated from the African American community. Conversely, if the individual identifies solely with African American values, he or she may not develop many of the necessary skills to survive in the occupational mainstream.

In order to resolve the ethnic identity issue, there are a number of possible outcomes that have been suggested: alienation, assimilation, withdrawal, and integration, which are affected by social factors such as discrimination, poverty, and education level for each individual (Phinney et al., 1990; Tajfel, 1978). Alienated individuals are those who accept the negative image that society presents, alienate themselves from African American culture, and do not adapt to the majority culture. These individuals accept that they are inferior as members of a minority group. Blackwell and Hart (1982) found that 8 in 10 Blacks from five large cities could be categorized as alienated. Assimilated individuals attempt to become part of the majority culture and do not remain connected with their minority culture. This can be a difficult task given that they are still easily identifiable as members of their minority group. However, they attempt to think and behave in ways that minimize, devalue, or deny their African American status. Withdrawn individuals become immersed in their own culture while withdrawing from contact with the dominant culture. In order to counterbalance negative images from the majority and to protect their self-esteem, they may overidentify with their own culture to minimize any loss of self-esteem resulting from comparisons to the majority group. Although this can be viewed as a healthy defense mechanism, it leaves individuals unprepared to cope with the reality of racism when they are not within the boundaries of the African American community. Immersion in the minority culture can often lead to a lack of ability to interact within the mainstream culture. Integrated individuals find a way of accepting their ethnic identity within the majority culture. They feel secure and confident with their African American identity while maintaining healthy contact with the majority. Integration can be a challenge; however, it is considered to be the healthiest outcome psychologically (Berry, Kim, Mindy, & Mok, 1987). This dual perspective of minority and majority culture allows persons to see themselves as ethnic and American and promotes more pluralistic attitudes and behaviors. It is important to note that integration is not an easy task, especially in situations when African American males are admitted to predominantly Euro-American schools. Also, the struggle to achieve a sense of ethnic identity typically begins in adolescence. However, individuals may "recycle" through various stages at different times during their development, depending on their recent experiences (Parham, 1989).

SHAPING IDENTITY THROUGH THE USE OF ROLE MODELS

Among the more important factors influencing identity development are those role models and significant others with whom the adolescent identifies. With new choices to be made in preparation for adult status, African American male youth are likely to search for useful role models that will provide avenues for experimentation, guidance, and direction. The tendency to rely on role models is most intense during late adolescence, as seen in teen fads, hero worship, and peer groups (Sebald & White, 1980). Youth need someone to believe in and look up to. In seeking a role model, males are influenced by many factors such as age, race, gender, future goals, and similarities with the model. Taylor (1989) identifies two types of role models that adolescents rely upon: exemplary and symbolic. Exemplary models are persons who provide technical knowledge, skills, or behaviors for general competence, demonstrating for the youth how something is done. Many different exemplary models can be utilized for different aspects of the identity and are typically associated with career aspirations. Symbolic models, on the other hand, can be seen as representing certain values or ideals. These values typically come from the adolescent's heroes, whether they are mythical, historical, or living. For example, symbolic role models can take the form of Malcolm X, Michael Jordan, or Snoop Doggy Dogg, and consequently, can be very motivating to that individual.

Taylor (1989) interviewed African American college males and found that they identified most often with familial role models. Parental models were seen as being key in their overall development, in both exemplary and symbolic fashion. Mothers are seen to be more important role models during early childhood and later in adolescence as a source of emotional support (Knoff, 1986). Fathers or father figures, however, appear to play a more significant role during adolescence, as in Taylor's sample. The nature of the father-son relationship largely determines how the adolescent will value and model the father's behaviors. For many males, the father's influence is often a function of his ability to provide support at critical times during the teen's development. The more valuable the support provided by the father was perceived to be, the more the adolescent identified with him as a positive role model and source of crisis resolution. For some, the father was not seen as a positive role model, but rather as a source of hostility. This was largely due to factors such as the father's shortcomings, low income, lack of power in the home, failure to live up to values and goals, and impersonal or hostile relations between father and son. These youth, however, report acting in opposition to the model provided by the father; thus the father as a negative role model was often just as influential in shaping identity as the positive models. In fact, Hunt and Hunt (1975) found that the father's absence had a greater effect on European American males than it did on African American males. This, they argue, is due to the fact that the nuclear family is not as much an expectation in the African American community; thus the effects of an absent father may be mitigated.

Other role models were observed to have significant influences on the college sample. In addition to the father model, others served as a work-related or value-related model. A work model is someone in a vocational area in which the youth is interested, and value models were ones that provided motivation, direction, and hope for the future through doing the right thing, or demonstrating what is worthwhile in life. The adolescent typically borrows traits from several models and condenses them into what Taylor calls the ideal identity (1989). As one youth responded: "You take Martin Luther King's articulation, Malcolm X's convictions and courage, and my father's physical strength and imagination, and that's what I want to be, that's my ideal" (p. 164).

Conversely, Taylor (1989) found that inner-city youth had a more difficult time identifying significant role models, a problem common to this population. Half of the subjects reported having no significant role models in their lives. The primary reasons for this lack of identification were a desire to be individualistic and a lack of trust in others as resources for knowledge, skills, and values. This individualistic attitude is seen as a response to the impoverished conditions of home and community. Their social environment is one that is unstable and fraught with realities such as death, incarceration, or illness, all factors that contribute to an unreliable or unpredictable social world. Taylor interprets this as the experience of failure and disappointment in themselves and others that directly affects their sense of self-worth, motivation to succeed, and confidence in exploring different life options. For example, many of the youths in the inner-city sample reported being frustrated with school. Education for them is an unpleasant experience compounded by their inability to perform well in academics. Their scholastic efforts were inhibited by work or family obligations and received little support from parents. Teachers further complicated their attitudes by maintaining lower achievement expectations and not encouraging exploration of worthy interests such as math and science. As a result, more than half of Taylor's inner-city subjects were dropouts who would only find employment in unstable jobs. One of the more relevant findings from Taylor's article was the lack of identification by the inner-city youth with their fathers. Less than one third mentioned the father as a positive influence, whereas another third viewed the father as a negative influence or were indifferent. Again, Taylor emphasizes the role fathers play in identity formation based on what they provide or fail to provide for their sons.

THE IMPORTANCE OF PEERS, COOLNESS, AND MASCULINITY

The tendency for African American males to become deeply embedded within their peer group has been noted by a number of writers (e.g., Kunjufu, 1986; Taylor, 1989). Such strong peer relations have been interpreted as a failure in parental authority, early dependency on siblings as caretakers, and normal expectations from adults in low-income communities (Jones, 1980). For Taylor's (1989) subjects, peers were seen as sources of security, achievement, social status, values, and self-validation. Belongingness is seen as a basic and fundamental human need (Maslow, 1954), thus for urban youth in particular, the peer group serves as a circle of social acceptance and support in a world where they feel isolated and pessimistic about the future and where positive adult role models are scarce.

To compensate for these feelings of insecurity in a Eurocentric world, African American male youth redefine what it means to be a man in their world. For most, this includes sexual promiscuity, machismo, risk taking, and aggressive social skills. Their noted mannerisms include physical posture, style of clothing, dialect, walking style, greeting behaviors, and overall demeanor (Harris, 1995). These attitudes and behaviors have been collectively referred to as the "cool pose" by Richard Majors and Janet Billson (1991). Through the attitudes and behaviors of the cool pose, African American males lay their own foundation for personal achievement and self-worth; however, they further separate themselves from the Eurocentric world (Harris & Majors, 1993). Furthermore, different peer groups emphasize different criteria for success. For example, some peer groups may value academic achievement whereas others value as indications of manhood deviant behaviors such as skipping class, fighting, sexual promiscuity, theft, drug use, "joning" (exchanging verbal insults) or even incarceration. Harris (1995) suggests that these behaviors manifest themselves because of unmet needs for security and belonging (Maslow, 1954). Males who exhibit competence in these areas will acquire status within the group.

Unfortunately, peer groups can discourage academic achievement as well. Many academic problems surface due to African American males' rejection of academic traits as being European or feminine. African American male adolescents are more likely to deny and devalue academic interests to avoid the ridicule and shame that accompany success (Harris & Majors, 1993). Others compensate for poor academic interest by hiding books, withholding truth about good grades, becoming the class clown, or dealing drugs. Others immerse themselves in interests outside of academia, for example, music, athletics, or entertainment. The influences of one of these areas, "hip hop" culture, will be briefly explored.

Hip hop culture goes beyond the music more commonly referred to as "rap." Rap music is one aspect of hip hop culture that is a part of the African American experience targeting African American males in particular. What is hip hop culture? It is music, fashion, and freedom of expression; it is cultural collectiveness in a seemingly divided nation. More important, it is something that young African American males can identify with, belong to, create, and call their own.

Hip hop culture is defined in part by famous rap artists such as Grandmaster Flash, Puff Daddy, Ice Cube, Tu Pac, Master P, Snoop Doggy Dogg, and Public Enemy, to name a few. This culture, as we know it, is less than 25 years old, but the rap artist sets the trends that Black males follow. The roots of hip hop music and culture stem from the "bebop" and "cool jazz" arena of the 1940s and 1950s. This was a time when frustrated African American musicians, males in particular, expressed their concerns over their place in society as Black males. This is the underlying theme of hip hop music. Hip hop culture provides a voice in society for African Americans. Some artists speak of violence whereas others promote peace. Some rap artists dress in baggy clothes and others don suits. These are the trends that African American adolescent males follow. Each male that considers himself to be a part of the hip hop culture follows the trends and incorporates the ideologies of rap artists who appear to share the young African American males' experiences.

It is this connection between the young African American male and rap artist that contributes to the development of the young African American male identity. Some adults have identified this connection and have worked to establish programs that promote positive identity development. These programs seek to get socially conscious Black youth to register to vote, stop the violence, and educate the community on AIDS by circulating messages of abstinence and safe sex. Individuals who do not wish to explore and learn about hip hop for themselves most often gain a negative and sometimes one-sided perspective from media sources. This perspective often sees a culture that promotes degradation of women and violence. These negative images overshadow a longer list of positives including the recent emergence of Christian rappers, stay-in-school (educated) rappers, and "take back the community" (social) rappers.

Hip hop is a language, dress, attitude and overall lifestyle that should not be ignored. It is very much a part of the African American experience, a place where frustration and anger can be voiced and received by sympathetic ears.

IDENTITY DEVELOPMENT, VIOLENCE, AND AGGRESSION

Another important factor that contributes to African American male identity development is the influence and practice of assaultive violence. Assaultive violence is defined by Hammond and Yung (1993) as "nonfatal and fatal interpersonal violence where physical force or other means is used by one person with the intent of causing harm, injury, or death to another." The numbers of African American males between 15 and 24 years of age who have died of homicide is staggering. Rodriguez (1990) reports that homicide is the second leading cause of death among children and adolescents across all ethnic groups and ages. Between 1978 and 1988, homicide was the leading cause of death for African American males. In 1988, 77% of homicides among teenagers 15–19 years of age were associated with firearms, and of this percentage, 88% were among African American males. A similar pattern exists for ages 20–24 in which 70% of deaths were due to firearms, and of this percentage, 81% were among African American males (Barrett, 1993). During 1987, murder accounted for 42% of all deaths of African American men between 15 and 24 years of age. Of these, 34% were a result of firearm assaults (Public Health Service [PHS],

1991). With this prevalence rate, the most at-risk group by age, gender, and ethnicity are African American adolescent and young adult males (Hammond & Yung, 1993; PHS, 1991).

According to Barrett (1993), Wolfgang and Ferracuti (1967) concluded that based on the overrepresentation of violence in American "ghettos," there must be unique dynamics inherent in this way of life that somehow foster violence. Implications from this theory have been made that one group is more prone to violence than another. This leads to the reasoning, when the theory is applied to African American males, that there must exist a gender-related sanctioning of assaultive violence (Roberts, 1990). Barrett (1993) and Wilson (1992) contend that the prevalence of African American male adolescent violence must be viewed in the context of the role of violence in American society's entire framework. Wilson (1992) makes the argument that violence is part of the American experience for those of African descent in America by virtue of slavery, racism, SES inequality, and cultural denial.

There are many different facets that contribute to African American adolescent male violence. First, adolescents have poorly developed coping skills to address anger associated with economic and discrimination-related identity issues. For example, according to Hammond and Yung (1993), resentment, anger, and frustration result from the awareness on the part of youth of the lack of material resources, which affects their self-esteem. Negative self-perceptions set the stage for environmental factors, such as accessible guns, to socialize the youth to act out aggressively. If, for example, the negative self-perception is self-hatred, then young African American men may lash out at those who resemble themselves. Aggression, which the individual can control and which provides immediate rewards, then is utilized to compensate for the males' inability to succeed in social arenas such as school, family, or work. The need for affiliation then encourages the bonding of like-minded adolescents into counterculture groups such as gangs (American Psychological Association Commission on Violence and Youth, 1993; Curry & Spergel, 1992). Individuals and gangs are likely to act out aggressively against those who are most conveniently situated geographically, economically, and in age, as they compete for the same local resources and attempt to establish individual and group identity through reputation (Hammond & Yung, 1993).

To summarize, too many young African American males incorporate violence into their developing identity. Given the amount of violence to which they are typically exposed, young African American males quickly learn that those of them who act out in the most violent manner are perceived by other young African American males to be "strongest" within the community. In short, they develop a reputation that leads others to begin to respect and fear them. Strong reputation reaps other rewards such as status, which promotes their level of social desirability and confidence as they are admired by young females in the community. Consequently, other young males in the community emulate the same aggressive behavior because they do not want to be perceived as "weak."

In short, young males want to be perceived as strong, and thus get drawn into the vicious cycle of violence against other young African American males. Connecting with similar others in groups or gangs only encourages more aggressive behavior as young men attempt to build and maintain reputations within the group, protect and be protected by the group, and seek revenge for aggressive actions taken by other groups.

A ritual factor that contributes to the incorporation of aggression into the male African American identity is the portrayal of violence in the media. In July 1991, the motion picture *Boyz 'n the Hood* began showing at theaters around the country. Although calm was the norm at the majority of theaters, many others became the setting for real-life violence, including several shootings. Movies often portray aggressive acts in which the actors are rewarded for their violent behaviors and perceived as heroes, not villains. Young African American males view these "heroes" in movies and television shows and emulate their behaviors with the expectation that they will receive the same social rewards as the actors in the movies.

Young males who exhibit aggressive competence acquire social status. Since identity development is largely socially defined, young males attempt to incorporate behaviors that reap them social rewards. The feedback that they gain from others in the community is that they need to be perceived as cool and strong. Thus, young African American males are more than willing to include aggressive attitudes and behaviors that promote their status and help them to define their identities.

SUMMARY, CONCLUSION, AND RECOMMENDATIONS

The task of identity development for African American males is a significant challenge that is impacted by how they define themselves ethnically in an oppressive society, whom they identify with and model, and by peer attitudes and behaviors. To know oneself through self-discovery can potentially discourage later maladaptive and dysfunctional lifestyle choices. Educational and community resources must be tapped to nurture the psyche of African American males. Healthy identity development, while an individual struggle, is the collective responsibility of teens, parents, and educators. What is critically important to this struggle is the need for African American males to receive continuous reinforcement for academic progress and success. Parents, role models, peers, and educators must transmit the belief that these teens can succeed, and then insure that it happens. The following recommendations are made in an effort to effectively achieve this goal.

Parent Training

Parent training workshops can be established to meet the needs of the parents relative to improving communication between the parent and adolescent male. Workshop topics should include adolescent issues, conflict management, communication skills, and tutorial training. It is essential that the program be nonthreatening and interactive. Where possible the workshop should be conducted by parents, giving greater validity to the program content. Support groups can also be utilized for sharing insights and strategies.

For example, positive self-esteem and emotional support can be taught to parents as components of effective coping. Parents would be encouraged to be available for companionship, to discuss issues, and to let their teenagers know that they care. Discussion ahead of time of ideas such as sex, peers, social conduct, drugs, and curfew will help to prevent parent-teen conflicts from reaching intense levels.

Parents need to be actively involved in their teens' academic progress. This becomes particularly critical during adolescence, when teens are attempting to become autonomous while still being dependent on parents. Schools can establish regular dialogue sessions for adults and teens. Dialogue with African American adolescent males must be open, frank, and honest. Educators and parents must learn to distinguish between what young males want and what they need. These sessions should allow African American males to openly speak their minds. Open-ended conversations can help them discover what they are really thinking and feeling. Adults' use of personal experiences will add to the dialogue while building rapport, trust, and a sense of connectedness. Parents should also be prepared to move from an autocratic decision-making position, which will likely create resentment and inhibit youth from developing independent, responsible behavior, to one that is collaborative and participatory.

Mentoring

Mentors are more experienced persons who agree to develop a one-to-one relationship with a less experienced person and serve as a competent role model. Mentors should be selected from the school or community and should be Black males, if possible. They should be established in the community, model appropriate social behaviors, and most important, be reliable and accessible to the mentee. Training should be given to the mentors so they can effectively guide the youth's development into young adulthood. Mentors should select activities that include things that are mutually rewarding. Mentors should be trained to have open-ended discussions that allow the youth to talk freely. Exposure to social, occupational, and educational opportunities is essential. It is through this exposure that the mentor facilitates intellectual/emotional growth and development.

Curriculum Development

Much of learning and the development of solutions to complex problems lies in the ability to integrate separate bodies of information. The task is for middle school teachers and interdisciplinary teaching teams to identify the most important concepts and principles within each discipline and integrate these main ideas into a meaningful curriculum that is reflective of African American adolescent issues and experiences. Currently, emphasis is placed on covering large quantities of information rather than on the depth and quality of understanding its relevance and application. African American history and literature can be taught to dispel many of the myths about the Western experience while emphasizing mastery of the fundamentals (reading, writing, math). The curriculum should emphasize critical thinking and problem solving through the use of journals, small group and individual projects, portfolios containing drafts as well as finished work, and the use of interactive technological approaches (media, web site, laser disc, CD-ROM). Cooperative learning can provide African American males with an opportunity to succeed and can help them learn and retain information better. Great care must be given to insure that the curriculum is multiculturally sensitive. Multicultural education is important because it encourages identity, promotes development of self-esteem, and discourages isolation while encouraging integration and respect for others.

Enrichment Programs

Enrichment programs must be accessible to African American males within the schools. Program content and methods should match their interests. Partnerships and collaborations with local community organizations and businesses should be encouraged. Integration of families, schools, and other community partners is necessary to foster a strong community support system. Enrichment programs must identify and nurture the participant's skills while matching that interest to available community resources.

Professional Development

Professional development must prepare teachers and administrators to teach as part of a team. Furthermore, they must be taught to design and assess meaningful interdisciplinary curricula while understanding the development of African American adolescent males. Specific training in working with African American males and their families must be included. Equally important is the acceptance of African American culture, which includes style of dress, music, and language. Creative methods for incorporating these cultural differences into daily classroom life will foster a sense of achievement and inclusion. Additionally, African American students need to learn something of their history and cultural heritage. They need to be exposed to African American achievers such as lawyers, politicians, teachers, doctors, news anchors, military officers, and so on. This puts African American achievement closer at hand. Then it is the responsibility of educators to believe and to instill in African American youth the belief that they can achieve the same professional goals. Teens are not likely to thrive academically unless they first believe themselves to be worthwhile individuals.

Guidance Counseling

Guidance counselors must begin to play stronger roles in elevating the academic and career aspirations of African American male adolescents. This is critical given that many of them live in impoverished conditions and seek to compensate for this through illegal means. The more guidance skills the counselors possess, the better they will be able to assist and direct students toward assessing and obtaining their educational needs and goals. Counselors should be adequately trained and prepared to teach psychosocial competency skills such as self-concept building, anger control, problem solving and interpersonal relationship skills, as well as goal setting and values assessment. Counselors can encourage students to seek out and utilize stress-reducing support systems when they feel angry or depressed so that maladaptive coping behaviors can be avoided. Students will turn to guidance counselors for help if they feel that the latter are willing to listen and be nonjudgmental. For occasions when the problem is too great for the counselor to bear, an up-to-date list of local adolescent mental health professionals and community health agencies should be kept for making referrals.

Making It Cool to Be Educated

Implementing some or all of the aforementioned recommendations will provide a functional approach to making education "cool." Educators must keep in mind that coolness is relative to the student's experience. If educators and parents can provide a positive educational experience that is included in the male adolescent's sense of identity, then that child will be in a better place to influence his peers academically. This will have to begin with the diminishing of the belief that being educated is a European or feminine trait. Positive African American role models is one avenue that educators can utilize to dispel this perception. It is important for young African American males to see other African American males demonstrating the integration of educated and cool behaviors, and be able to build relationships with those individuals in a nonthreatening manner.

Responsive Teaching for African American Male Adolescents

Peter Murrell, Jr.

ONE OF THE MOST TROUBLING problems in urban education is that African American children, particularly males, have been categorically underserved by public schools. In particular, disproportionately large numbers of African American boys in our city schools are expelled, suspended, relegated to special education programs, and left with fewer personal resources than their European American peers. Clearly a combination of political, economic and sociological factors contributes to the inability of teachers, schools, and schools systems to uniformly promote educational success among urban African American children. A systematic pedagogical understanding of how these factors shape the culture of individual classrooms is essential for reversing these negative trends.

Educators are not likely to develop a pedagogical knowledge base of the critical aspects of class and culture for nonmainstream minority-group learners unless a theory is developed that addresses how these students make sense of the curriculum in the context of their unique racial, ethnic, cultural, and political identities. More specifically, teachers cannot fully interpret the developmental learning of these students without an analysis and synthesis of the students' experiences with the curriculum and knowledge of how they position themselves in the culture of the classroom. This necessitates that teachers acquire a deep understanding of the discourse routines and dynamics of the educational settings these students find themselves in.

Developing an understanding of these issues as they relate to African American male students' academic achievement in mathematics is compli-

African American Males in School and Society: Practices and Policies for Effective Education. Copyright © 1999 by Teachers College, Columbia University. All rights reserved. ISBN 0-8077-3870-0 (pbk), ISBN 0-8077-3871-9 (cloth). Prior to photocopying items for classroom use, please contact the Copyright Clearance Center, Customer Service, 222 Rosewood Dr., Danvers, MA 01923, USA, tel. (508) 750-8400.

cated by recent developments in mathematics curricula. A National Council of Teachers of Mathematics (NCTM) (1989) document titled *Curriculum and Evaluation Standards for School Mathematics* is presently transforming the instructional practices and classroom dynamics of mathematics learning in significant and positive ways. These standards emphasize developing learners' abilities to use mathematics in problem solving, reasoning, and communicating by engendering a greater emphasis on understanding mathematics concepts than on achieving computational competence. They explicitly promote educational outcomes that include dispositions such as self-confidence in doing mathematics and valuing it as a discipline. They further call for instruction that encourages students to

1. articulate their reasons for using a particular mathematics representation or solution;
2. summarize the meaning of data they have collected;
3. describe how mathematical concepts are related to physical or pictorial models; and
4. justify arguments using deductive or inductive reasoning.

Thus, the NCTM standards influence an important dimension of the classroom culture: the discourse of learning or "math talk." Gee (1991) defines a discourse as "a socially accepted association among ways of using language, of thinking, and of acting that can be used to identity oneself as a member of a socially meaningful group or 'social network'" (p. 3). However, to the degree that many urban African American students do not share mainstream,[1] middle-class perspectives or assumptions about learning and teaching, these students may construct profoundly different subjective worlds from those anticipated by the teachers who teach to these standards (Kochman, 1981).

The recent curricular innovations in calling for greater emphasis on communication in mathematical reasoning (as articulated in the NCTM standards, for example), together with the fact that most instructional time is teacher-initiated talk (e.g., Goodlad, 1981) underscore the importance of classroom discourse as the foundation of children's classroom learning. Because the uses of language and forms of discourse are critical determinants of the degree to which children can participate in the social-interactional dynamics of learning, it is important to understand how new forms of classroom discourse may marginalize those who do not already have access to them (Bowers & Flinders, 1990).

In this chapter I synthesize results of a critical ethnography of classroom practices of mathematics instruction. Specifically, I analyze the discourse patterns and speech events[2] that evoke qualitatively different learning experiences for African American male students in urban schools. The purpose of this synthesis is to systematically account for the ways that particular teaching practices that are intended to promote deeper understanding of mathematics for all children actually diminish African American students' opportunities to understand, communicate, and apply mathematical ideas. From this account, a pedagogical framework of responsive mathematics instruction for African American males will be described.

CULTURE AND CLASSROOM DISCOURSE

Increasingly, teachers whose backgrounds are middle class and mainstream are being called upon to promote both conceptual understanding and communication skills among urban school children of color. Preparing teachers to work effectively across boundaries drawn by culture, racial/ethnic, and class differences continues to be a problem (Murrell, 1991, 1993). However, as most students in American public schools are increasingly children of color in urban settings, the stakes are high with regard to finding ways of providing these students with teachers who can promote their learning, development, and intellectual growth.

Classroom learning is a social process requiring considerable communication, coordinated action, and common understanding (McDermott, 1977). Recent ethnographic research findings make connections between cultural and social-class differences on the one hand, and educational achievement on the other hand. In particular, this body of research suggests that differences in the way in which the social context of the classroom is construed by culturally mainstream teachers in contrast to students from historically marginalized groups (e.g., African American, Native American, Mexican American) often result in diminished academic success for the latter; including African American (e.g., Foster, 1989; Heath, 1983; Ladson-Billings, 1989; Lubeck, 1985), Mexican American (Diaz, 1989; Erickson, Cazden, & Carrasco, 1983), Native American (Erickson & Mohatt, 1982; Phillips, 1972), and Pacific Islander (Au & Jordan, 1981; Kawakami, 1991).

The growing ethnographic research literature revealing how cultural incompatibility diminishes school success of culturally nonmainstream children in mainstream schools has provided the impetus for efforts aimed at transforming current pedagogical practices. However, findings from this research literature do not constitute a basis for formulating a pedagogical theory for improving the academic fortunes of those children.

As Ogbu (1986, 1992) forcefully argues, cultural and language differences between African American children and mainstream culture are insufficient to account for the diminished quality of these children's schooling experiences. He reminds us that culturally linked perspectives, abilities, and ways of knowing do not exist in a vacuum; and that the historical, political, and economic fortunes of an ethnic or cultural group determine the extent to which their cultural and linguistic distinctiveness from mainstream American culture becomes an educational disadvantage. For African Americans specifically, the utility of the cultural-incompatibility concept is voided because multiple concepts exist regarding what constitutes African American culture. Moreover, even if there were a single, agreed-upon conception, no culture or cultural form exists in unaltered form; rather, this almost always arises out of contact or contestation with other forms. Similarly, many of the culture differences that create problems for children of particular ethnic or cultural groups arose out of their contact with the dominant culture engendered by public schooling. Among these differences, which are called secondary cultural differences, are those that emerge as opposition and resistance to the dominant culture.

There are several reasons for the limitation of cultural incompatibility in the formulation of theory. First, use of the concept has the unfortunate effect of dichotomizing cultural background into two categories: mainstream and "other." This bifurcated notion of culture recapitulates the problems of diversity as faced by public schools—namely, reductionistic and stereotypical thinking about what constitutes the culture of the other, and the conceptualization of African American culture only according to the ways in which it differs from mainstream cultural sensibilities. Implications for practice are left hanging at that point because "difference" too has become reified without a practical understanding of the meaning and significance of cultural differences.

Second, the use of the concept retards the critical understandings teachers need to develop about their own culture relative to those of the students in their classrooms. The cultural-incompatibility notion presupposes an understanding of both school culture and a home culture that rarely exists in practice. Without a deep understanding of which aspects in a student's cultural background support learning and which do not, the culture of a student becomes a self-fulfilling category in the process of schooling. Without first providing a means of making commonly sensible the important elements of culture with respect to schooling in both locations, there really is no foundation on which to build a pedagogy of culturally responsive teaching and learning.

Many African American students, for instance, are unavoidably "bicultural" (Darder, 1992) in these contexts because they must learn to negotiate the cultural world of school and reconcile it with that of their homes and communities. Culturally Black students in "culturally White" school settings may be subject to more than the typical interpersonal conflicts around issues of race and belonging: they may be subject to intrapersonal conflict as well, as they struggle with the choice between not "selling out" their racial identity on the one hand and achieving academic success on the other (Fordham & Ogbu, 1986).

The identity struggles that students of color face are complex, and complicated beyond the simple bifurcated choice of whether to participate in mainstream culture represented by the institutional structure of schools on one hand, or to claim one's own ethnic/racial heritage on the other. Students do both. For example, the cultural expressions of African American students "representin' contemporary 'hiphop'" culture (Perry, 1995; Powell, 1991; Rose, 1991) or the demonstrative expressions of ethnic pride (e.g., as illustrated in the 1994 PBS airing of *School Colors*, as a *Frontlines* segment), emerge, in part, as oppositional expression and resistance to the dominant culture.

Clearly, the oppositional cultural markers adopted by African American students may not represent culture in conventional ways such as ethnic or national heritage, and they often combine aspects of ethnic and youth cultures. Therefore, the pedagogical problem to improve teaching and learning for children of color, particularly African American males, is not how to improve their assimilation into the mainstream culture. Rather, the problem is how to structure school cultures so that the quality of nonmainstream students' educational experience or the integrity of their identity development does not depend on the degree of assimilation to mainstream culture.

Bruner (1996) framed the question this way: What are the theory-informed practices for organizing the culture of school in ways that help young learners access those resources and acquire those tools necessary for full and effective participation in the broader culture? The public school classroom is the critical place to begin scrutiny of practices for organizing cultures of learning for the purpose of revising instructional practices, pedagogical decision making, and classroom interactional routines in ways that promote understanding among African American male students.

Deeper scrutiny of the discourse of mathematics classrooms may provide insights regarding how African American students construe the purposes of mathematics learning differently from their classmates. The distinct patterns of discourse among African American male students in the context of a new learning discourse termed "math talk" is examined next.

MATH TALK

The phenomenon of math talk denotes the types and amounts of discourse that occur during mathematics instruction, particularly the oral-reasoning performances of learners during teacher-led mathematics inquiries in the classroom. It consists of students' public talk and public display of mathematics reasoning, in both on-task and off-task situations, as well as their sense of the purpose of mathematics discourse.

Math talk can be seen as a variation of the typical IRE discourse sequence described by Cazden (1988), who contends that nearly all classroom discourse can be interpreted according to a basic pattern or concatenations of this pattern. According to Cazden, the IRE sequence consists of (I) teacher initiation, (R) learner response, and (E) teacher evaluation. The first step usually occurs in the form of a teacher's question about a solution to a problem; however, these questions most often are used to elicit from students a specific response. For example, a teacher might ask, "How many values can X take on here?" (I), to which the called-upon student might answer, "Two" (R), and obtain the teacher's evaluation of "Correct" or "Good" (E). Teacher initiation queries can take three forms: (1) open questions (e.g., "Can we treat a ratio the same way we treat a fraction?"), (2) request for information (e.g., "Now, what did we call these?"), and (3) invitation to initiate a math-talk sequence (e.g., "Well, let's see what we can figure out about this, shall we?").

Conversely, learners' responses can also take three: (1) choral responses (several students responding together in unison), either to open questions or calls for information; (2) overlapping talk, such as that which takes place in small-group problem-solving teams, or when the teacher purposely delays an evaluation to see what the class as a whole comes up with when students "have the floor" in the dialogue of inquiry; and (3) sequenced talk—that is, student discourse offered concurrent with the activity or task, such as when each student supplies part of an answer or negotiates the task procedure with a partner.

Because the teacher controls both the development and direction of the inquiry during math talk, there are two important variations in the mathematics IRE patterns that stem from teacher implementation of the NCTM standards' pedagogical emphasis on learner participation, ownership, and communication of reasoning in the learning processes. One of these is the length of the learner's "turn." The NCTM standards are based on the expectation that students will elaborate answers with supporting reasoning, and that their responses will include both a position and a rational for their positions. In such math talk, responses will include both a position and a rationale for their positions and learners are encouraged to provide rationales for every solution they generate. Therefore, relative to other kinds of directed discourse in the classroom, students are expected to do more talking. They are encouraged, and often prompted, to provide a rationale for their problem solving (e.g., "How do you know that?") or

Table 6.1. Percentage of 7th-Grade Students Scoring at or Above the National Average on the Iowa Test of Basic Skills in Mathematics by Race/Ethnicity, 1990–1991

	Alston	*Easton*	*Norton*	*Sutton*
Black	18	31	10	17
Hispanic	45	71	15	17
White	65	67	38	71

to evaluate another student's answer/reasoning (e.g., "Do you agree with what X came up with?"). An additional variation of the mathematics IRE pattern wrought by the NCTM standards is that teachers may suspend their evaluations of student responses until after several students have spoken (e.g., "Who has still another idea?").

METHOD

The method of investigation employed in the present study was modeled after the interpretative-research framework of the QUASAR Project on mathematics run by the Learning Development and Research Center at the University of Pittsburgh (Stein, Grover, & Silver, 1991). The initial observations of one of the classroom sites were performed by the researcher as a member of the QUASAR field observation team. The aspects of the QUASAR design adopted for this study were the one-week immersion of the researcher into the school life at each site, including formal interviews with the principals and with site coordinators (curriculum directors), and group interviews with the students. Another adopted aspect was the notion of a focus group, a selected group of four students upon whom classroom observations were focused. These students' classroom discourse was recorded electronically and their completed class work was analyzed. Structured group interviews were conducted with members of this group, as were informal interviews. Three target groups of African American male focus students were formed.

The Schools

Four urban middle schools—Alston, Easton, Norton, and Sutton—were selected for this study.[3] At the time of the study, all of the schools had African American populations near or exceeding 50%: Alston (58%), Easton (49%), Norton (56%), and Sutton (59%). All four schools had total enrollments exceeding 800 students. Table 6.1 compares mathematics achievement at the schools as indicated by the percentage of students who scored at or above the national average on the Iowa Test of Basic Skills. As depicted in this table, the standardized-test results of seventh graders in each of the middle schools on mathematics achievement reveal a discrepancy in the performance of White and African American students. In all four cases, the academic mathematics achievement for Hispanics and African Americans is significantly lower than that of Whites.

Four mathematics classrooms, one in each school, were selected for observation and its occupants selected for periodic, in-depth interviews exploring the focus students' emic experience of the mathematics curriculum. Each class was taught by a regular classroom teachers with the assistance of a student teacher for whom the researcher served as the college supervisor.

Sample

Twelve African American male students (6 sixth graders and 6 seventh graders) were selected as the focus students for the study. The students were selected on the basis of their being designated as "low ability" in mathematics by the classroom and student teachers.

Procedures

As part of an assignment routinely given to student teachers by the researcher, the four student teachers participating in the present study were required to (a) select from each of their classrooms three students who seemed to be having difficulty learning mathematics, (b) frame the nature of the students' learning problem or difficulty, (c) reflect on the contributing causes, and (d) generate an appropriate intervention. In the tradition of microethnography, the student teachers were to record in their teaching journals observational data consisting of continuous handwritten accounts of classroom interactions and activities during instruction. They were to note the frequency and types of IRE interactions that occurred in the classroom, the kinds of inquiries and responses that took place in group work, and the tropes of teacher talk and student talk (e.g., giving direction, providing information, displaying knowledge, etc.). Additionally, classroom artifacts, curricular materials, teaching materials, student class work, and homework in portfolios were analyzed in order to construct the conceptual landscape of the enacted curriculum. The researcher also observed and recorded informal interactions with students and school personnel outside the focus of the class period during which mathematics instruction took place.

Data gathering consisted of classroom observation and interviews, both formal and informal. The focus students in each classroom were interviewed as a group. Interviews with the principal and the curriculum coordinator were conducted individually. Interviews with teachers were informal, impromptu, and unscheduled. The bulk of the field observations were conducted during biweekly visits to the school sites. These visits included classroom-visitation sessions as well as meetings with the participating teachers.

Interpretation of the intended instructional goals in each of the four classrooms were also obtained through three-way conferences among the cooperating classroom teachers, the student teachers, and the researcher. This permitted a triangulation of perspectives as to what constituted the learning goals, how well instruction brought about these goals, and how well the instruction represented the NCTM mathematics standards. In addition to conferences evaluating the student teachers' performances, the researcher also assessed teaching practice through an evaluation of the student teachers' lesson plan designs and their analytical teaching journals.

Structured postobservation group interviews were conducted with the three focus students nominated from each classroom. The group interview focused on the students' perceptions of (a) the classroom experience in general, brainstorming answers to interview questions (e.g., "What does it take to get a good grade in Ms./Mr. _____'s class?"); and (b) the instruction (e.g., "What do you think was the main thing you were supposed to learn during this activity?"). As the three students brainstormed, all of their responses was recorded by the researcher on a drawing pad mounted upright on the table in front of the group.

RESULTS

All 12 of the focus students most frequently entered the mathematics discourse in their respective classrooms following request-for-information types of initiating questions. Only rarely did they respond to open questions, unless their responses were part of a unison response or responses to the teachers' invitations to initiate math talk. The infrequency with which the focus students participated in the class inquiry following these latter types of initiators suggests that the participation of the African American focus students was limited to the classic IRE role of supplying information. Table 6.2 summarizes the distinctions in the inquiry discourse of the present study's focus students contrasted with those intended by the NCTM curriculum standards. As this table shows, the contrast between the math talk roles intended by the instructional outcomes of the teacher and those assumed by this sample of African American male students differs markedly.

Table 6.2. Learning Goals and Learning Roles

	Intended Learner Role	*Role Assumed by Students*
Math talk goals	Manipulation of ideas and information	Manipulation of situation and people
Achievement goals	To understand the conceptual content	To meet performance requirements

All students (African American and White, male and female, sixth and seventh graders, etc.) tend to limit their explanations to the point at which they sense the other members of the class may conclude they are saying too much, showing off, or otherwise "acting like a brain." In public math talk during whole-class instruction, students almost always supply information to supplement their initial responses to the teacher's question. Typically, they merely await the prompts offered by the teacher's probe-type questions. In this manner, the IRE pattern is a familiar and frequently enacted discourse frame. In situations when a student continues talking and does not await the teacher's prompt of either an evaluation (E) or new initiating question (I), other students will exchange looks or make subtle comments.

In the present study, however, the African American male focus students were not at all influenced by such cues from peers. For example, in each of the classrooms it was customary for the teacher to require a representative from a group to come to the front and illustrate a set of solutions they had generated for an activity or problem. However, in such situations, the focus students frequently tended not only to hold the floor in the front of the class but also to insert ideas of their own that were not necessarily those of the group. They proceeded to "hold the floor" in front of the class for as long as they could, even after they had exhausted their set of meaningful things to say. Thus, the identifier "controller" was selected to designate the prominent features of the focus students' math talk participation in whole-group settings.

Moreover, in many instances it was obvious that the focus students were attempting through their discourse merely to "get over"—that is, respond in such a way, particularly when called upon, that they appeared to have a grasp of the subject matter when, in fact, they did not. To disguise their inability to answer a request for information, the students would often engage in superficial aspects of math talk. Although their responses monetarily satisfied their teachers, assessments of the students' mathematics performance reveal that the students did not attain the conceptual understanding that math talk is presumed to engender. What seemed to the students to be of greater importance than the inquiry and the need to understand mathematics concepts and ideas was their participation as a talker. The focus students seemed to regard verbal adroitness, whether or not it was substantive in terms of mathematics learning goals, as the criterion for doing well in mathematics class.

The focus students also frequently attempted to reframe the nature of the interactions with teachers during small-group interactions. They seemed to relish discovering small mistakes in the teachers' discourse, and often became obstinate just when they appeared to be on the verge of a critical point of understanding. Some discussion of the basis for this resistance and obstinacy is merited here. The data suggest that the teachers and focus students operated from two different frames in their math-talk interactions. Kochman (1981) would describe this as a classic example of a contestation of interactional styles: The teachers sought to engage in the kinds of discourse called for by the NCTM standards. The focus students, on the other hand, drew from their cache of verbal verve and adroitness to engage in discourse that allowed them to disguise the fact that they did not fully understand the concept at hand and avoid appearing dumb. The students were operating from the frame of maintaining face, or, as Majors and Billson (1991) would contend, they were more concerned about not losing their "cool pose," or sense of masculine identity. Thus, at one level, the focus students' resistance and obstinacy was a result of interpersonal conflict. That is, to admit that the teachers helped them get the answers or that they even needed help was, for these students, an admission of inadequacy. As though their identities as mathematics learners contradicted their racial, personal, and masculine identities, participating in math talk constitutes an approach-avoidance conflict of the motive to be assisted versus the motive to maintain a cool pose.

In general, the African American male students in this sample did not construe discourse-laden, inquiry-based mathematics instruction to represent a greater emphasis on understanding mathematics ideas. As teachers engaged in more math talks as a means of exploring and elaborating mathematics principles and concepts, these students did not regard the discussion as an increased focus on mathematics learning. Rather, they tended to regard the emphasis on math talk simply as a new regimen to be mastered to meet their teachers' requirements as a string of operations and concepts with little or no thematic coherence. As they acted on these perceptions, their learning performance differed dramatically from that intended by the curricular innovations. These differences are summarized in Table 6.3.

Comments offered during the group interviews reveal that in their perception of mathematics instruction, the sampled African American male students did not distinguish between behaviors of compliance and personal conduct from mathematics concepts, principles, and ideas. Table 6.4 presents a composite list of brainstormed items generated by the sixth graders

Table 6.3. Distinctions in the Learning Actions of African American Males

Intended Learner Role	Role Assumed by Students
Shorter lengths of turn-taking during public math talk	Longer length of turn-taking during public math talk
Monitoring of the quality of one's own rationale	Monitoring the effects of one's performance on the audience
Teacher evaluation taken as informational feedback regarding the concepts to be learned	Teacher evaluation taken as performance feedback regarding the quality of the performance
Rate of volunteering answers consistent throughout the public math talk inquiry	Rate of volunteering dramatically increases during the suspended evaluation during public math talk
Volunteers equal proportion of base-level information, as well as risking putting forth own ideas	Volunteers base-level information and not a risk taker in areas of uncertainty

in response to the questions "What do you think of when I say mathematics?" and "What does it take to get a good grade in this class?" What is significant about this list is that the number of items associated with conduct and classroom behaviors nearly matches that of items associated with mathematics concepts. The students generally did not distinguish mathematics achievement from behaviors associated with compliance, control, and classroom routine (e.g., turn in homework, listen to the teacher, do not talk, do your work, etc.), and their responses were far afield from the intended curricular goals (also shown in the table).

DISCUSSION

What understandings about responsive teaching for midlevel mathematics instruction can be gleaned from the study described in this chapter? Responsive teachers must act with the understanding that the relationship that students construct with their teachers, as well as with the subject matter, is shaped by the degree to which discourse routines and speech events promote interest, social participation, a sense of efficacy and industry, and a sense of purpose. As such, responsive teachers recognize and capitalize on

Table 6.4. Comparison of Student Responses and Intended Curricular Goals

Student Responses		
"What Do You Think About When I Say Mathematics?"	"What Does It Take to Get a Good Grade in This Class?"	Intended Curricular Goals
Pattern blocks	Come to class	Communication of
Worksheets	Listen and learn	reasoning
Fractions	Following directions	Organization of
Subtraction	Reading carefully	reasoning and ideas
Multiply	Getting an A	Communication of the
Decimals	Turn in all your work	appropriate concepts
Borrowing	Do your best	Development of ideas
Adding	Work real hard	Accurate computation
Carrying	Work with your partner	Problem comprehension
Blocks	Working nicely	
Building	No talking when	
Checking	someone else is	
Thinking	talking	
Learning	No walking in the	
Numerator	classroom when we	
Denominator	are working	
Whole numbers	Pay attention	
Bringing necessary	Be cooperative	
supplies	Do extra credit	
Listening	Don't talk back	
Solving problems		
Hard work		
Talking		
Not talking		
Discussing		
Cooperating		
Understanding		
overhead projector		
The sheets of work		
Not being late		
No talking		
Bringing homework		
on time		

the frames of discourse within which African American male students routinely operate. These include

1. a question-posing, teacher-challenging approach;
2. a preference from request-for-information teacher inquiries;
3. an eagerness to show off the knowledge they possess;
4. a penchant for extended explanation; and
5. a preference for "getting over" rather than admitting ignorance.

This requisite cultural knowledge for effective teaching with African American children was acquired through careful, systematic observation, not from any teacher-education tracts on "Black culture" or "learning styles" or "multicultural teaching and learning." The point demonstrated by the findings of the reported study is that to teach more responsively, teachers must not only understand their curriculum, but the manner in which their enacted curriculum structures the culture of their classrooms and children's experience of the curriculum.

CONCLUSION

An important principle for responsive teaching for African American male students is that the instructional practices designed to bring about conceptual understanding must be grounded in the organization of activity settings in the classroom, not merely in classroom discourse. Learning activity should be structured by actions and community building, not merely by verbal direction and public discourse. This means that teachers must (a) realize that learning requires a context of social interaction—learning by doing in a context of peer relationships—and relinquish the assumption that conceptual understanding can be imparted to youngsters through talk, (b) require that learning achievements be based in the demonstration of understanding rather than merely the display of knowledge through talk, and (c) find ways to align the high achievement motive of African American children with authentic demonstrations of understanding.

NOTES

1. Although the term "mainstream" has been ill defined in both popular and scholarly literature, I adopt it herein to coincide with the specific meaning given it by Heath (1983) in her now classic ethnography *Ways With Words: Language, Life, and Work in Communities and Classrooms.* As she states: "Mainstreamers

exist in societies around the world that rely on formal educational systems to prepare children for participation in settings involving literacy. Cross-national descriptions characterize these groups as literate, school-oriented, aspiring to upward mobility through success in formal institutions, and looking beyond the primary
networks of family and community for behavioral models and values orientations"
(pp. 391–392). In the United States, mainstream individuals and populations tend to
be white, middle class, and politically moderate to conservative. See Ogbu (1992) for
a discussion of why the historical experience of African Americans as "involuntary
minorities" virtually guarantees them nonmainstream status in America.

2. Gumperz (1982) defines speech activities as "a set of social relationships
enacted about a set of schemata in relation to some communicative goal" (p. 166).
What is argued here is that responsive teachers actively define and make explicit
the expectancies and rules for a speech activity, and, in a sense, define the speech
activity of mathematics learning.

3. Names of schools and students are pseudonyms.

Combating Educational Neglect in Suburbia: African American Males and Mathematics

Vernon C. Polite

THIS CHAPTER PROVIDES a case study of the mathematics-related experiences of a cohort of African American males who attended a suburban high school in the class of 1989. The outcomes of this case study remain important for parents and students today. The work is centered on the former students' reflections of their experiences in the mathematics department of a large public high school.

SETTING AND BACKGROUND

The Metropolitan Public School District[1] is located in a predominantly African American, midwestern, near-central-city suburb—one of many such typical, middle-income communities in the United States that are contiguous to a core city or are situated within the first and second geographical rings surrounding it (Farley, 1983; Grier & Grier, 1983; Kain, 1985; Stahura, 1987). Metropolitan City is approximately three square miles in size, predominantly populated by African Americans, and situated on the first geographical ring surrounding a large industrial city. The core city, not unlike other older and primarily African American cities across the country, is encircled by scores of incorporated municipalities, as Massey and Denton (1988) have demonstrated.

African Americans began moving to Metropolitan City during the mid-1970s. In 1970, only slightly more than 100 African American stu-

African American Males in School and Society: Practices and Policies for Effective Education. Copyright © 1999 by Teachers College, Columbia University. All rights reserved. ISBN 0-8077-3870-0 (pbk), ISBN 0-8077-3871-9 (cloth). Prior to photocopying items for classroom use, please contact the Copyright Clearance Center, Customer Service, 222 Rosewood Dr., Danvers, MA 01923, USA, tel. (508) 750-8400.

dents, or less than 9% of the total student body, attended Metropolitan High School (MHS). The majority was made of middle-income Jews and ethnic Whites. Between 1970 and 1990, the school lost an average of 90 White students each year while it gained approximately the same number of African American students annually. As African Americans moved into the Metropolitan Public School District, resulting in larger overall percentages of African American students, middle-income Whites in the district fled to the exurbs.

In 1970, MHS was reputed to be one of the best secondary schools in the state. However, within a relatively short period of time (20 years), MHS changed drastically in the areas of student socioeconomic status, achievement orientations, and attitudes toward schooling. The teachers remained relatively unchanged. The most obvious change, however, the racial makeup of the school, was apparent to teachers, parents, and students alike. By the close of the 1980s, the school was controlled by layers of rules and structure designed to control student behavior, primarily that of African American and Arabic males (see Polite, 1994).

Peer culture, with its heavy emphasis on drug trafficking and use, had an adverse impact on the overall school climate at MHS. Particularly among the class of 1989, it emerged as a consequential factor influencing the educational opportunities of many African American males at the school, second only to the importance the students placed on the role of "caring" on the part of teachers (Polite, 1994). There are those in the MHS community who would argue that the oppositional and oftentimes confrontational behaviors exhibited by the school's African American males were the central casual factors explaining their widespread underachievement. However, through my observations, document analyses, and interviews with students and teachers at MHS, it became apparent to me that the school—despite its status as a suburban school with a proven history of academic success—lacked a serious academic focus. Consequently, there may have been some justification for descriptions of the school as a "zoo," a "drug school," a "joke," and a "prison"—the metaphors most often used by the African American males whom I interviewed to describe their alma mater.

A cohort ($n = 115$) of lower-middle- and low-income African American males were enrolled in the 10th grade at MHS in the fall of 1986. These students comprised the sample for the present study. African American males have only rarely taken advantage of the more rigorous academic opportunities, especially those higher level courses within department of mathematics, traditionally available at MHS, and teachers and counselors have most often failed to direct them to these opportunities. Their parents most often self-effaced from direct involvement in the educational choices made by their sons, feeling less prepared to help (Polite, 1995). Conse-

Table 7.1. Courses Completed Within MHS's Mathematics Department by African American Male Students in the Class of 1989

Semester Course	Number of Students Who Completed Course	Percent of Students Who Completed Course
Pre-Algebra I	65	61
Pre-Algebra II	62	58
Algebra I	36	34
Algebra II	31	29
Geometry I	21	20
Geometry II	14	13
Trigonometry I	4	3
Calculus I	2	2

Notes: N = 107. The original number of 115 was reduced by 8 to reflect those students who transferred to other schools because of a change in residence.

quently, the school's African American male students have overwhelmingly enrolled in the lower-level and introductory courses in mathematics. Not more than 1 out of 15 of the MHS African American male alumni cohort was actually prepared for college-level work. Although the school offered the same higher level mathematics and science courses in the 1980s that were provided during the 1970s, my review of the subjects' individual transcripts revealed that few of these 115 students elected or successfully completed the traditional college-preparatory courses, particularly in the areas of mathematics (algebra, geometry, trigonometry, and calculus) (see Table 7.1). Corresponding shifts away from the prerequisite higher level courses for traditional college entry were observed in the sciences, English, social studies, and foreign languages departments as well. What became evident to me as the researcher was a strong correlation between the nonchallenging school environment and the increased incidents of class truancy, suspensions, violent behaviors, and classroom disruptions, particularly for the African American male cohort. In other words, the school became more socially oriented than academically oriented as the percentages of African American students increased with each passing year between 1976 and 1986.

Only about half the cohort (60) completed their high school education. Only 4 of these graduates earned a grade point average (GPA) above 3.0 (on a 4.0 scale), whereas 40 of them achieved GPAs below 2.0. Twenty-eight of the 115 subjects were administratively dismissed from school for nonattendance, 8 were expelled for violent and aggressive behaviors, 23 (20%) were incarcerated between September 1986 and June 1989, and 3 were killed due to their direct involvement in the drug culture.

It is therefore not surprising that only 15 out of 115 African American male students were college bound at the end of their senior year. Nor is it surprising that these few met with little success in getting admitted into 4-year colleges and universities, most of which commonly require all applicants to take either the ACT or SAT college entrance examination and submit their test scores as a prerequisite for admission. Only 17 of the 60 African American males who graduated from MHS in the class of 1989 even took the ACT examination.[2] Moreover, none scored within the highest interval and only three scored within the upper-middle interval.

PROCEDURES

I returned to Metropolitan City during the summer of 1992—3 years after the class of 1989's graduation anniversary (even though some of the non-graduates left MHS as long as 5 years prior)—to conduct semistructured interviews with 39 former students (29 graduates and 10 nongraduates). The 39 respondents accounted for 34% of the original cohort of 115. I used a telephone protocol to interview five former students who had relocated to other sections of country and were accessible only by telephone. I also interviewed five others who were imprisoned for drug-related crimes, whom I visited in three state prison facilities. All interviews were transcribed and topic-coded. Like codes were aggregated to facilitate analyzing the content across the respondents. Each respondent's answers were initially analyzed separately. Three levels of analysis were performed on the data. The first considered only the information provided by the respondent in direct response to a specific question; the second compared and contrasted the respondents' answers on related questions; the third was performed to disclose general patterns across multiple answers (Bogdan & Biklen, 1992).

The interview questions reported on here queried the respondents about their specific secondary school experiences in area of mathematics and related sciences including their perceived relevancy of the curriculum at MHS in preparing them for higher education, the work world, or both.

RESULTS

Reflections on MHS Teachers as Caring Professionals

Each respondent was asked to reflect on his secondary-schooling years at MHS, highlighting where possible the strengths and weaknesses of the school's mathematics curriculum, teachers, and counselors. There was overwhelming consensus among the former students with regard to issues of caring, academic challenge, effective teachers, and strengths and gaps in the curriculum. The social distancing between teachers and students reported by these students who attended MHS at the close of the 1980s stands in sharp contrast to the atmosphere of caring informality reported by students and teachers during the early 1970s, prior to the arrival of large numbers of African American students.

The lack of caring teachers and counselors at MHS emerged as a critically important issue for these African American males. Teachers and counselors were remembered as principally failing to create a challenging academic climate, particularly within the mathematics department, and generally lacking in their ability or desire to provide a caring school environment. By and large, the teachers at MHS were not well regarded by this cohort. On the other hand the respondents readily pointed out, with explicit details, those atypical teachers, both African American and White, whom they remembered as effective, supportive, and caring. Remarkably, these respondents' comments also reflected a sense of regret about and personal acknowledgment of the role that they themselves played in their poor schooling outcomes and their failure to take advantage of the academic opportunities available to them through the more rigorous curriculum offering. They commonly reported that they had "free choice" in deciding what courses to study and generally selected their courses based solely upon the minimum graduation requirements, not based upon their career goals. Consequently, they admitted that they themselves, as human agents, played a role in the nonacademic nature of the overall school climate during their high school years and in adversely affecting both teachers' attitudes and students' achievement.

The two excerpts that follow were typical sentiments shared by the African American males regarding their relationships with their teachers. There was a sense that they were left pretty much to their own demise, a fate that later caused them significant barriers when attempting to make the transition from secondary school to college, work, or both.

> Well, to me, I just wished—well, it's my fault, too—but I wished
> that the teachers would have cared more. For example, I went
> through like my senior year carrying a 3.4 [on a 4.0 scale]. I never
> brought books home, and everything was just easy. You know, no
> teachers cared. And then when I got to college I found out that it
> was a lot different. . . . 'Cause you know, I was real good friends
> with Mr. Peterson [back in high school], so I could leave any class
> any time and go to the gym. We used to play basketball. . . . The

teachers didn't care. I think my senior year, two of my teachers gave us open-book tests the whole year. Like Ms. Davidson, she gave us open-note tests, and then she'd basically—she gave us a review the day before the test. So you know, we just take in all our notes. And in her class, if you finished with all your tests, you just hand your notes back to one of your friends. [Ricky, attended a historically Black college for 2 years and returned to the local community college due to financial problems.]

I think the classes were offered there, but I don't think the students took them and nobody made [encouraged] them. The challenging courses were offered, but nobody took them. . . . I don't think that's service to kids. All that school had was more rules and [they didn't] give you anything on the other hand. That doesn't work very well. [Billie has worked in an unskilled position on the assembly line with a major factory. He has also attended the local community college part-time for 2 years.]

Reflections on Mathematics Instruction

When I was assigned to the school in 1986 as an assistant principal with complete access to course and enrollment records for each student in this cohort, I was concerned that the upper-level mathematics courses rarely included African American males. It became clear to me in this retrospective study that this cohort, in their postsecondary school lives, had begun to realize the importance of mathematics foundation courses as "gatekeeper courses" to college and ultimately to higher-paying jobs in the workplace. Their individual accounts exhibit their awareness of their lack of direction during their high school years and of the unwise choices that they themselves made while in high school. Similarly, the respondents were aware that the lack of good guidance and counseling support services at MHS resulted in many of them intentionally shying away from the more challenging mathematics courses in high school. The comments that follow provide important insight into the mathematics-related issue:

No one ever told me that I needed Algebra 1, 2, and 3; and geometry and trigonometry, calculus, and then all those sciences. I see now with my computer science classes [college classes] that you need to have a lot of math. I stopped at geometry. So it would have helped if I had gone a little farther, but I really didn't know that. I have to go much higher than geometry in my major now. [Benny]

If I were back in high school now, I would study advanced mathematics and electronics . . . electronics and computers. 'Cause that's the field that everything is moving towards: computers or electronics. I really didn't pay attention to it in high school. [Andrew works part-time for a major factory and a clothing store. He attended the community college for one year.]

I had Ms. Bonnelli's class for math. I like math. I still do like math to this day. I didn't get to trig [trigonometry]. I took geometry and then I took algebra [2]. My counselor stuck me in a pre-algebra class. I wasn't supposed to be there, but it was too late! I got put into pre-algebra because those tests they had gave us during freshman year I had missed [was absent]. So they just stuck me in general math, and then once I got up in there, the work was too easy. It was A's and everything. I don't know who my counselor was at the time. I took trig when I got into college. [Jimmie]

Rubenstein, that's who I had. He was a good teacher. Dr. Rubenstein, I had him for geometry. I used to come home every day, and my sister would help me with geometry. I got a B [the first semester]. And then, from there on out, I got C's. And then it started going down, because I got a new teacher, Mr. Black. Mr. Black, to me, didn't teach me. I mean, he taught, but he didn't really teach. I know that sounds stupid but he wasn't serious. [Dre' has served 2 years in the military. He joined the service because he could not find work or acceptance at a 4-year college.]

Math, I was always a little weak in that subject, so I never wanted to journey off too far in the math. Now I get mad at myself, but I think I did well. Science is another one, I don't know why. I liked math more than science. But I never was that good in math. . . . I enjoy math. It's a challenge to me. I think that I needed more support in those subjects back in high school. [Bill works on an assembly line at a major factory 20 hours per week.]

The majority (85%) of the members of this cohort built their high school programs around courses that had little relevance for their futures. For example, it was common for members of this group to have taken Ceramics I, II, III, IV and V or Photography I, II, III, IV and V, or both, whereas their mathematics courses, for example, consisted only of Pre-Algebra I and II and Algebra I. It was shocking to me, yet common, for these young men to articulate during the interview sessions their lack of knowledge about the prerequisites for specific college programs and jobs. Many reported that while in high school they had postsecondary plans for careers in mathematics, electronics, the sciences, health careers, and so forth, yet the overwhelming majority had enrolled in courses that were clearly unrelated. Fewer than 10% had enrolled in traditional college preparatory courses in mathematics.

DISCUSSION

The deplorable findings reported in the present case study are not surprising. The opportunities to learn available to African American males in this suburban community were foiled by the students' individual resistance to schooling as well as the clear lack of structured support from the school community in the form of effective teaching and counseling. It is fair to say that the members of this African American male suburban high school cohort meandered through secondary school, rarely if ever being academically challenged or sufficiently prepared for postsecondary schooling or work in the areas of mathematics. My findings also lead me to conclude that these students' opportunities to excel were stifled by a lack of direction from their counselors and teachers as well as their individual resistance to schooling. Consequently, I am compelled to refer to their high school experiences as an ecology of educational neglect.

By the late 1980s, the nature of the relationship between teachers and students, that in the 1960s and early 1970s was described as "caring informality," had been transformed to one of "high formality." The latter scenario was characterized by pronounced social distancing between teachers and African American male students, poor student achievement and attendance, high drop-out and expulsion rates, lack of caring White teachers, and negligible attention on the part of school personnel for career counseling and test-taking preparation for these students. Given the outcomes for African American males at MHS, the academic opportunities for African American males in other predominantly African American suburbs are also suspect.

These outcomes are not at all unlike findings on the education of African American males reported nationwide. Of the most recent examples, Garibaldi (1992) reported that within the New Orleans (LA) Public Schools, African American males accounted for 58% of the nonpromotions, 65% of the suspensions, 80% of the expulsions, and 45% of the dropouts, while accounting for only 43% of the school population. Leake and Leake (1992) research with the Milwaukee (WI) Public Schools showed that only 2% (or 135) of 5,700 African American males enrolled in that city's public secondary schools achieved cumulative grade point averages between 3.0 and 4.0, and 80% of the African American male high school students performed below average. Similarly appalling outcomes are reported annually by public school systems in Atlanta, Baltimore, Chicago, Cleveland, Detroit, and Washington, D.C.—all cities largely populated by African Americans.

In the case of Metropolitan High School as the racial social class compositions of the school changed, the quality of the educational outcomes, especially for African American males, declined drastically. Thus, the only conclusion that can be drawn from examination of these outcomes is that the school's mission, to provide a quality education to all students through effective teaching, was not being met for the population of students it presently serves. As the social-class composition of the school changed, so did the nature of the school environment and academic outcomes experienced by the students, most of whom were African American. As the school became more oriented toward an order-and-discipline atmosphere, most of the students, including the 115 African American males I studied, left MHS unprepared for the demands of college and university work in the mathematics areas and ill prepared for the postindustrial workplace of the Midwest. As a result, the path of education, formerly seen as a way out of the working-class situation in which most of these students found themselves, was closed off at MHS, particularly for African American males.

CONCLUSION AND RECOMMENDATIONS

How can the cycle of miseducation in the mathematics disciplines observed at this and other high schools in urban-fringe school communities be broken to ensure greater opportunities for African American males in particular and all students in general? Since the mid-1980s, when this study was begun, MHS has been the target of various school reform activities under the direction of its principal. In the past 6 years, numerous curricular changes have occurred at the school. For example, special remedial assistance and counseling are now provided to all incoming students, and students are now required to take and pass courses in algebra and geometry, as well as sciences, prior to graduation. Academic and career planning have also become a central focus of the counseling staff's activities. The school and community have begun addressing the special needs of African American male students, and issues related to cultural and racial differences between the teachers and students are now part of a new ongoing discourse within the school. As a result of these and other school-reform efforts, incidents of violence and crime within the school have diminished significantly.

There is, however, still much work to be done within the Metropolitan Public Schools before trenchant and systemic change will effect the education of African American males at MHS. My recommendations are that the following factors become part of the systemic change at the school:

1. Ongoing career planning and in-service training for counselors and teachers should be provided. There should also be a clear focus on encouraging students to set career goals. Students must clearly understand the importance of mathematics in the workplaces of the future and the nexus between mathematics and technology.
2. All students, particularly African American males, should be required to develop career objectives including career goals, specific achievement strategies, and a plan of action for fulfilling the course requirements needed to realize those goals. Students should review and adjust their goals and strategies annually under the support of teachers and counselors. Again, higher level courses in mathematics should not be presented as options but as requirements for high school graduation.
3. Semester reports displaying mathematics-course enrollments by course title, grade, gender, and race should be generated and disseminated to parents, elected officials, students, teachers, administrators, and counselors. School administrators should be held accountable for the underrepresentation of any particular group within the school's higher level mathematics course, especially African American students and girls.
4. Administrators should insure that the content offered in the various courses in mathematics meet the national standards. In the case of MHS, where too many African American students excluded themselves from the higher level mathematics courses, many of the courses had been "watered down," meaning that for those students enrolled in the higher level mathematics courses, the content received was less than adequate.
5. A continuing education program for all teachers must be developed and implemented. This program should provide teachers with skills in multicultural learning, communication, cultural, and social styles, with an emphasis on African Americans.
6. As teaching vacancies occur, qualified African Americans (and non-African Americans) who are sensitive and responsive to the cultural, social, economic, and educational conditions and aspirations of African Americans must be hired.

In this chapter I have described some of the important mathematics-related experiences of the African American male cohort of the class of 1989 at Metropolitan High School in an attempt to explore the consequences of demographic change on the quality of educational outcomes. Given the similarities between the outcomes of the students at MHS and other African American males across the country, it is hoped that this discussion will lend insights into the process by which African American males become underprepared in the area of mathematics in this society and how this condition of underpreparation can be eliminated and reversed.

NOTES

An earlier version of this article was presented at the annual meeting of the American Educational Research Association, April 1993, Atlanta, Georgia. The author gratefully acknowledges the financial support used for the completion of this project provided by the Spencer Foundation of Chicago, Illinois.
    1. This name and other names referring to the school, its locale, and the former students are pseudonyms.
    2. Most college-bound students throughout the midwestern states traditionally took the ACT examination, whereas the SAT is generally taken by those students residing in the northeastern section of the country.

8 An Absence of a Talented Tenth

Joseph A. Hawkins

THE SUBURBAN DRAW has not escaped African Americans. In 1996, according to the U.S. Bureau of Census, 70% of African Americans in the nation lived outside central cities. For many, however, the image of Blacks in the suburbs is a strange one. Certainly, the image requires many to suspend nearly everything they recognize about "Black pop culture," which always seems framed by "the urban"—rap music, Hollywood gangster films, and the evening TV news broadcasts.

Regardless of race or ethnicity, most individuals moving to the suburbs do so for similar reasons—safe neighborhoods, better jobs, affordable homes, and modern schools. Over the past 20 years, as a full-time researcher in a large suburban school district, I have referred to this move as the search for the "land of milk and honey" that pie-in-the-sky place where all dreams come true. Such expectations, however, do not seem so far fetched for Blacks moving into wealthy school districts from poverty-stricken inner-city school districts. When it comes to schools, especially the resources, most suburban school districts simply are light years ahead of their neighboring urban districts. For example, many suburban school districts benefit from generous capital-improvement budgets, assuring students, at a minimum, modern school facilities. Many neighboring urban school districts, however, barely can afford to put new roofs on their aging school buildings.

It also has been my experience, over years, that for Black youngsters, their mere physical presence in the suburbs does not translate into anything automatic when it comes to schooling outcomes. In fact, in spite of the wealth and the abundance of resources it brings, Black youngsters struggle in the suburbs. And without question, Black males struggle much harder

African American Males in School and Society: Practices and Policies for Effective Education. Copyright © 1999 by Teachers College, Columbia University. All rights reserved. ISBN 0-8077-3870-0 (pbk), ISBN 0-8077-3871-9 (cloth). Prior to photocopying items for classroom use, please contact the Copyright Clearance Center, Customer Service, 222 Rosewood Dr., Danvers, MA 01923, USA, tel. (508) 750-8400.

than do Black females. In this chapter, with particular emphasis on Black males, I explore some of the major factors that contribute to this disturbing reality.

THE COMMUNITY

Montgomery County, Maryland, located directly outside of the nation's capital, Washington, D.C., is one of the wealthiest counties in the nation. In 1995, the county's wealth per pupil stood at an astounding $394,980. In comparison, Baltimore City's, just to the north of Montgomery County, per pupil wealth stood at $124,290 (Maryland State Department of Education, 1995). The Montgomery County 1990 U.S. Census report indicated that the median household income stood at $54,089. In 1990, there were only seven other counties in the entire nation with higher household incomes. Many of the county's nearly 100,000 Black Americans participate in this wealth, and Blacks are very well represented among the county's professional ranks. In the Montgomery County Public Schools (MCPS), the 15th largest public school district in the nation, it is extremely common to find Black students coming from homes where both parents are present and employed. It also is rather common to find Black parents who are college graduates.

When one considers all these factors together, it becomes difficult to argue against the notion that all the key ingredients are not present to foster academic success for the nearly 25,000 Black students enrolled in the county schools. Nevertheless, the right social and economic conditions do not translate automatically into the right outcomes. If it is a *good* academic thing—Scholastic Achievement Test (SAT) scores, grades, honors course work—Black students generally come in last place. If it is a *bad* academic thing—suspensions, special education placements (i.e., overrepresentation)—Black students generally come in first place. When academic measures and outcomes are disaggregrated further by gender, the picture worsens, with Black males nearly always coming in dead last.

AN ABSENCE OF BLACK MALE SCHOLARS

In the spring of 1997, when my daughter graduated from Walt Whitman High School in Bethesda, Maryland, she departed with a distinguished academic record. Across 21 senior high schools in my school district, the Montgomery County Public Schools (MCPS), a mere 6% of the seniors from the class of 1997, approximately 435 out of 7,100 seniors, matched my daughter's academic record. Few exceeded her with an earned academic grade point average of 3.5 or better, SAT scores of 1300 or better, and 18 or more earned honor/advanced placement credits.

To graduate from a public Maryland high school, a senior must earn 22 total credits. My daughter left high school with a total of 29 credits. More than half her credits were earned in honor/advanced placement course work.

If one were to sit this exclusive group of academic achievers down in the same school auditorium, one would notice very few Black students among the hundreds of faces. In fact, my daughter, and roughly nine other Blacks—practically all females, would take seats in the auditorium. The MCPS Class of 1997 graduated more than 1,200 Black students.

But even if we lower the standards, it still is unlikely that significantly more Black students would find seats in the auditorium. We could drop the SAT score down to 1200 points and about 50 more Black students would show up. That's 50 out of more than 1,700 seniors scoring 1200 points or more on the SAT. Dropping the honor/advanced placement credit requirement down to 15 credits would have a similar impact: about 50 more Black students would show up. That's 50 out of more than 1,300 seniors accumulating 15 or more earned honor/advanced placement credits.

The situation I described for my daughter—the rarity of her academic record for a Black student—is not a fluke. Over the years, study after study has demonstrated with absolute clarity that Black students in MCPS do not participate in the county's abundance of academic excellence. For example, in 1990, A. Wade Boykin and Lawrence Johnson conducted a study commissioned by MCPS on school suspensions and had this to say: "Black students are less involved in their schools and are more likely to see their schools as problematic places" (Boykin & Johnson, 1990, p. 46). That same year, a different commissioned study, undertaken by Edmund Gordon, observed, "Ethnic minority group students tend to be over-represented in special education and less demanding classes and under-represented in classes for able and gifted students" (Gordon, 1990, p. 7). In their 1996 book, *Dismantling Desegregation: The Quiet Reversal of Brown v. Board of Education*, authors Gary Orfield and Susan Eaton (1996) disagreed with claims by MCPS that it has eliminated the racial gaps in educational attainment. They wrote, "Data fail to corroborate the MCPS's argument that racial gaps in educational attainment have narrowed considerably. . . . Clear and large gaps remain on tests of higher order skills and on success rates in important college preparatory experiences" (p. 237).

To a great extent, these rather sobering assessments—all conducted by respected researchers—have been ignored by school officials. The district's

Table 8.1. Number of Honor Credits Earned at Montgomery County Public Schools by Race/Ethnicity

	Class of:							
	1990	*1991*	*1992*	*1993*	*1994*	*1995*	*1996*	*1997*
Asian	6.1	6.8	7.7	8.0	8.6	8.6	9.4	9.3
White	4.3	4.8	5.4	5.7	6.3	6.9	7.1	7.5
Hispanic	1.7	2.3	2.0	2.4	2.3	2.6	2.4	2.8
Black	1.6	1.7	2.1	2.3	2.3	2.8	2.8	2.9
Black males	1.3	1.4	1.3	1.8	1.5	1.8	2.0	2.2

superintendent—a Black man—is fond of communicating a reality that is clearly at odds with the facts. In 1995, writing to the county's board of education about "marvelous" academic achievement gains, earned by "all" students, he wrote, "With nearly the same number of students overall, but within a significantly different racial and ethnic mix and a larger percentage of students receiving economic assistance, we are sending more students to college, with significantly higher average scores of the SAT. Increasingly higher levels of academic performance have been achieved among all racial and ethnic groups of students" (Montgomery County Public Schools, 1995, pp. 2–3).

Table 8.1 clearly illustrates that Blacks, especially Black males, leave MCPS less prepared than do their White counterparts. With some certainty, MCPS knows the fate of its less prepared graduates. A 1996 study conducted jointly by MCPS and Montgomery College revealed that the less prepared graduates—those with very few earned honor credits—entering the county's community college system are more likely to be placed in remedial programs, earn lower grades, and accumulate fewer college credits (Larson, Garies, & Campbell, 1996). This is not a formula for success, and most of the poor performing graduates end their education at Montgomery College without a degree.

WHY ARE THINGS THE WAY THEY ARE?

It is difficult to remember a time when MCPS has not had a special effort under way to address the academic needs of Black students. When I started working for MCPS in 1979, the "Black Action Steps" had just gotten started. This initiative outlined 32 strategies to address underachieving of Black students. The Black Action Steps died quietly in the early 1980s when a conservative school board majority came into power.

In the mid-1980s, with a new and more compassionate school board, "Priority 2" (also referred to as the Minority Student Achievement Plan) came into existence. This initiative was very similar to the Black Action Steps; however, this time around the academic rescue mission was expanded to include the rapidly growing Hispanic student population. Priority 2 did not die as quickly as its 1970s counterpart but it did die nonetheless. It is important to point out here, however, that an active and critical African American community aided in Priority 2's death. Politically, this was an easy call for the Black community, since Priority 2 produced few concrete successes (e.g., higher test scores or fewer suspensions for Blacks).

But a county with lots of resources, and a reputation for being "a progressive moral leader in social policy and education" (Orfield & Eaton, 1996, p. 207), did not give up after failing a second time to eliminate the achievement gap. In 1989, the school board turned to an outside Black consultant, Edmund Gordon, to assess the status of minority-student achievement in MCPS. In November 1990, Gordon delivered to the school board his report, *A Study of Minority Student Achievement in Montgomery County Public Schools* (Gordon, 1990). Essentially, the Gordon report concluded that Priority 2 was a failure. The report noted that

> (1) the present Minority Student Achievement Plan included several elements needed for the improvement of minority student achievement, but that those elements present are insufficiently comprehensive, insufficiently distributed, and inconsistently implemented; and (2) the initiatives for each of the existing elements are unevenly planned, and in some instances, are unenthusiastically implemented and insufficiently communicated to staff and students. (p. 3)

MCPS, however, took its "medicine" and used the Gordon report to begin anew, creating another special initiative—*Success for Every Student* (SES)—to eliminate the achievement gaps (in the end, the achievement levels of Blacks would match those of Whites and Asians). The 1990s initiative is interesting because as the school board adopted SES it also appointed its first Black superintendent of schools, Paul Vance. No image could be better—new plan, new Black man, welcome to the promised land of milk and honey. Miracles were certain to happen now.

But the achievement data presented earlier (see Table 8.1), all under Superintendent Vance's tenure, reveal that since 1990 no real miracles have occurred. In fact, in many ways things have worsened for Black students, especially the males. Besides the politics, there are a variety of explanations for why MCPS fails to eliminate its achievement gap, and in the remainder of this chapter I discuss what I believe are six of the more important reasons for academic failure among Black males.

"Old-Fashioned" Racism Is Alive and Well

There is an abundance of evidence suggesting that a consideration of racism still plays a significant role in an understanding of why Blacks lag so far behind. In MCPS, racism plays itself out in peculiar ways. For example, take MCPS's increasing dialogues about poverty. Poverty is offered as an explanation for why things are the way they are for Blacks. Yes, poverty is on the rise in the county. The percentage of students receiving free and reduced-price school meals has increased noticeably over the past 20 years, climbing from 6% in 1975 to 22% in 1995. Nonetheless, poverty alone cannot explain away the large racial disparities. As noted previously, when one accepts the reality that Blacks in Montgomery County, on average, are one of the best educated, and perhaps wealthiest Black populations in the world, it is not possible that only poor Black students attend the county schools.

The poverty explanation gets more "play" than it deserves because like others around the nation, county residents when given a chance also exaggerate "poverty status" for Blacks. After all, it is the perfect escape hatch—everyone knows you can't save poor Blacks. A recent study by Giles (1996) demonstrates that "the public thinks Blacks make up an even larger share of the poor" than is known to be consistent with actual U.S. Census data (p. 594). For example, in one opinion poll the median guess was 50% when respondents were asked, "What percent of all the poor people in this country would you say are Black" (p. 595). Currently, according to U.S. Census figures, about 28% of poor Americans are Black.

However, racism in MCPS, especially the kind directed at students, is not always as indirect as the poverty explanation. The way we treat Black students is perhaps much more insidious. Consider the following words, written by a 1992 Black female graduate:

> It has been very upsetting, not just the school in general but the county as a whole. Once I do get established and have a family, my children will not attend a county school. The system has no place for Black students. The Black students that do attend are disappointed and angry just like me. This has to be the most racist county in the State, and I must have attended the most racist school in the county.

Dismiss this comment if you like, but the feelings expressed here are not rare. Results from a 1994 telephone poll of county high school students suggest that racism plays a significant role in the lives of young people in MCPS (Montgomery County Committee on Hate/Violence, 1995). Some highlights from the survey are as follows:

1. Insulting name-calling and joke telling are common. Twenty percent of the Blacks surveyed said they had been called a name (e.g., Nigger); 54% of the White students surveyed said they had either seen or heard name-calling based on race or ethnicity.
2. Witnessing hate produces lots of anger. More than 70% of the students who witnessed an incident at school (e.g., insulting name-calling or joke telling) said they felt angry and upset about what had happened.
3. Ignoring hate is common. Nearly half of the students who witnessed an incident at school knew the offender; however, the largest percentage of students (48.6%) said they either did nothing about the incident or ignored it. The majority (two thirds) of those who said they did not report the incident to a school official said they took no action because they thought that reporting the incident would cause more trouble.

Racial Disparities Remain Because MCPS Avoids Discussions of "Race-Related Issues"

To make matters worse, MCPS rarely engages itself in any meaningful, and lasting, dialogues about its racism. School officials will do anything to avoid open and honest discussions about race. This action, however, clouds how we view conditions. Black boys are not a problem if we decide not to discuss them. In the end, MCPS avoids making the right decisions that could make conditions better for all students.

Let me offer a real example of this thinking. Years ago, I was handed the research task of finding out why Black students were suspended from school more often than their White counterparts. Publicly, school officials insisted that race played a role in these outcomes. I agreed, and over a 3-year period I asked students a lot of questions about the role that race and racism played in the suspension process. In the end, school officials were right: Racism played a major role in who was suspended. School officials, however, did not want this message heard, fearing the implication that the system would be branded racist by the local news media. So, in the end the study was quietly filed away. That decision still haunts me.

My suspension study asked students some fairly direct questions about fighting in school (Hawkins, 1991). The response to a question about fighting still captures my attention. When faced with a fight at school, Black males (67%) find it hard to back down. Yet White males (47%) find it easy to walk away. Others have documented similar outcomes. In her 1993 book, *Deadly Consequences: How Violence Is Destroying Our Teenage Population*, Deborah Prothrow-Stith reports that many teenagers simply do not have the skills to back down from fights. Her successful antiviolence curriculum work in the Boston city schools, however, shows that it is possible to teach youngsters the skills to walk away from fights. My school district could have done the same thing. All the adults had to do was get past their fear of talking about race openly.

But MCPS could not get beyond its fears. No open, honest dialogue about suspensions and Black males occurs. In addition, there is no honest dialogue about teachers' perceptions of Black boys. Many MCPS teachers believe that Black boys are more likely to cause trouble at school than are other groups of students. In some schools, more than half the teachers believe that "Blacks commit more offenses (e.g., fighting, insubordination, etc.) and react with more aggression" than do other groups of students (Hawkins, 1991, p. 8).

Racial Disparities Remain Because the Game Plan to Eliminate Achievement Differences Is Not Radical Enough

Several years ago, a group of teachers, parents, and interested educators (myself included) approached the school board (the more compassionate one mentioned earlier in this chapter) with a simple request: Let us take one of the worst high schools in the county (there are several) and experiment with real educational change and reform. Using the reform model developed by the Coalition of Essential Schools, one of the nation's best-known school-reform organizations, we had high hopes that the school board would seize the opportunity. Board members listened, but in the end no one stood up and said, "Make it happen. We'll support you 125%."

This brief encounter sums up perfectly this county's attitude about changing the educational lot of those who consistently come in last. MCPS hesitates to invest in the structural changes that lead to better outcomes for Black students, especially the low-achieving ones. MCPS remains convinced that "business as usual" gets the job done for Blacks. On the other hand, it could be argued this is not the case for Whites. For example, MCPS has never hesitated to create a "world-class magnet." As a rule, Blacks' participation in these programs is severely limited. This does not have to be the case. There are lots of Black students who could benefit from the participation in these programs.

Let me add here one other very significant observation. As a system, MCPS always has been willing to listen to what the "experts" have to say about Blacks; however, MCPS rarely uses the advice to create new ways of doing business. And the list of experts who have come through MCPS over the years reads like a Who's Who of African American scholars: Edmund Gordon, A. Wade Boykin, Carol Camp Yeakey, Reginald Clark, James Comer, Sylvia Johnson, and so on.

Racial Disparities Remain Because the Game Plan for Eliminating Disparities Is Not Focused on Those Who Need Help the Most

MCPS requires that all school do SES—the minority-achievement game plan for the 1990s. This too is the result of avoiding specific discussions about race. It is politically incorrect to identify any school as a "low-achieving colored school"—a school with lots of low-test-scoring Black and Brown students. Of course, the reality is there are lots of these schools. Nevertheless, MCPS avoids targeting its limited resources on those schools that need help the most. As MCPS allocates fewer resources to SES, targeting becomes extremely critical. At the beginning of the 1990s, MCPS was sinking nearly a million dollars annually into efforts to improve minority achievement. For example, activity busses for after-school programs for minority youngsters alone got a line item of $13,000. Not any more. Even rich Montgomery County has downsized. A quick review of the FY97 budget identifies less than $0.3 million dedicated to SES (Montgomery County Public Schools, 1995).

Racial Disparities Remain Because (Some) Black Boys Are Afraid of the Academic Challenge

Racism plays a significant role in why Black boys are not academically achieving in the county schools. However, as I wonder about how to lessen racism's impact on Black boys—this is critically important—I also wonder about an issue that I believe is just as important. Are Black boys willing to become better students? Are they willing to go beyond the limited expectations most of us hold for them? Sadly, perhaps, not enough are!

Let me give you an example of what I mean. My job frequently gives me the opportunity to engage Black males in dialogue on all sorts of issues. Several years ago I had a chance to talk in length to a group of 20 Black males who all identified themselves as MCPS students. Fifteen of the 20 also identified themselves as seniors. Our conversation was not about college but somehow the discussion shifted to the subject when one of the students began talking about how important college is.

There was no argument from me, and regardless of racism, for Blacks, higher education still usually translates into higher quality of life (Oliver & Shapiro, 1995). Yet the behaviors of this limited group of Black males didn't match their beliefs. I'd seen this mismatch between beliefs and behaviors before while working with Black high school students at Howard University. Recently, researchers at the University of Chicago and the National Opinion Research Center discovered that this mismatch, which may exist for all high schoolers, is more common than we believe (Olson, 1996).

When I asked how many planned to attend college, every hand in the room went up. When I asked the seniors how many had actually applied to a college, just six hands went up. It was late March. Typically, by late March or early April many seniors have already been accepted to college. Of the six seniors in the room who had applied, only one had been accepted to college and was willing to give its name.

Have the county schools, a mostly White institution, failed these Black boys? To a certain extent they have. However, those who dream, and obviously Black boys dream too, must themselves do very specific things to help their dreams come true. Those who plan to go to college must begin by first applying to college. County statistics show that college acceptance rates for Black boys, when they apply, are fairly high.

Racial Disparities Remain Because (Some) Black Parents Who Know Better Do Not Necessarily Do Better

Which of the following scenarios is more likely to upset the typical Black parent?

- Scenario A. A Black child is called a "nigger."
- Scenario B. A Black child isn't placed in the honors track.

In all fairness, either of these events should bring Black parents to school. The harsh reality of both is unmistakable. We know that name-calling is a very serious problem in our high schools. We also know from data presented in this chapter that when it comes to participating in honors course work, Black high schoolers lag way behind Whites.

Regardless of how real each scenario is, I'm not so sure that Black parents in Montgomery County respond to their children's "dumbing down" with sufficient outrage. When Blacks express outrage it is generally aimed at Whites and their old racist ways. Blacks seldom look in the mirror and see the enemy within. There are times when I can shame Whites into acting on behalf of Black children. Guilt works. It frequently fails to work with Black parents.

Another true story: About a year ago I ran into a good friend on the street and we got into one of those comfortable conversations about our high schoolers. Everyone was doing fine. Being curious, I asked my friend *about the kinds of courses his son was taking.* I specifically asked, "Are his courses honors and advanced placement?" My friend froze for a moment but responded, "I'm not sure. He's happy. His grades are good. But I'm not sure about honors. He might be in one honors class."

I'm sure I came off sounding like the unwanted expert but I fired back, "I'm glad he's happy but man, you've got to know something about the level of the work. One honors class is not enough. If a Black boy isn't enrolled in all honors he's half-stepping. Get the boy's classes changed as soon as possible."

Now, the friend I'm talking about here is a very well-educated Black man with a great job—the type of professional you'd think would be so-phisticated enough to demand that his child be enrolled in all honors. Yet for reasons unknown, this is not the reality for most Black students. OK, a few Blacks are concerned, but still the vast majority appear content—per-haps some even smug.

Now I do not use the word "smug" lightly. So let me tell one final story to hammer home my point. I attended a Black social function in Montgomery County attended by no one but highly educated profession-als. The parking lot was full of very expensive Japanese and European luxury cars. As always, the chitchat turned to the common denominator, our children. The conversation centered around college scholarships and how to obtain one. Finally, one parent offered the following piece of god-awful advice. "I've made sure my son's grade point average has remained high by making sure his academic course load wasn't too demanding." Of course, I asked, "And how exactly is that done?" I get back, "Everything doesn't have to be honors. Too many demanding courses brings down the grade point average."

Wow—goes my brain to itself! What planet is this parent on? Why would any parent demand less? Expect less?

Social psychologist Jeff Howard claims that Black people generally adopt a problem-solving ideology "that says that the way to solve the prob-lems of the Black community is to hold White people's feet to the fire because they started these problems. Now, that has validity; that has truth to it. White folks are the original source of these problems. But the fact is that, right now, White folks don't have a clue about what to do about these problems, and given any other priorities they can switch their attentions to, they will. So if these problems are going to get solved, they have to get solved by a mobilized Black community" (Olson, 1994, p. 39).

If Blacks are serious about closing the academic-achievement gap, here in Montgomery County and elsewhere, they can't look to Whites for salva-tion. Certainly, operating on blind faith alone is out. That's too dangerous a gamble for our students. Howard sees just one way (Olson, 1994). His prescription: "Think you can. Work hard. Get smart. Smart is not something you just are. Smart is something that you can get."

And under this scenario there are no shortcuts. No watered-down curriculum. No more half-stepping our way to tomorrow, even if we do live in wealthy suburbia—the land of milk and honey.

A SOLUTION

Several school years ago, when the Black male student suspension problem—the disproportionate suspension rates of Black boys, made its way back into the local news, and school and community leaders demanded that we study the issue (again), I started having flashbacks. As a school system staff researcher, I had studied the suspension problem from nearly every conceivable angle.

I oppose studying the issue further. Everything we need to know about suspensions we already know. Another study would reveal the same things uncovered years ago. For instance, a 1988 study (Hawkins, 1988) that I conducted on students suspended numerous times over a 4-year period (1982–1986) concluded that frequently suspended students, compared to their classmates who are never suspended, are more likely to

- move frequently (within the county);
- have only one parent at home;
- have received special education services;
- have high absenteeism;
- earn lower grades and have repeated a grade;
- fail basic competency exams; and
- be suspended for fighting, insubordination, or both.

Another MCPS suspension study (Boykin & Johnson, 1990), conducted over a 2-year period (1988–1989) by two Washington, D.C., Black psychologists discovered that for Blacks, especially males, the most important thing related to not being suspended was how well they were integrated academically. Academically integrated and involved Blacks were less likely to get suspended from school than were their counterparts who struggled through school. Of course, this makes absolute sense. But remember, traditionally, when compared to others, greater numbers of Blacks struggle through MCPS.

I believe that a continued lack of substantial academic progress by Blacks, the struggling characterized by our two psychologists, is the major reason that Blacks are suspended more than Whites, Asians and Latinos. Institutional racism, still present, plays a role in who is suspended, but the county's consistent failure on the academic front is the primary reason we revisit this issue again and again.

MCPS wants us to believe that in more recent times (1990–1994) Black students have made major academic strides. I'll concede improved performance by Blacks (both boys and girls) on the Maryland Functional Tests (reading, mathematics, citizenship, and writing skills). I'm just as happy as the next guy when Black students master the basics, but I refuse to get excited about it. Mastering Grade-7 basic skills is a given in a school district that touts itself as one of the nation's best public school systems. Anything less is a sham!

My bottom line is simple. I'm interested in how Black students, especially the males, stack up against others when it comes to the serious academic issues that we know leads to college acceptances, academic scholarships, and successful completion of college. It's SAT scores and advanced placement (honors) courses that count the most in this county. This is where it is hard to convince me that MCPS has made major strides for Black students. And frankly, it is difficult to interpret the data any other way.

Perhaps it's unfair to characterize Black achievement in MCPS as a total bust. When compared to Blacks elsewhere MCPS Blacks do better. But when compared to others within the district too many Blacks are stuck in the slow lane.

I know I'm making it sound easy, but that mass of alienated Black students stuck in the slow lane are targets. That's exactly what our two psychologists told us years ago. At county high schools that suspend lots of Black students, they learned that Black students, especially the boys, are the most alienated from their educational environments whereas in contrast White students are the most connected.

Years ago in a focus group with suspended Black boys, I asked the group what they thought was the most constructive thing the school could do to help them overcome misbehaviors. "Stop assuming I'm up to no good," noted one boy. "The principal needs to worry less about what's on my head (a hat), and more about what was in my head," noted another.

Apparently, the school waged a relentless campaign against wearing hats inside the building. The campaign produced a lot of friction between Blacks and the school's administrators. Clearly, the campaign didn't help the school's high suspension rate.

I'm not here to pass judgment on a "no-hat policy." I've really never thought much about its merits. I am, however, interested in what these Black boys had to say about academics. Nearly everything they said on that front confirmed my belief that their academics were not the school's number-one priority. When it comes to eliminating school problems that face Blacks we still consistently fail to use our best weapon—academics. Put more Black boys in the fast lane, keep them there, and I guarantee you that the Black suspension problem, as well as other significant school-related problems, will disappear.

CONCLUSION AND RECOMMENDATIONS

Nearly a century ago, writing about the need to develop the academic talents of Black youngsters, W. E. B. Du Bois wrote, "The Negro race, like all races, is going to be saved by its exceptional men. The problem of education, then, among Negroes must first of all deal with the Talented Tenth; it is the problem of developing the Best of this race that they may guide the Mass away from the contamination and death of the Worst, in their own and other races." Throughout his life, Du Bois, again and again, returned to this theme, never faltering in his belief that a tireless devotion to developing Black minds was the key to Blacks' survival and progress worldwide.

However, in my county—a suburb with everything—the insistence that Black people, at a minimum, develop a Talented Tenth falls flat on its face. My daughter and a few other Black students, mostly females, come closer to representing a Talented One Percent. To me this outcome is inexcusable in a community that has more resources than most, including a large population of highly educated Black parents.

Also, the absence of a solid Black Talented Tenth in a society moving quickly to no affirmative action seems like a sure formula for disaster (e.g., lower undergraduate college enrollment rates for Blacks). But Black people cannot simply sit back and say they play no role in this disaster. Commenting on the future of "Negroes" (his "masses") in 1947, Du Bois said, "The uplift of the masses cannot be left to chance." And if we do? Then perhaps Black students always will come in last place in the academics race. And perhaps deservedly so!

9   Ebony Men in the Ivory Tower: A Policy Perspective

M. Christopher Brown II

THE ISSUE OF EQUAL educational opportunity for African American males has significant implications for public policy and educational law. After decades of litigation and legislation, it is an appropriate time to examine the legal and educational history that revolves around how higher education attempts to attain and maintain equal educational access. What follows is an account of ongoing political activity that threatens both the future and success of African American males in higher education. This account will be joined by critical analyses of the possible implications of the current assault on educational practices and policies designed to insure access. Therefore, in this chapter I will explore the historical and present position of African American males in higher education, the current attacks on their access to equal educational opportunity participation in higher education, and the implications for educational policy and practice.

TRUISMS: AFRICAN AMERICAN MALES IN HIGHER EDUCATION

There are a number of truisms that can be offered about the African American male student in the predominantly White institutions of American higher education. These manifestations include, but are not limited to, assertions that Black men in the ivory tower are nearly always in need of academic remediation, that their greatest concentration is in campus athletic programs, and that they lack critical and higher-order thinking skills. As a result, higher education initiatives focus primarily on White and Afri-

African American Males in School and Society: Practices and Policies for Effective Education. Copyright © 1999 by Teachers College, Columbia University. All rights reserved. ISBN 0-8077-3870-0 (pbk), ISBN 0-8077-3871-9 (cloth). Prior to photocopying items for classroom use, please contact the Copyright Clearance Center, Customer Service, 222 Rosewood Dr., Danvers, MA 01923, USA, tel. (508) 750-8400.

can American women, other locally and globally disenfranchised groups, and underrepresented populations. There is also the pervading untruth that there are more African American males involved in the criminal justice system than in institutions of higher learning (Miller, 1996). This mythological research statement lacks veracity and has immeasurable implications for the future of Black men in postsecondary education. What is the role of legal/political happenings, governmental power structures, intellectual curricular traditions, and historic intent in influencing the future of African American males in higher education?

By employing the term "truism," I mean to suggest not a fact or reality, but an obvious and self-evident situation. The term as used here is not intended to denote falsehood, but rather a stereotyped remark made as though it were an unquestionably absolute notion. For example, in a recent newspaper article there is an account of a young, African American male who is struggling to find his way in the academic and employment markets. The article, titled, "Improved Economy Doesn't Help Everyone," explores the ways in which the expansion of the American employment market as a result of the mandate for increased academic credentials and higher profit margins has left many African American males in the lurch. The current condition of African American males is consistent with the nation's celebration of economic prosperity and record-breaking low unemployment rates. The author states:

> Economic reports are full of good news these days—the strongest growth in a decade, the lowest unemployment in a quarter-century. It can seem a bitter irony to young unemployed Black men. . . . The good times are not good for everyone. Joblessness is higher for city dwellers than for suburbanites, higher for teens than for adults, higher for Blacks than for Whites. And, among Blacks, it's significantly higher for young Black men. (Skidmore, 1997, p. 6B)

The preceding statement takes on a whole new meaning when we acknowledge that the majority of all African American males are teenage city dwellers. Consequently, if this population is to participate in the national economic, political, and social structures, there is a prerequisite for increasing levels of educational attainment. Sadly, there are political forces that seek to close the doors of educational opportunity for these young, African American males.

With the most recent Supreme Court appointments and national election results, there has been a conservative shift in the American ideology. Consequently, there is unrelenting erosion of policies, programs, and principles of law that have constituted the spirit of progress in higher education, particularly for African Americans. During this retrenchment, only a rededication to effective policies rooted in the original letter and spirit of the law can safeguard African American males from the pernicious effects of recent attempts to decimate Black admissions, destroy race-based scholarships, dismantle affirmative action, disestablish historically Black colleges, and decentralize African American studies. The current conservative backlash is the result of social hostilities largely birthed by the rage and paranoia of some who fear a loss of their historic station. These legal battles involve the access of African American males to higher education, especially as it pertains to those opportunities protected by law, legislation, or both.

HISTORY OF AFRICAN AMERICAN MALES IN AMERICAN HIGHER EDUCATION

Historically there were few mainstream educational opportunities for African American males with the exception of historically Black institutions established by abolitionists for nonslaves. With the postwar shift to industrialization, America recognized the need to educate its former slaves and their progeny. However, after years of significant progress, the races still remained separate and their education unequal.

In 1954, the U.S. Supreme Court's ruling in *Brown v. Board of Education* (347 U.S. 483 [1954]) overturned the prevailing doctrine of separate but equal introduced by *Plessy v. Ferguson* (163 U.S. 537 [1896]) 58 years earlier. By the time *Brown* was decided many southern and border states had created dual collegiate structures of public education, most of which operated exclusively for Whites in one system and African Americans in the other. Although *Brown* focused the nation on desegregation in primary and secondary public education, the issue of disestablishing the duality and limited educational access existing in public systems of public higher education had yet to come to the forefront.

African American males and their European American counterparts have generally had dissimilar experiences regarding the acquisition of higher education. From slavery through Jim Crow, African Americans were categorically excluded from collegiate participation except at a few northern liberal arts institutions (e.g., Berea and Oberlin). In fact, during slavery, educating chattel or their offspring was a criminal offense (Klingberg, 1941). In some states these "ignorance" laws included emancipated slaves. Despite the existing laws, punishments and hardships, a small percentage of southern Black men and boys still sought a knowledge of reading, writing, and arithmetic. Although "clandestine schools" and Christian education provided them with an opportunity to read, memorize, and recite biblical passages (Woodson, 1968), when the Civil War commenced, less than 5% of the 4.5 million Americans of African descent were literate; even fewer knew the three R's—reading, writing, and arithmetic (Fleming, 1981).

The aftermath of the Civil War brought a proliferation of Black-founded, -operated and -populated institutions. More than 200 Black educational institutions were founded in the South during the interval between 1865 and 1890 (Jencks & Reisman, 1968). By and large these institutions were established and funded by the Freedman's Bureau, Black churches, local communities, private philanthropists, and northern missionaries. Although they were called colleges or institutes, many of these institutions began as secondary schools. According to Hill (1982), only 2,600 students (nearly all of whom were male) in 33 Black institutions engaged in college-level work in 1915, five decades after the genesis of Black higher education.

Additionally, during postwar political shifts, state governments were added to the list of financial patrons of Black education. The southern states were mandated to provide a public school education for all citizens after 1865, in keeping with the Thirteenth, Fourteenth, and Fifteenth Amendments (Roebuck & Murty, 1993). The new mandate to subsidize Negro education was not received well in the states south of the Mason-Dixon Line. The legislators of the postwar South would utilize all of the strategies within their means to delimit Black higher education (Pilgrim, 1985). This state-level inequality was bolstered by the loose wording of the Morrill Act of 1890 (Ch. 841, 26 Stat. 417). The act specifically prohibited payments of federal funds to states that discriminated against Blacks in the admission to tax-supported colleges or that refused to provide separate but equal facilities for the two races. It was this latter clause that led to the immediate establishment of dual public, land-grant institutions in 17 of the 19 southern states. Hence, although unintentional, the Second Morrill Act played a central role in cementing and expanding the separate-but-equal standard in collegiate education in the South (Hill, 1982; Roebuck & Murty, 1993).

Beginning in the 1930s, however, the National Association for the Advancement of Colored People (NAACP) launched a campaign to reverse social, political, and educational inequality. Despite the NAACP's efforts, the public Black colleges continued to exist in a closed and segregated educational structure up until 1954 (Law & Clift, 1981). However, the U.S. Supreme Court's 1954 *Brown* decision declared that separate but equal was unconstitutional. Although the legal theory utilized in *Brown* was premised on higher education precedents, *Brown* was a primary and secondary education ruling. The mandate to desegregate did not reach higher education until *Florida ex rel. Hawkins v. Board of Control* (350 U.S. 413

[1956]). The *Hawkins* ruling, however, failed to generate any significant changes in the Black and White colleges of the South (Preer, 1982). It was not until one decade after *Brown* that President Lyndon B. Johnson signed the Civil Rights Act of 1964, which was designed to eliminate discrimination against Blacks and other racial and ethnic groups. This new law empowered the federal government to bring lawsuits on behalf of Black plaintiffs. Moreover, Title VI of this act specifically restricted the spending of federal funds in segregated schools and colleges. The desegregation mandate had finally arrived at the door of America's colleges and universities.

There is no debating the fact that both Title VI of the Civil Rights Act of 1964 and subsequent litigation brought the issue of dismantling dual systems of public higher education to the attention of postsecondary education policy makers and federal enforcers of laws and statutes related to the educational enterprise. Not only did it bring to bear the notion of a unified system of higher education, it also paved the way for a series of initiatives designed to promote educational access and equal scholastic opportunity. It was this coagulation of initiatives that brought the African American male to his present status in academe. Those enterprises include, but are not limited to, the following: (a) the use of race in collegiate admissions, (b) the implementation of scholarships to support educational access, (c) affirmative action in faculty and staff hiring, (d) the development of Black colleges, and (e) the creation of academic units focused on issues related to Americans of African descent.

BARRIERS TO POSTSECONDARY EDUCATION
FOR AFRICAN AMERICAN MALES

In *Regents of the University of California v. Bakke* (438 U.S. 265 [1978]), the Supreme Court enjoined the use of racial quotas but sanctioned the use of race as a factor in admissions decisions. In *Bakke*, the Court struck down separate admission processes for Blacks, but not affirmative initiatives to recruit and admit minority students. This case is often improperly cited in reverse discrimination suits. In actuality, the Court ruled five to four that although numbers or ratios could not be set, race could be taken into consideration in developing future admissions programs. Additionally, in 1979 the Department of Health, Education, and Welfare's Office for Civil Rights issued its *Policy Interpretation of Anti-discrimination Regulations Under Title VI, Including Affirmative Action for Clarification in Light of Bakke.* The policy statement outlawed the use of race as a sole determinant of admission, in addition to banning admission of predetermined numbers of underrepresented persons. However, the policy statement did not restrict the voluntary recruitment of underrepresented students, only the establishing of set numbers to hire or admit.

This discussion has recently reemerged and its focus and authority been usurped in *Hopwood v. Texas* (78 F.3d 932 [5th Cir. 1996]), a case involving four White students seeking admission to a Texas law school. The result of that discussion was the devastating affirmation of the U.S. Court of Appeals that race may not be used as a criteria for admission. Many say the ruling in *Hopwood* may lead to the resegregation of higher education. It also without doubt will drastically worsen the enrollments, particularly in the most elite public institutions, of African American male students, who are already an endangered species in academe.

In *Beyond the Ivory Tower*, Derek Bok (1982), a past president of Harvard University, said that the vital question is not whether preferential admission is a success, but whether it has made more progress toward overcoming the legacy of discrimination than other strategies that universities might have pursued. Universities should stick by their conviction that a judicious concern for race in admitting students will eventually help lift the arbitrary burdens that have hampered Blacks in striving to achieve their goals in our society.

After years of modest progress, *Hopwood* is just one of the assaults on educational access and opportunity. Another major attack comes from *Podberesky v. Kirwan* (38 F.3d 147 [4th Cir. 1994]). This case involves litigation brought by a Hispanic student challenging the constitutionality of the Benjamin Banneker merit scholarship program for African Americans at the University of Maryland. The court ruled that there was a strong evidentiary basis for the university to utilize race-based scholarships in remedying the effects of past discrimination. However, the Supreme Court's denial of certiori in this litigation may ultimately signal the death knell of scholarship programs that target African American males and other persons of color.

The Supreme Court's failure to review *Podberesky* merely delays the inevitable national discussion regarding African Americans, ethnic and economic minorities, preference, equity, and remedy. For the first time in the history of our country a major academic institution—the University of Maryland—stepped forward to admit a legacy of discrimination and racial prejudice. The University of Maryland confessed that their policies and practices were unjust and violated the Equal Protection Clause of the Fourteenth Amendment. Recognizing this tragic past, they instituted a scholarship program to remedy their prior race-biased policies that favored majority students. The Court, however, said that the university had no right to correct its errors in judgment using this procedure. The ruling held that only the Court can initiate a remedy for racial injustice. Only the Court could say that racial discrimination existed in the institution's past.

In the 3 decades since the enactment of the 1964 Civil Rights Act, predominantly White universities have not been particularly successful in recruiting and retaining African American male students, much less Black male faculty. Institutions throughout the country have initiated a variety of programs and policies to promote the recruitment and retention of students of color. Unfortunately, these initiatives have not achieved their intended goals. The disparity between the numbers of faculty of African and European descent entering the higher education workforce is widening, with the upper hand in favor of European faculty. In almost every region of the country and in most universities, African American male faculty are seriously underrepresented across all ranks (Brown, 1996).

Notwithstanding, according to the February 3, 1995, *Federal Register*, a Senate bill (S. 318) that was introduced by Jesse Helms (R-NC) would bar the use of affirmative action in all college and university hiring practices. This legislation is designed to eradicate the guidelines that have opened the doors of academe to African Americans, women, and other populations. Senator Helms leads the parade of those individuals who believe that affirmative action is just another instance of government interference in higher education; affirmative action, however, has been the icon in broadening the pool of prospective employees through enlarging the number of qualified personnel.

As an outgrowth of the Civil Rights Act of 1964 and presidential Executive Order 11246, affirmative action had the initial intent of prohibiting discrimination in programs utilizing federal funding. Simply stated, affirmative action was a plan whereby an institution could set forth its commitment to equal educational employment opportunity or admissions or both for all qualified persons, in an attempt to eliminate any possible discrimination.

Affirmative action's numerical goals are often confused with quotas. Quotas are illegal because they exclude individuals. Goals, on the other hand, merely establish benchmarks for the number of qualified minority applicants that one desires to have in the pool. This benchmarking provides institutions with information regarding the number of qualified minorities and women available. The mere acknowledgment of a goal is in no way a carte blanche to hire less qualified individuals.

The primary purpose is not to force institutions into hiring faculty from underrepresented groups, but to eliminate the tenuous and obtuse practices of the "good old boy network"—those informal associations in which recommendations about faculty hiring decisions are made. The realities are, minorities and women have not, by and large, had access to this network, and it has served as their nemesis and a source of angst for decades. Even more onerous are the vague employment requirements, such as the best-person criterion. The best-person criterion is totally subjective and the requirements for the job are nondescript and are decided on solely based on abstract measures.

Likewise, an increasing number of researchers are criticizing higher education for its refusal to educate African American males and other historically marginalized persons on their own terms (i.e., modifying the curriculum to include the African diaspora) (Allen et al., 1991; Bennett & Okinaka, 1984; Edmonds, 1984; Fleming, 1984; Garibaldi, 1984; Gosman et al., 1983; Hytche, 1989; Jones, 1971; Stikes, 1984; Thomas, 1981; Willie & McCord, 1972). Until recently, with the inclusion of departments of African American studies, decisions about what was worth teaching and what counted as culture was relatively homogeneous and significantly Eurocentric.

This Black studies option will no longer exist at the City College of New York. Only one year after Leonard Jeffries, an African American male professor, won his battle to be reinstated as chair of the Black studies department at City College (*Jeffries v. Harleston*, 21 F.3d 1238 [2nd Cir. 1995]), the institution's response was to downgrade the department to an interdisciplinary program. Irrespective of whether Jeffries's scholarship is viewed as credible, this action endangers African American studies programs across the country—these will be the first to go when universities are faced with financial exigencies or other difficulties. The end of this progressive, Africa-centered construction of knowledge may well be imminent.

THREATS TO POSTSECONDARY EDUCATIONAL DIVERSITY: A POLICY PERSPECTIVE

The courts have continually expressed the opinion that state systems of higher education have an affirmative duty to utilize race-conscious initiatives to remedy the continuing effects of de jure segregation. After decades of work to insure equal educational opportunity, especially for African American males, the essence of current national attempts to revoke the promise of educational equity disarms and nullifies the acceptability of race-conscious efforts at equality. Hence, there are no standards that acknowledge integration or inclusion of all into the American landscape of higher education. Nonetheless, in an effort to reverse the growing underrepresentation of African American male students and faculty in academe, the notion of equal educational opportunity must be praised and upheld as a necessity. If successful, the nation and the world stand to benefit through the engagement of human potential that might otherwise have been wasted. Is our nation rich enough to ignore the talents of African American males and other persons of color?

Let us look retrospectively at the legal steps being made to dismantle the spirit of progress for African American men and other underrepresented groups in college. First, as a result of the 1996 *Hopwood* ruling, those borderline African American male students (as assessed subjectively) who could have contributed to the diversity of our collegiate racial makeup will no longer be afforded such an opportunity. Granted, some of these students will be admitted; however, for those economically unable to meet the rising cost of tuition, *Podberesky* insures that no specially targeted monies will be available. This notwithstanding, for those Black males who are able to pay the tuition, S. 318 alludes that there will be few African American male faculty or administrators (much less others of color) working in these institutions to mentor them. Further, if the disengagement of ethnic studies becomes a trend, these young Black males will find limited venues in which to explore their respective roles in the construction of social knowledge and history.

This policy perspective is not intended to suggest that the majority of America's White male dominated higher education structure is intentionally malicious, but that the pervasive, pernicious, ill-conceived, mean-spirited educational policies and court decisions issued in the past several years are detrimental to many African American males. Consequently, higher education is without consensus or lucidity regarding how to define equal educational access and opportunity. Academe is even further away from outlining any meaningful criteria for achieving this integrative and illusory goal. This ambiguity prevents postsecondary institutions and policy makers from establishing and attaining achievable goals relative to equal access and equitable educational practices. The uncertainty over the prevailing academic goals, standards, or timetables results in a lack of logical, consistent, or sound practices for insuring the participation of African American men in higher education. This void in consciousness is partially resultant from the holistic phobia of a "tanning," much less "browning," of the academic tower of learning.

All of these phenomena—*Hopwood*, *Podberesky*, and S. 318—represent not only a massive reduction in both African American male student and faculty access to the "poisoned"-ivy-covered walls of academe, but attempts to kill the spirit of social progress in higher education. The most frightening retrenchment involves the massive efforts to eliminate historically Black institutions from the landscape of higher education (or, as it is more technically called, collegiate desegregation, the dismantling of dual systems of higher education, or both).

HISTORICALLY BLACK COLLEGES AND UNIVERSITIES

After 40 years of race-neutral mission statements and admission requirements, the Supreme Court has declared that the mere existence of historically Black institutions in several states (particularly Alabama, Louisiana, Mississippi, and Ohio) delineate segregation. The Court's focal question is whether the states have disassembled their previous dual systems of postsecondary study. The Supreme Court's decisions in these cases have the potential of establishing judicial precedents that could ultimately eliminate the historically Black institution as an institutional choice (Brown, 1995a).

The *United States v. Fordice* (505 U.S. 717 [1992]) case and Mississippi's attempts at compliance will establish the precedent for the "desegregation" of higher education across the country. In the most recent *Fordice* ruling, Judge Neal Biggers outlined a plan that has the potential of creating an atmosphere for the eventual elimination of predominantly Black enrollments in three of Mississippi's institutions of higher learning. The alleged goal is to maintain only those programs and entities that are educationally justifiable and cannot be practically eliminated. Interestingly enough, at the same time that there is a dismantling of the historically Black institutions, the admissions requirements are being raised statewide at the predominantly White institutions. Prior critical commentary on the latest ruling contends that this trend ultimately reduces access for significant percentages of the African American male student population in Mississippi colleges and universities (Brown, 1995b).

Although higher education initiatives have been attempts to establish benchmarks for access by African Americans to higher education, these benchmarks have not necessarily succeeded in guaranteeing perennial and unmonitored equal educational opportunity (Thomas, 1981). Examples of these aforementioned enrollment aids include affirmative action programs; governmental grants and incentives; offices of minority affairs; university directorships for equity; and gender, ethnic, and cultural centers. It should be noted that historically Black colleges continue to produce a significant percentage of all African American baccalaureate degree recipients. Presently, historically Black colleges produce 28% of the bachelor's degrees awarded to African Americans, and as such a considerable proportion of the bachelor's degrees awarded to African American males (U.S. Department of Education, 1996a).

The existence and productivity of historically Black colleges does not absolve higher education of the responsibility to explore the sociocultural, socioeconomic, political, and familial backgrounds that contribute to collegiate attrition by African American males, and the function of the larger society in perpetuating these characteristics (Lang & Ford, 1988). This notwithstanding, the historically Black college remains the academic home of the lion's share of the legacy of scholastic achievement by African American males (e.g., Dr. Martin Luther King, Jr., Booker T. Washington, W. E. B. Du Bois, Thurgood Marshall, George Washington Carver, Ernest Just, William Julius Wilson, John Hope Franklin, and others). Quoting Vernon Jordan, Roebuck and Murty (1993) state that "the historically Black college is the undergraduate home of 75 percent of all Black doctorates, 75 percent of all Black army officers, 80 percent of all Black federal judges, and 85 percent of all Black physicians" (p. 13). Research also shows that historically Black universities have been the primary educators of African American males (Allen et al., 1991; Edmonds, 1984; Fleming, 1984; Garibaldi, 1984; Hytche, 1989; Jones, 1971; Stikes, 1984; Thomas, 1981).

Although it is true that these Black colleges are of great value, some in society are not convinced of their importance. As a result many questions are being raised about the need to continue their current configuration or even existence during this era of retrenchment to educational access. Thompson (1973) writes, "Black colleges constitute an indigenous, unique, most challenging aspect of higher education in this society, and as such are still badly needed" (p. 284). Hence, it is apparent that the historic successes and continuing contribution of historically Black colleges and universities should be documented and stressed in the battle to maintain a space for African American men in higher education and in academe writ large.

NEGOTIATING THE FUTURE OF EBONY MEN IN THE IVORY TOWER

Academic researchers and policy makers must begin to pay more attention to the ongoing legal and political battles that affect African American males and their ability to enter postsecondary education, as either faculty or students. The time has come for all of us to tell one another the truth regarding the ominous forces that have brought us to the current crossroads in academic and social progress. The presence of African American males and other academicians of color are not only endangered, but potentially will be extinct in postsecondary institutions. The structures, norms, practices, and personnel of White-dominated and populated universities may ultimately govern whether African American male student, faculty, and staff outcomes at their institutions are positive or negative. These universities have failed to establish environments like that of the historically or pre-dominantly African American campus, which consistently fosters African American male persistence across categories. Although many African American male students in these institutions must endure financial hardship, overcome academic deficiency, and transcend social isolation, they still succeed. While there are African American male faculty who lack lengthy vitae documenting years of prolific writing, their devotion to teaching and student intellectual progress is often unparalleled. And granted the fiscal endowments of many historically Black institutions average below 10 million dollars, their administrators manage to keep them operating in the face of declining fiduciary support.

As the academy reacts to the problems, debates the solutions, and studies the inclusion of African American men in institutions of higher education, we encounter at every turn more questions and fewer answers. One thing, at least, is clear: To recruit and maintain a diverse campus population that values the role and function of African American males is only a beginning, albeit an essential one. The educational opportunities—and obligations—that must follow over the upcoming years will test the commitment, energy, resources, and imagination of the ivory tower in profound and enduring ways.

10

What Does Gender Have to Do with the Experiences of African American College Men?

James Earl Davis

IN THIS CHAPTER, I focus on different higher education contexts for African American males and explore research on the complexities of Black males' relationships and experiences within these contexts. I challenge colleges and universities to consider race *and* gender in their attempts to address the needs of African American males. Finally, I present findings from a study about social support and its influence on Black male academic achievement. This discussion is framed by one fundamental assumption: There is virtually no race- or gender-neutral schooling context for Black males in higher education. Although this argument may appear inconsistent with the availability of and access to racially desegregated and sex-integrated colleges and universities, even these institutions present challenges for Black males that go beyond the seemingly placid surface harmonies of race and gender relations. Historically Black institutions and, to a much less degree, all-male college settings provide another lens from which to more closely examine how campus environments influence the experiences of African American males.

The research literature in higher education is replete with cases of the marginality that Black students endure in their quest for higher education. Studies of African Americans in higher education have by and large ignored gender as an essential component that frames students' experiences and relations. Race analysis in American higher education too often shadows gender and in doing so limits our understanding of how males and females negotiate their identities and roles on college campuses. Gender studies in

African American Males in School and Society: Practices and Policies for Effective Education. Copyright © 1999 by Teachers College, Columbia University. All rights reserved. ISBN 0-8077-3870-0 (pbk), ISBN 0-8077-3871-9 (cloth). Prior to photocopying items for classroom use, please contact the Copyright Clearance Center, Customer Service, 222 Rosewood Dr., Danvers, MA 01923, USA, tel. (508) 750-8400.

higher education are generally associated with women's experiences and outcomes; men, however, have gender too. Almost without expectation, the experience of African American male college students is absent from the discourse of Black students in postsecondary institutions, as well as from the research literature's attempt to illuminate differences and commonalties across gender and race. Indeed, gender has a lot to do with Black males' social and academic experiences in college. Hence, the rationale for this work is to look more closely at African American college men. By doing so, I hope to disentangle the differential effects of race and gender on these students' achievement outcomes and social experiences.

BLACK MALE VOICES ON COLLEGE CAMPUSES

Voices of African American males on college campuses echo their struggles. They struggle to become socially integrated in a community of peers who are supportive but often confining; they struggle to overcome academic hurdles created by inadequate precollege preparation; and they struggle against hostile schooling environments that marginalize their presence on campus. Further, Black men in college also wrestle with high expectations from their families and community, and low academic expectations of an understood campus code of behavior and acceptability. Out of these struggles, however, have emerged many Black men who are, although wounded, yet persistent in their reach for higher education. These shared experiences of racism and stereotyping have also forged a constructed identity of what it means to be an African American male in college. In a study of college students' constructions of manhood, one Black male, Rodney, a senior at a prestigious university in the Northeast, laments,

> "Being a man is very connected to my success in college. Black males *have* to do well. There is so much pressure and it makes it very difficult with relationships. Expectations are high. If I don't do well in school it does not mean that I am not a good Black man. However, your attitude is important, that's what counts." (in Davis, 1995, p. 2)

Often these voices are not heard, misunderstood, or simply ignored. The same is true for the experience of Black women in college, particularly on predominately White campuses; there is evidence, however, that suggests that Black males experience more racial hostility and are more disadvantaged by racial stereotypes (Davis, 1994). One possible exception may be African American student-athletes who have high social profiles on campus and are "respected" and sometimes privileged because of their special athletic contributions. In contrast, Harrison (1998) posits a competing argument focusing on the negative campus climate experienced by Black student-athletes that is created by the social construction of African-American males in sports. On the basis of a study of Black male scholarship athletes at two predominantly White universities, Harrison finds that these students suffer from internalizing negative stereotypes and low expectations of Black males athletes. These social constructions are grounded in a campus culture that intentionally isolates, exploits, and objectifies African American males. I contend that the social construction of Black men on college campuses regardless of their athletic status is steeped in the hegemony of Black masculinity and how it frames the experience and affect of African American males enrolled in college. For instance, Jamal, a college sophomore from the Midwest, reflects on his college experience and his consciousness about his racial and gender identity:

> "Black men on campus are constantly in transition. There is a constant need for us to transform to the community. How one speaks, how you talk is very important—it's an indicator whether you are part of the community. . . . There is high expectation to talk like a 'Black man,' with that attitude and manliness. Being a good proper guy is not always important, it doesn't get you very much. On campus, it's important to appear very sexual, you get man points. . . . And if you play basketball, you are cool as hell. I don't play, so I have to make up for it in other ways." (in Davis, 1995, p. 3)

AFRICAN AMERICAN MALES IN HIGHER EDUCATION

The participation and experience of African American males in college has become a major source of concern and challenge for many institutions of higher education. Discussions of the "gender gap" have recently occupied the agenda of many educational research and policy analysts. Currently, Black men make up about 37% of all African Americans enrolled in higher education. Even at historically Black colleges and universities, Black males constitute less than 30% of total enrollments (U.S. Department of Commerce, 1996). Overall, African American males account for 3.5% of the total enrollment in college, however, they are disproportionately represented among students who are forced to withdraw, those with relative lower academic performance and generally negative college experiences (Carter & Wilson, 1997). There has been an overall increase in the enrollment of African American males in college during the 1990s. Since 1990, the college enrollment rate of Black males actually increased by 14.6% percent. Ironically, this quantitative increase belies some underlying declines in the quality of the collegiate experience for Black males during this time.

Generally, research on the experience of African American students in higher education has been concentrated in two areas: (a) differences in academic and social experiences in college relative to White students, and (b) differences in the outcomes of students attending predominately White versus historically Black institutions. Very little work, however, has focused on the role of gender in the higher education experience of Black students and specifically how gender informs the experiences of African American males on campus. The research on gender that does exist primarily examines declining participation and increased attrition rates of African American males in higher education (Green & Wright, 1992), with scant attention given to the quality of these students' higher education experiences. In this literature, institutions of higher education are too often studied without consideration of how their gender and racial environment affect student experiences and outcomes. One recent exception is provided by Hrabowski, Maton, & Greif (1998), who chronicled the success of African American males who participated in an academic support program at predominantly White University of Maryland-Baltimore County.

PREDOMINANTLY WHITE VERSUS HISTORICALLY BLACK COLLEGES AND UNIVERSITIES: DOES IT MATTER FOR BLACK MALES?

Increased educational opportunities for African Americans have been witnessed since desegregation policies changed the demographics of most higher education institutions. However, 3 decades after legally mandated corrective reforms began, the nation still has not come to grips with the importance of educational opportunity and its manifestations through a diversity of higher educational institutions. Indeed, many challenges are presented to Black students in higher education and these challenges are often dictated by the racial context. For instance, Black students at predominately White colleges have lower grade point averages than their peers at historically Black campuses (Allen, 1992; Thomas, 1981). Although students at historically Black colleges and universities (HBCUs) perform better academically, they are often dissatisfied with the facilities and organizational structures of their college institutions (Allen, 1987; Nettles, 1988; Roebuck & Murty, 1993).

Indeed, the rapid movement of African Americans into predominantly White institutions of higher learning has spawned some concern. Contemporary merits and outcomes of attending traditionally Black colleges and universities are being voiced, with some suggesting that Blacks receive greater support at Black institutions, report greater levels of satisfaction, and therefore perform better academically. Although the results of this debate have been inconclusive, most research indicates that historically Black colleges provide a more supportive and nurturing environment (Nettles, 1988; Thomas, 1984). Fleming (1984) reports that students at Black colleges perform better academically and do, in fact, report a greater degree of satisfaction in their social and academic endeavors. Other findings suggest that Blacks at White institutions report greater satisfaction with peer relations than White students, but they experience less academic integration and satisfaction. Consequently, it is suggested that the social needs of Blacks, particularly males, are different and that predominantly White institutions may simply not provide the needed social support that Black students require in order to succeed academically (Nettles, 1987). A final, and perhaps most important, finding is that compared to their White peers, Black students generally see a need for increased numbers of formal programs, informal contacts with faculty members, and a greater number of social activities. Additionally, students report that these programs would be useful in helping them to deal with the academic, racial, and social problems that they were experiencing on campus (Lewis, 1987). Very little gender analysis among African American students has been done to disentangle the differential experiences of African American males in diverse college settings. Likewise, differences between African American males attending historically Black and predominately White colleges are given little attention.

The few studies in this area have found that African American males gain more, both social and academically, at historically Black colleges. Predominantly White colleges appear to retard the development of African American males (Fleming, 1984). In these interracial environments, Black males experience more negative feelings and unhappiness about college life. They feel they are unfairly mistreated, experience academic demoralization, and think less of the academic ability. Moreover, academic interaction during college did not have a positive effect on the academic self-concept of African American males (Pascarella, Smart, Etherington, & Nettles, 1987). Other factors that negatively affect the academic self-concept of these students include secondary school achievement and social interaction during college.

BLACK MALES AT HISTORICALLY BLACK COLLEGES

The contemporary role of historically Black colleges has been a point of intense discussion in the academic literature and within public policy debates. Research in higher education has documented a link between the social and academic experiences of African American college students and whether they attend historically Black versus predominantly White institutions (Gurin & Epps, 1975; Fleming, 1984; Nettles, 1987; Allen, Epps, & Haniff, 1991). Still, uneasiness surrounding public endorsement of these institutions, particularly the financial linkages to state-supported public historically Black colleges, continues to persist. However, HBCUs remain viable options for many African Americans, and in fact there has been a recent increase in enrollments at HBCUs—about a 15% increase between 1986 and 1990. Interestingly, female students account for the bulk of this increase, while Black male enrollment experienced a slight decline during this period (Hoffman, Snyder, & Sonneberg, 1992). While the rolls at HBCUs continue to increase, the overall share of the total enrollment of African Americans in higher education continues to decline. In 1995, HBCUs enrolled 15.6% of African American college students, down from 16.6% in 1990. Unfortunately, fewer African American males are enrolling at HBCUs (American Council on Education, 1994).

Research on the benefits and outcomes of attending a historically Black college may be mixed, yet there are some consistent findings about how these schools structure and influence students' experiences. Recent studies offer some evidence of Black colleges' unique abilities to effectively structure environments that lead to greater achievement outcomes for their students. For instance, future wages of Black college alumni are at least equal to the wages of other students (Constantine, 1994). This finding is very significant when compared to previous expectations that students attending HBCUs would actually have lower future wages. Additional analysis of labor market outcomes for students attending HBCUs found little to no effect. Although students from HBCUs were more likely to receive a BA degree, they did not garner labor market benefits such as additional wages (Erhenberg & Rothstein, 1993). In a related economic indicator, African American men who attended HBCUs were more likely to be married. Two thirds of graduates of historically Black colleges were married in 1986 compared to about half of non-HBCU Black men. However, there were no differences in the marriage rates for women who attended Black institutions. Additionally, recent studies are inconsistent concerning graduate school attendance of HBCU students. In some fields, however, such as medicine, there appears to be an advantage in attending a historically Black institution when students seek admission to medical schools (Erhenberg & Rothstein, 1993). These data are insightful given that men are disproportionately represented in the sciences at HBCUs.

Research using the National Post-secondary Aid Study of 1990 found that African American HBCU students are more likely to pursue postgraduate education and become professionals than are Black students at predominantly White colleges and universities (Wenglinsky, 1996). To the contrary, other studies have found that HBCU graduates were no less likely to continue on for graduate degrees than were non-HBCU graduates (Ehrenberg & Rothstein, 1993). Even with these recent studies, there still exist conceptual problems and limitations in examining how historically Black colleges provide and structure these benefits to African American students, particularly for Black males.

SOCIAL SUPPORT AND BLACK MALES IN COLLEGE

The idea that positive and nurturing social environments influence the educational experiences of college students is a consistent thread through research on African Americans in higher education. Of particular importance has been the notion of social support and how it influences academic achievement. Social support has been shown to have significant consequences for educational outcomes, but there has been little attention given to differential experiences of African American males in college. Better understandings of the relationship between background factors, academic performance in college, and college social support factors are required to uncover how these factors affect Black college males.

Social support, in particular, has been shown to have significant consequences for educational outcomes (Allen, 1985; Jay & D'Augelli, 1991). Whether considered a positive or negative influence, social support provided by colleges and universities is a critical ingredient in the educational experience of African Americans (Allen, 1992; Hershberger & D'Augelli, 1992; Hughes, 1987; Oliver, Smith, & Wilson, 1989; Sedlacek, 1987).

Despite the work on the differential effects of college context on African American students, we know surprisingly little about how, or even whether, gender circumscribes Black student outcomes. Although the potential importance of the context has been noted, investigation of the effects of social support within differentially racialized campus environments for Black males requires much more focused attention.

In addition, a number of studies suggest that there are two salient factors that differentially affect Black college student performance: a lack of positive social support, and discrimination imposed by professors, administrators, and peers (Allen, Epps, & Haniff, 1991; Hughes, 1987; Oliver et al., 1989; Sedlacek, 1987). African American students at predominantly White institutions report that racial discrimination occurs with much greater frequency. Similarly, it has been found that on self-reports of academic achievement, social integration, and campus race relations, the responses were at best neutral but usually negative for this group. Here again, there was demonstration of a positive relationship between social support, racial discrimination and academic achievement (Allen, 1992). We also know that when students feel that members of the faculty are racially discriminatory, they do not perform as well academically as a consequence of their not fostering relationships with the faculty. These data further suggest that academic achievement is significantly related to student satisfaction with general college life. Even African American males who are doing well academically on predominantly White campuses exhibit a marked decrease in performance from their high school grades—over and above what is expected for adjustment to college-level work (Allen, 1986). Many African American students, particularly Black males, report that their relationships with faculty members and peers are negative, and that they avoid interaction with them outside of the classroom at predominantly White colleges. Additionally, these students report that they rarely attend Black-sponsored events and were generally not socially active on campus (Allen, 1986; Fleming, 1984; Nettles, 1988).

The student-faculty relationship has long been noted as a significant predictor of academic achievement as well as of a number of other outcome variables such as educational aspirations, attitudes toward colleges, academic achievement, personal development, and persistence (Tinto, 1993; Tracey & Sedlacek, 1985). Pascarella and Terenzini's (1991) review of the literature on student-faculty contact and college outcomes suggests that the quality of the contact between student and faculty should be examined in greater detail to determine the academic benefits to students. A student, for instance, may have very little contact with the faculty, but the periods of contact may be so positive (or conversely so negative) that the limited interaction may still somehow demonstrate a significant relationship with academic performance. Indeed, previous findings clearly suggest that the perception of social support that Black students receive from their institutions of higher learning has a significant effect on achievement related outcomes.

According to other findings, students who are better off academically report that they are on better terms with faculty members. In addition, they found the institution to be generally supportive of their educational endeavors and consequently seemed to make a greater effort to interact with their professors (Nettles, 1988; Tracey & Sedlacek, 1985). Allen (1985) posits that there is a mutual-attraction relationship that exists between students and faculty members. In essence, students who perceive higher levels of support from the university will be less reluctant to avoid informal contact with faculty and administrators than will students who do not perceive this support. Professors will respond more actively to students who have fostered informal contact with them outside of the classroom setting, and this relationship quite reasonably will affect academic performance and engagement.

BLACK MALES IN COLLEGE:
FINDINGS FROM MULTICOLLEGE DATABASES

During the past decade, two major databases have disproportionately influenced the literature and discussion on African American college students' experience and outcomes. In turn, these data sets have more specifically informed the higher education community about Black males at colleges and universities. First, the National Study of Black College Students (NSBCS) is a multiyear survey that includes the questionnaire response of 2,531 African American students. About 38% of these students were enrolled at eight historically Black public universities ($n = 953$) and the remainder ($n = 1,578$) attended eight predominantly White college campuses (Allen, 1992; Allen, Epps, & Haniff, 1991). NSBCS is by far one of the most important and comprehensive databases on Black college student life. Another data set of importance is the Student Opinion Survey (SOS) that includes responses from African American students attending 30 public and private colleges and universities (18 predominately White and 12 historically Black) (see Nettles, 1988). All of the institutions participating in this study were selected on the basis of geographic diversity and accessibility. Both of these databases provide a comprehensive examination of information about the higher education experience for a substantial number of Black college students.

Without question, these two data sets represent the most complete information currently available on characteristics, attitudes, experiences, and achievement of African American college students. In the previous sections of this chapter I have cited heavily from published findings of the National Survey of Black Students (NSBS). In doing so, I give credit for the immense informative value these data have had on the field's particular understanding of Black males' college experiences and outcomes. I turn my attention now, however, to findings from the Student Opinion Survey. This data set offers a diverse collection of information from students attending both historically Black public and private institutions. These findings compliment results from NSBS and serve as a window to our awareness of how the relationship between race and gender plays itself out in various higher educational settings.

RESEARCH USING THE STUDENT OPINION SURVEY

In a study using the SOS data base (Davis, 1994), I have assembled a set of research findings by systematically focusing on African American male college students. This study explores how the racialized and gendered environments of college campuses affect the academic and social lives of these students. Specifically, this work focused on attitude about social support and whether it is a significant predictor of achievement over and beyond other academic and nonacademic factors. Since previous studies suggest that the experiences of African American males attending predominantly White versus historically Black colleges may differ (Fleming, 1984), analyses were performed to examine the relationship between college environmental type and student achievement.

The conceptual framework used in this study is adapted from educational studies of college impact. This framework distinguishes between students' social capital variables such as precollegiate and background characteristics (e.g., parents' educational levels) and the characteristics of the college they are attending (racial makeup). These predictor variables are often referred to as input variables and have been shown to be correlated to student achievement outcomes. Although other outcome data about the college experience have been investigated, these recent studies are confined to college academic achievement. The independent or predictor variables used in the multivariate analyses in this study can be placed in three groups: academic- and personal-background factors, racial-congruency factors, and college-level experience and institutional factors, including social support.

Measuring Social Support and Other Variables

Although there were a number of different responses that SOS was designed to elicit, the most recent analyses were only concerned with a subset of the variables aimed at understanding African American males' college outcomes. The variable social support is derived from items measuring the attitudes and perceptions of students on questions dealing with general satisfaction with social support issues on campus. Specifically, social support is derived from questionnaire items (e.g., satisfaction with counseling services, and faculty-study relations) that are factor analyzed to create a factor score that represents African American men's overall attitude about institutional social support. Age and socioeconomic background of students are included in the analysis. Socioeconomic background is a factor score that provides an index of the student's socioeconomic status by obtaining a weighted sum of all items loading significantly on the SES factor. SAT, the composite of the students' verbal and quantitative sections on the Scholas-

tic Achievement Test, is one of two academic background variables entered
as predictors of student college achievement. HSGPA (high school grade
point average) is the other academic variable included in the analysis. Several nonacademic, attitudinal variables are also investigated to test their
significance over and beyond academic variables used to predict college
success. Degree aspiration is a variable that measures the highest degree
aspired to by Black males. Two racial congruency variables, high school
and community, are also considered. These variables indicate the racial
fit of students' previous school and home environments with their current
predominantly White college environment. College-level variables, academic integration, and study habits are also included in these analyses.
Academic integration (Pascarella & Terenzini, 1991) is a factor score that
indicates students' integration in and satisfaction with their academic environment. Scholastic practices is a variable that represents a summary of
study habits, dispositions, and academic motivation of African American
males in this study. This variable is a factor score consisting of several
items on the questionnaire that are all loaded on the scholastic practices
factor. Peer relations is a factor score that reflects students' relations, social
and academic, with other students on campus. The dependent variable,
academic achievement, is the student's cumulative college grade point average measured on a 9-point scale.

These studies examine differences in college racial context (HBCU vs.
predominantly White college or university [PWCU]) for all variables of
interest. For these samples of African American males, separate racial-con-
text group analyses are performed using hierarchical regression to investigate relationships between outcome variables and sets of predictor variables, including social support.

Findings and Discussion

All variables in this study are significantly different for Black males enrolled on predominately White and historically Black campuses with the
exception of peer relations. Regarding academic performance, African
American males at HBCUs reported significantly higher grade point averages than their peers on predominately White campuses. Similarly, African
American males attending Black colleges had a higher mean age, lower
socioeconomic status, lower high school grades and SAT scores, and higher
degree aspirations. There were also differences in the continuity of Black
males' high school racial context and that of their current college campus.
For instance, African American males on predominately white college campuses have less racial congruency of their high school and the community/
neighborhood in which they grew up than their peers attending historically

Black colleges. That is, African American males at Black colleges were more likely to come from predominantly Black high schools and communities than were Black males at predominately White colleges to come from predominantly White high schools and communities.

Focusing on college-level variables, Black males at HBCUs are significantly more integrated academically at their institutions and receive more social support that their brothers at PWCUs. Further, African American males at predominately White colleges report having better study habits. Black males from the two campus environments have comparable levels of peer relations. When multivariate analysis is performed, some interesting findings follow. Contrary to expectations, African American males' perceptions of social support are not significantly related to their academic performance on predominantly White campuses. The same is true for study habits and peer relations. Interestingly, African American males with better feelings about social support, who study harder, and who have stronger peer relations, do not necessarily have higher levels of achievement. However, males who have higher levels of academic integration appear to perform better academically.

Both racial congruency variables are significantly related to academic achievement, however in opposite directions. When there is a closer match of the racial composition of the students' neighborhood/community to the college environment, there tends to be a positive effect on achievement. Interestingly, there is a negative effect of congruency with high school racial composition. Grades are lower for Black males whose high schools are not predominantly White. Students who were high achievers in high school are significantly more likely to be high achievers in college. Similarly, Black males with high degree aspirations have higher college achievement.

African American college men's negative perceptions about an institution's social support need not be interpreted as being automatically detrimental to a student's academic performance. Interestingly, an equally persuasive explanation may be that those students who fare well academically may correspondingly interpret their social support as being more meaningful than their less academically successful peers. In fact, Allen (1985) suggests that the student-faculty relationship is a mutually reciprocal relationship that is complex and equivocal.

A strong connection between social support and achievement was not supported in these data. Further, the relationship between social support and college academic achievement was not moderated by the predominant race of the institution that Black males attend. It seems as though social support is as important to the success of African American males at Black colleges as it is for their brothers attending predominantly White colleges and universities. It was my initial contention that African American males who hold racial-minority status at their institution would view their minority status as more salient and would feel an inevitable sense of alienation as well, thus relating to feelings about social support. The literature suggests, in fact, that students at predominantly White institutions experience a number of psychosocial problems that have demonstrated themselves as significant predictors of the students' academic outcomes. Nevertheless, the findings here support the view that Black males in general—regardless of the type of college they attend—have unique needs for social support and that universities should provide services that can meet these needs more effectively.

To a large degree, advisement, counseling, administration, faculty-student relations, and faculty's sensitivity to student problems underlie the satisfaction that a student has with the level of support offered. Many of these students are encumbered with a number of family, financial, and personal problems that may interfere with their ability to function effectively in an academic setting. Perhaps the perception that the faculty members understand and are willing to support students' educational endeavors serves as a buffer to the African American males' college stresses and facilitates their attempt to negotiate the complexities of multiple responsibilities and expectations.

Since the interaction that was proposed between social support and achievement was not obtained, the consequences of the well-documented finding that African Americans males at White universities do not get the social support that is obtained at Black universities may require clarification or qualification. The failure to find a connection between social support and achievement, however, is not a denial of the difference in how Black men experience social support within difference college context. Rather, these findings provide interesting fodder for Cheatham, Slaney, and Coleman's (1990) claim that traditionally Black colleges do not necessarily facilitate the psychosocial development of African American students more than do White universities. These findings are in contradiction to what previous education literature seems to suggest. For instance, Allen (1992) is unequivocal in his following assertions:

> Black students on Black campuses have advantages over Black students on White campuses in many respects. For instance, they display more positive psychological adjustments, more significant academic gains, and greater cultural awareness and commitment. (p. 32)

Perhaps the variations between Black and White colleges that are so often reported, as in Allen's findings, need to be further explored differentially for males and females in order to reinforce the idea that Black colleges are exceptional in providing social support. It may be the case that African American males at predominantly White colleges have no illusions about these institutions' supporting them in meaningful ways, so their low expectations of support are not completely captured in how social support is usually operationalized. Black students often perceive predominantly White institutions as providing better facilities and services than Black colleges and these benefits may somehow offset the perception that the university does not provide the social support that they desire and need. The conceptualization of social support may need to be broadened to include other facets such as views about facilities and services.

CONCLUSIONS AND IMPLICATIONS FOR HIGHER EDUCATION

In presenting the research findings in this chapter, I attempt to draw conclusions about the mediating nature of social support on the academic experiences of Black men in college. Although the results of this study can in no way serve as a panacea for problems that are faced in educating African American males in higher education, the implications of this study are numerous. It is true that colleges and universities provide uneven levels of support for African American males; however, it's not important for achievement outcomes. If social support is in fact not significantly related to Black male college achievement, should the urgency of addressing the crisis in higher education be reexamined? Irrespective of such a relationship, it would be advantageous for educators, policy makers, and administrators in higher education to adopt effective strategies to deal with the unique psychosocial and cultural needs of African American males on these campuses. Given the volatile rates of college enrollments for Black males, the provision of a supportive academic environment that may be a protective factor against attrition is essential.

These findings should be also viewed in a larger policy context. Certainly, collegiate desegregation has increased higher educational options for African Americans. However, only 3 decades after these corrective reforms began, through assaults on affirmative action and cutbacks in economic support, the nation is witnessing again a distressing ebb in the tide of educational opportunity for African Americans, particularly young Black men. This occurs paradoxically at a time when higher education desegregation policy is connected to continued increases in Black males' attending predominately White institutions (Carter & Wilson, 1997). In order to undermine policy and institutional shifts that create a precarious positioning of African American males in the higher educational landscape, more direct attention should be paid by universities, and by those who study these institutions, to how race and gender influence the quality of students' experiences in these settings.

Although considerable attention has been directed toward understanding gender and racial differences in higher education, little of that effort has centered on the intersection of race and gender. Namely, the important and unique collegiate experiences of African American men and women have been omitted because of an exclusive focus on race or gender. The current plight of African American males attending college demands much more focus, both theoretically and methodologically.

From the current discourse has emerged an urgency to address the education problems Black males face in postsecondary institutions. Given the recent concerns about college enrollment and completion rates, it is rather ironic that scant attention has been given to the perspectives of African American college men concerning their own plight and experiences in higher education.

Findings from this study and other relevant research challenge colleges and universities to reconsider traditional approaches to exclusive race-based or gender-based strategies for developing community and integrating students into the mainstream of campus life. A recent study by Jackson (1998) on African American college women also offers a complimentary critique. Placing the responsibility on institutions' traditional effort provides some rationale for shifting their strategies:

> Colleges and universities should reexamine their diversity efforts and consider their students as multifaceted people whose school experiences are not affected only be either their race or their gender buy by both their race and their gender. (p. 361)

Black males' negative college experiences and limited social support are usually viewed as by-products of structural institutional factors and entrenched college culture. However, these experiences may be linked to how Black men adapt to systemic pressures and expectations—usually undermined by maladaptive definitions of masculinity (Hunter & Davis, 1994). These issues are potentially points of departure and direction for higher education institutions as they try to provide more supportive academic environments. Both historically Black and predominately White colleges are being held more accountable for providing conducive learning communities by acknowledging gender's role in the social and academic lives of Black males. Ultimately, success is accomplished by truly valuing the presence of African American males on campus and supporting these students as they learn to negotiate their identities in these environments.

11

African American Achievement and Socioeconomic Collapse: Alternative Theories and Empirical Evidence

Patrick L. Mason

ECONOMISTS (AND OTHER SOCIAL SCIENTISTS), policy makers, and layper-
sons are all in general agreement on the relationship between education
and inequality: closing the intra- and interracial gap in education will also
close the intra- and interracial gap in socioeconomic outcomes. That is to
say, as African Americans and low-income individuals become relatively
more educated, their wages, marriage rates, and occupational status will
improve while unemployment, crime and imprisonment, divorce, and the
rate of out-of-wedlock births will decrease. With more and better education, African Americans, particularly males, will make both intertemporal
and interracial gains in their socioeconomic status. This individualist and
meritocratic theory of socioeconomic status forms the unquestioned hard
core of the most common explanation of inequality and intertemporal differences in well-being. Unfortunately, explaining the precarious socioeconomic condition of Black men within this framework further victimizes this
group.

The economic history of the last quarter of the 20th century offers a
serious challenge to this perspective. Instead, the past 2½ decades provide
substantial evidence that relative increases in education, both intertemporal
and interracial, represent a necessary but not a sufficient condition for
achieving social and economic parity. The dominant perspective, perhaps
shared by a substantial majority of African Americans, Whites, and other

African American Males in School and Society: Practices and Policies for Effective Education. Copyright © 1999 by Teachers College, Columbia University. All rights reserved. ISBN 0-8077-3870-0
(pbk), ISBN 0-8077-3871-9 (cloth). Prior to photocopying items for classroom use, please contact
the Copyright Clearance Center, Customer Service, 222 Rosewood Dr., Danvers, MA 01923, USA, tel.
(508) 750-8400.

Americans, incorporates an understanding of racial discrimination as the outcome of individualist bigotry and individualist prejudice and thereby misunderstands the interaction between racism and class conflict in economic processes. Indeed, this approach misunderstands the very nature of race.

I do not wish to challenge the proposition that economic improvement, education, and other outcomes (e.g., marriage rates) have a positive relationship, while the rates of out-of-wedlock births, divorce, welfare receipt, and imprisonment are negatively related with education. Rather, in this chapter I challenge the individualist and meritocratic explanation of these phenomena and the direction of causation implied by the dominant perspective. Specifically, I argue that there are continuous material incentives for racial exclusion in economic processes. Further, these racial exclusions have effects on African American males far beyond the labor market in such areas as family formation (marriage, divorce, and childbirth) and social policy (imprisonment of economically unneeded and socially unwanted persons).

The job competition and human capital theories offer alternative explanations for the dramatic changes in inter- and intraracial male wage inequality that began to increase after 1979 and the stagnation and eventual decline in male earnings that began one half decade earlier in the mid-1970s (Darity & Myers, 1995a). For example, Mason (1995a) shows that among heads of household, the average African American male wage as a fraction of the average White male wage was 0.72 for 1973–1975. By 1988 it was 0.71, 0.72 for 1989 and 1990, and 0.68 for 1991. Similarly, for all male heads of household, ages 18–64 with positive earnings (and converting all wages to 1992 dollars), the average wage rate was $14.64 per hour in 1973 but only $12.52 per hour in 1991—$0.33 per hour below the 1967 hourly wage rate. Using the standard deviation of the natural log of average hourly earnings as a measure of inequality, wage inequality among male heads of household rose from 3.11 in 1975 to 3.99 in 1991—a 28% increase in male earnings inequality (by this measure).

This chapter provides both theoretical and empirical evidence that suggests that neither the general increase in inequality and the concomitant decline in the average wage rate nor the increase in interracial inequality can be related consistently to impersonal market forces increasing the rate of return to skill. Both forms of increasing inequality and the associated decline in the average wage rate are quite consistent with the notions that the bargaining power of workers as a whole has declined and that workers have differential abilities to protect themselves against the substantial economic restructuring and contemporary public policy changes that may have had their origins in the mid-1970s, and that accelerated—to the detriment of workers—after the 1979–1981 period. Finally, in order to be consistent with the theme of this volume, both the theoretical and empirical content of this chapter are focused on African American male socioeconomic outcomes.

This chapter is divided into three main sections. I first present alternative perspectives on the nature of inter- and intraracial changes in socioeconomic well-being. In particular, I discuss human capital theory and job competition theory. The former provides the theoretical background for the dominant understanding of race, markets, and social outcomes, while the latter provides the theoretical background for an alternative (and, I argue, a more relevant) perspective. The next part of the chapter provides descriptive statistics on the nature of socioeconomic changes that have occurred over the past half century. The chapter concludes with a summary of the discussion and its implications.

ECONOMIC THEORY AND RACE

Human Capital Theory

There is a remarkable consensus among human capital theorists: Competitive markets are not compatible with persistent discrimination in economic life. Within the human capital framework, isolated and nonsystemic incidents of racial discrimination may occur, but continuing and systemic racial discrimination is not a problem when competitive markets exist. To the extent that interracial differences in economic well-being persist, they reflect persistent interracial and intraracial differences in the behavior of individuals and families. Hence, racism is not a relevant factor within competitive markets. Racial differences in individual behavior are explained by racial differences in family and community "culture," racial differentials in individual responses to the incentive structure of public policy, or other phenomena beyond the reach of competitive market forces. In short, the new conventional wisdom among neoclassical economists boldly asserts that race per se has no consequence for market outcomes in the presence of competitive markets. Accordingly, policies such as affirmative action are quite superfluous and may be injurious to Whites (males) as well.

Call this the market power hypothesis: racial discrimination and market competition are inversely correlated. Discriminatory behavior will persist only in those sectors of society where the competitive forces of the market are least operative. The argument in brief is that agents (firms and individuals) who engage in discriminatory behavior are limiting their own range of choice, in other words, reducing their access to a particular good or service. However, the intended victims of discrimination will not be harmed (when competitive conditions exist) because they will exercise their option to engage in market transactions with other nondiscriminatory agents. Because limits on free choice are costly, discriminating agents will be forced to pay a higher price for what they buy, or receive lower compensation for their work (if they do not wish to work alongside members of particular subgroups of the labor force, e.g., an African American male).

Those who regard race as irrelevant can buy some things more cheaply as a result, thus nondiscriminating agents will have a competitive advantage in the market. Hence, discriminating agents will be faced with two choices: to change their discriminating behavior so as to become competitive in the market, or to continue to discriminate and be driven out of the market because of higher costs. So, discriminatory costs cannot persist in the marketplace in the long run because of the competitive environment of markets in a capitalist economy. Neither racial identity (or racial culture) nor racism (which orthodox economists define as differential treatment of individuals) influences the accumulation of productive attributes; and neither has an impact on market processes. Moreover, neither racial identity nor racism is influenced by socioeconomic outcomes. Both intraracial and interracial variations in market outcomes are the result of variations in individual attributes.

Yet it is difficult to reconcile the naive version of the market power hypothesis with regularly observed empirical outcomes. After adjusting for observable and individual-specific characteristics, researchers have consistently found the following outcomes: (a) African American men earn less than White men and have less access to stable employment, (b) African Americans have poorer health status and receive lower quality of treatment than Whites, (c) African Americans are less likely to be granted a housing loan than Whites, (d) if they do receive a housing loan it is more likely to be of a lower amount and have a higher interest rate than a loan made to an otherwise identical White person, and (e) African Americans have a lower entrepreneurship rate than Whites and among those who are self-employed African Americans obtain lower earnings. Finally, analysis of aggregate data has shown that African American males have a greater probability of criminal participation than White males, whereas analysis of microdata has found no significant race effect.

This pattern of outcomes is certainly consistent with the notion that racism is a strong determinant of the life-chances of African American men. Therefore, it would seem that there is sufficient evidence to reject the market power hypothesis. Yet there is considerable resistance among neoclassical economists to taking this bold step and this resistance has rather deep roots in economic theory. The notion that competition levels the playing field is the faith-based and nearly impenetrable hard core of orthodox economic theory, despite empirical evidence on race and socioeconomic outcomes that is simply not compatible with the naive market power hypothesis.

Specifically, the orthodox economic argument is that there are unobserved individual attributes that influence market outcomes and these unobserved attributes are not equally distributed across racial groups. These unobserved attributes are primarily accumulated at home, in school, in the neighborhood, or through interpersonal relations and thereby are not fully subject to the equalizing tendencies of the competitive process. Further, these attributes have a positive correlation with earnings and income and (inexplicably) Whites have a greater amount or higher quality of all unobserved attributes (Neal & Johnson, 1994).

If racism is relevant, at all, it may affect some aspects of the accumulation of productive skills, since education, marriage, and community background (for example) are not subject to fully competitive markets. However, the primary cause of interracial inequality is the interracial differences in unobserved attributes that directly affect productivity and that also indirectly affect it, through their impact on the accumulation of observable productive attributes.

Racism may influence the accumulation and quality of productive attributes, but neither race nor racism is relevant within market processes. There are, then, many affiliation networks (marriage, friendship and extra market personal relationships, etc.) that are not fully subject to the competitive discipline of the market but have economic consequences (Loury, 1984). So, from this perspective, racial identity and racism may influence the accumulation of productive attributes because of so-called cultural differences across groups and because there are interracial differences in the ability to draw on affiliation networks to strengthen the accumulation of productive attributes. But, within the market, both inter- and intraracial differences in socioeconomic well-being are determined solely by differences in observable and unobservable individual attributes.

Culture, in this instance, refers to market-functional individual attributes: future orientation, deferred gratification, disciplined behavior, strong family bonds, socioeconomic status of one's neighborhood, and degree of access to individuals in positions of power and authority (role models). Individuals who possess a greater portion of these cultural attributes will tend to acquire a greater quantity and a greater quality of the set of skills (such as education) that are most desired (and, thereby, more highly remunerated) in the economy.

The labor quality hypothesis has spawned a cottage industry of explanations that focus on various aspects of (presumed) African American inferiority. For example, Loury (e.g., 1984) argues that African Americans have a disproportionate number of individuals with market-dysfunctional culture. And, because individuals tend to live in communities that are segregated by race and socioeconomic status, African American cultural behavior will transmit interracial inequality in perpetuity—even when there is no racial discrimination in the market and when one is observing an African American male and a White male of equal socioeconomic status. The heart of the problems confronting the African American community is individual values. Loury argues that (low-income) African Americans are not morally inferior, only that they, as a group, have a disproportionate share of values that are economically dysfunctional. From this perspective, cultural (racial) differences have led to differential levels of acquisition of human capital. Hence, measured quality-adjusted differences in labor market earnings are a reflection of differences in cultural acquiescence to the income-earning requirements of the market, not of discrimination.

But why is African American culture more market dysfunctional than White culture? Sowell (1984) and Williams (1982) have put forth the thesis that the primary barrier to African American economic progress is governmental policies that have a deleterious effect on both African American culture and the competitive environment of the market. They claim that governmental interference with the market mechanism, in other words, welfare and a collection of alleged race-specific privileges such as affirmative action and minority set-aside programs, has reduced entrepreneurial drive and the incentive for African Americans to work hard, save, and invest. Also, governmental sanctions of private barriers to competition (e.g., license fees, unions, etc.) have tended to make African Americans less competitive in the marketplace.

Murray and Herrnstein (1994) have argued that heredity is the crucial unobserved variable. In particular, the distribution of inherited cognitive skills is the single most important factor for determining a host of generally observed social outcomes. For example, they assert that the distribution of wages is determined by meritocratic assessment of inherited cognitive ability within the context of impersonal market forces. Neither culture nor socioeconomic status nor racial and gender discrimination represents an important element of earnings inequality in competitive labor markets. This perspective challenges the necessity and the efficacy of all public efforts to eradicate poverty, discrimination, or other socioeconomic inequities.

Empirical Evaluation of the Labor Quality Hypothesis

Among human capital theorists, differences in productive ability are the result of individual optimizing decisions by agents, faced with a competitive labor market and noncompetitive markets for skill acquisition. Proponents of this hypothesis assert that the post-1975 slowdown and eventual deterioration in male interracial wage equality has occurred because of a market-driven increase in the price of cognitive skill, which is differentially distributed across racial groups. Starting at or about the mid- to late 1970s, there was an increase in the demand for more highly skilled workers. This increased demand for more skilled workers generated a rising wage premium for skill, thereby increasing the extent of earnings inequality among the least- and best-paid White male workers. Since the median African American male earns substantially less than the median White male (placing at about the 31st percentile), interracial inequality also increased. Hence, increasing interracial inequality is not due to rising discrimination against African American workers but is part of the more general increase in inequality resulting from a competitively induced rising skill premium.

However, there are points of agreement between human capital theory and the biogenetic approach of Murray and Herrnstein. One, both relied upon the use of Armed Forces Qualification Text (AFQT) scores to explain interracial inequality. Two, both explicitly deemphasize an important role for racial discrimination within the labor market. Again, for the proponents of the labor quality hypothesis it is the allegedly inferior family and community backgrounds of African Americans that mitigate against skill acquisition. AFQT scores are presumed to capture unobserved ability or skill that is derived from family and community background but that is not captured adequately by the standard specification of the earnings process. Rodgers and Spriggs (in press), however, have shown that the AFQT has measurement bias that is associated with race. Therefore, human capital theorists have implicitly accepted the notion of African American cultural inferiority whereas the proponents of the cognitive skills meritocracy explicitly argue for the biological inferiority of African Americans (Ferguson, 1995; Maxwell, 1995; Neal & Johnson, 1994).

An additional empirical problem within the literature concerns the relationship between completed years of schooling and cognitive skills assessment. More able individuals obtain more years of schooling, but additional years of schooling also increase cognitive skill. This simultaneous relationship between schooling and cognitive ability implies that a wage equation that includes both variables may yield misleading results. In this case, the coefficient on the cognitive skill variable does not provide an estimate of the rate of return (payment) to unobserved ability.

Third, previous empirical studies have not been taken advantage of panel data techniques to account for individual heterogeneity. Cognitive skill may not be the sole unobserved ability variable. For example, Mason (1996a) challenges the commonly held assumption that unobserved labor quality among African Americans and Latinos is lower than unobserved labor quality among Whites. I proceed by simultaneously examining the relationship between observed individual attributes and educational and income attainment. In the initial step of the investigation, I find that for a given set of background characteristics, African American men are more likely and Latinos are at least as likely to obtain the same level of education as White males. Next, I find that after adjusting for observable characteristics, African American men and Latinos receive a lower wage rate than White males. The interracial differences in the patterns of educational attainment and earnings are consistent with the claim that interracial earnings differentials are evidence of discrimination, rather than higher quantities of unobserved characteristics among Whites.

Darity, Guilkey, and Winfrey (1995) and Mason (in press) also present evidence that discredits the labor quality hypothesis. Darity et al. find that after adjusting for differences in years of education, number of children, marital status, years of work experience, language fluency, health status, extent of assimilation, region, location, occupation, and industry, African American men earn 13–15% less than the national average for otherwise identical men. Since African American male wages are 79% of the national average, the Darity et al. results imply that the vast majority of the wage gap is due to discrimination. Moreover, Mason's (in press) findings do not support the labor quality explanation of wage differences between Black and White men.

Inadequacy of Human Capital Theory

Despite widespread acceptance, human capital theory does not provide an appropriate framework for examining intertemporal changes in interracial earnings. Neither the naive market power hypothesis nor the labor quality hypothesis can explain recent (post-1973) changes in interracial wage inequality. Nor can either of these hypotheses explain the decline of the average wage rate. The choice-theoretic framework of human capital theory is ill suited for seriously understanding the persistence of racism. Indeed, human capital theory suggests that persistent discrimination cannot happen when markets are competitive. As such, much of the research flowing from this approach has been a continuously futile search to find the crucial flaw in African American male behavior and culture that permits sustained African American–White economic inequality. We turn now to examine an alternative approach that attempts to incorporate both racism and class conflict as important elements in its analysis.

Job Competition, Class, and Persistent Discrimination

The job competition model of discrimination (Darity, 1989; Mason, 1993, 1995b, 1997; Williams, 1987, 1991) explores the economic incentives for firms to engage in discriminatory behavior and for workers to engage in racial conflict. The impact of racial identity and racism is not limited to the acquisition of observable and unobservable attributes. Racism and race are also major explanatory variables within competitive markets. In turn, socioeconomic outcomes contribute to the development of racial identity and the economic environment that allows racism to flourish.

The details of the job competition model are presented in two stages. First, regardless of race or gender, identical workers will not necessarily receive identical pay for identical work in the job competition model. Intra-group differences in pay is the norm within this approach. Competition does not level the playing field. The competitive attempt by firms to earn the average or normal rate of profit produces dissimilarity in the treatment of otherwise identical workers. Remuneration for the job depends on the average quality of labor (education, experience, on-the-job training, etc.), the competitive structure of firms, job desirability, whether firms are operating at expected capacity utilization, and the bargaining power of workers. Those workers employed at identical work within the same firm may receive identical pay; however, those workers within the same occupation but employed at different firms within the same industry or who may be employed at the same occupation in a different industry are unlikely to receive identical pay. Wage differentials will occur because firms operate with differential competitive structures and face workers with differing degrees of bargaining power.

Race matters in the formation of inter- and intra-industry wage rates because racial conflict is one of the factors that determine the strength of worker bargaining power. As racial conflict increases (decreases) the bargaining power of workers as a group decreases (increases). Employers then have a strong economic incentive to adopt personnel policies or tolerate working conditions and working environments that discourage interracial coalition building among workers.

Second, given the distribution of wages, workers use racial identification as one of the means for obtaining the best job available. In effect, this attribute of the job competition model takes the focus on culture from the labor quality hypothesis and stands it on its head. Interracial differences in access to individuals in positions of power and authority may lead to differences in skill acquisition, but these differences in access also produce preferential treatment for Whites in the allocation of the most desirable employment opportunities.

The important point here is that race and class interact to transmit socioeconomic status from the group to the individual. Race (or, alternatively, family and community background) influences the acquisition of productive attributes, whereas class is an important determinant of whether and where a worker with a given set of productive attributes will find employment. Hence, the average socioeconomic status of a racial (or ethnic) group is a determinant of individual wage rates. A specific prediction of this model is that regardless of race (or gender), individual wage rates increase with White male employment density. That is to say, all other things being equal, an individual's compensation will increase if (s)he moves from a "low" White male employment-density job to a job where White male employment density is "high." Additionally, persistent intra-group wage differences are also a normal outcome of the competitive process, since job wages vary with the competitive structure of jobs. Finally, reductions in bargaining power will lower the wages of all workers—regardless of race, gender, or skill level. Thus, theories that suggest that the distribution of income is solely a meritocratic outcome of optimizing decisions by individual agents (in the face of impersonal market forces) lack both theoretical and empirical support.

Mason (in press) presents a cross-sectional evaluation of alternative theories of interracial inequality and discrimination. The weight of evidence from this study is consistent with the job competition analysis of discrimination: after adjusting for interracial differences in cognitive ability and observed attributes, I find that access to White- (especially male-) dominated jobs increases an individual's employment stability and earnings. Specifically, utilizing the most conservative set of assumptions, if a White male moves from a job with the average White employment density for Whites to a job with the average White employment density for African American males, his wage rate would decline by over 14%. If an African American male moves to a job with the average White employment density for White males, his wage rate would increase by about 3%. Moreover, these segregation effects are independent of the wage discrimination effects encountered by African Americans. As reported earlier, this study shows that African American men received a 16% wage discrimination penalty—regardless of the racial-gender composition of the job.

Extension of Job Competition Model

The job competition model of discrimination in the labor market is conformable with the African American structural model of transitions in family structure (Mason, 1996b). Consider Darity and Myers's (1995a) explanation of the dramatic rise in the presence of female-headed households. They argue that the rise in these households and the rise in the fraction of never married African Americans are strongly determined by the economic marginalization—social rejection and economic redundancy—of African American males. Their economic model of household formations conforms to Bowman's (1988, 1989, 1995) social-psychological model of intrafamily relations. He argues that deindustrialization and socioeconomic discrimination and isolation creates provider-role strain among young and blue-collar African American males. Provider-role strain discourages marriage among unmarried men and contributes to divorce among married men.

Besides premature deaths due to violent crimes and accidents, marginalized males also have a lower probability of entering into or remaining in marriage because of involuntary institutionalization (incarceration or mental hospital), low or unstable earnings, current participation in illegal activities, and poor health. Racial discrimination within the labor market, then, contributes to marginalization of African American males because it is an important cause of employment and earnings security, as well as access to more or less secure jobs. Since it reduces the supply of marriageable males, marginalization is a major contributing factor to the rise of female-headed households.

Indeed, as I discuss below, there is solid empirical evidence that for African American men, limited legal earnings opportunities are the primary determinant of drug dealing (Myers, 1992), and increases in joblessness tend to be associated with increases in the incarceration rate of African American men (Myers & Sabol, 1987). So, in the Darity-Myers-Bowman model of transitions in the African American family structure, short- and long-term shifts in the macroeconomy combine with racial discrimination within the labor market to strongly influence microeconomic decision making in the marriage market. In particular, these social forces have lowered the ratio of marriage-eligible males to females.

For example, Mason (1996b) reports that marginalization has severely reduced both the male-female sex ratio and the fraction of marriage-eligible men. Among the findings summarized in that study, a 25% increase in a husband's income reduces the probability of divorce by 8%. Among women ages 23–28, African American women are 51% as likely to enter first marriage as White women if there is no statistical control for male marriageability. However, after controlling for male marriageability, young African American women are 71% as likely to enter first marriage as young White women. Similarly, if the sample is restricted to women who expect to marry within 5 years the relative probability of marriage increases from 46% to 59% when the pool of full-time employed men is included as an explanatory factor.

CYCLES, TRENDS, AND LONG-TERM CHANGES

We turn now to investigate how the job competition and human capital approaches measure up against recent empirical evidence of changes in African American socioeconomic status, including education, wages and income, incarceration, and out-of-wedlock births. Looking back from the vantage point of today, we can now see clearly that the train to the promised land of racial equality crashed at precisely the point in time that Freeman and Wilson made their optimistic announcements. Indeed, by the close of the 1980s prominent economists openly pondered, "What went wrong?" (Bound & Freeman, 1992).

Education

From the standpoint of educational attainment and achievement, nothing went wrong. African Americans made stunning progress. During 1954–1974, African Americans made impressive strides in completed years of schooling (U.S. Department of Commerce, 1979). In 1940, 25- to 34-year-old African Americans had a median of 6.9 years of completed schooling, 3.5 years less than the White median. By 1960, 25- to 34-year-old African Americans had a median of 10.3 years of education, just 2 years less than the White median. In 1970 and 1975, young African Americans averaged 12 and 12.4 years of completed education, respectively, or 0.6 and 0.4 years less than the White median. The largest gains were among southern African Americans during the 1960s. By 1975, southern and nonsouthern African Americans had virtually identical median years of completed schooling.

In 1968, 30% of all African Americans age 25 and above had completed high school. By 1994, 73% of all African Americans age 25 and above had completed high. Among Whites of the same age group, 55% and 82% had completed high school in 1968 and 1994, respectively. So, the racial gap in high school completion rates declined from 25 percentage points to 9 percentage points during the 24-year period from 1968 to 1994.

College enrollment among 18- to 24-year-old African Americans also showed impressive gains. In 1967, 16% of African American men and 10% of African American women were enrolled in college. Among Whites, 35% of men and 20% of women were enrolled in college. By 1976, the racial gap among men was only 7 percentage points as 22% and 29% of African American and White men, respectively, were enrolled in college. Among women, 23% of African Americans and 26% of Whites were enrolled in college, a racial gap of only 2 percentage points. Due to the rising cost of education, cutbacks in the availability of student assistance, and the decrease in the rate of return to education, African Americans began to lose ground in the late 1970s. Yet by 1993, 23% of African American men age 18 to 24 were enrolled in college versus 34% of White men, whereas 26% of African American women versus 35% of White women were enrolled in college.

The period from 1970 to the early 1990s has been one of substantial improvement for African American performance on standardized tests (Bernstein, 1995; Jencks, 1993). Summarizing the literature, Jencks reports the following results. Among 17-year-old high school students in 1970–1971, 98% of Whites and 82% of African Americans read at or above the "basic" reading level, whereas 51% of Whites and 8% of African Americans read at or above the two highest reading levels, i.e., "adept" and "advanced." By 1987–1988, these numbers were 99% and 97%, respectively, for the basic reading level and 52% and 28% for the adept and advanced reading levels, respectively. During 1977–1978, 96% of White 17-year-old high school students and 70% of African American 17-year-old high school students performed at the "basic" level of mathematical competency, whereas the numbers for "moderately complex" level of competency were 84% and 40%, respectively. By 1987–1988, these figures were 89% and 46%, respectively, for White students, but 76% and 26%, respectively for African American students. Bernstein (1995) shows that the gap in science scores among 17-year-old students on the National Assessment of Educational Progress test declined by 17% during 1977–1990. Similarly, Bernstein (1995) shows that the ratio of African American to White Standard Achievement Test scores increased during the 1976–1993 period. Hence, one cannot reasonably argue that the decline in African American–White education gap simply reflects lower promotion standards at schools and colleges attended by African Americans.

The impressive gains of African Americans in educational achievement and attainment illustrate an important point. For a given set of background characteristics, African Americans tend to achieve a higher level of educational attainment than otherwise identical Whites (Bernstein, 1995; Grissmer, Kirby, Berends, & Williamson, 1994; Haveman & Wolfe, 1994; Mason, 1996a). And statistical evidence suggests that this racial differential cannot be explained away by the massive intervention of the federal government into the educational and social structure of the South during the civil rights movement (Jaynes & Williams, 1989). Rather, Jaynes and Williams are suggesting that race-specific factors have also had a positive impact on African American educational gains. To the extent that this racial differential is related to cultural, family, and community attributes that are difficult to capture in statistical models, it provides rather strong evidence that something very positive is occurring among African American families, communities, and cultural roots—despite the persistence of negative myths to the contrary.

Wages and Income

As high school graduation and postsecondary education for African Americans became the norm between 1960 and 1975, there were paradoxical changes in the interracial gap in family income. For example, in 1947 African American families obtained 51% of the income obtained by White families. In 1959 African American families obtained only 52% of the income accruing to White families. By 1970, African American family income was 61% of White family income. By 1974, this statistic had declined back to 58% and continued downward thereafter to 52% by 1993 (Mason, 1996b; U.S. Department of Commerce, 1979). So, despite the tremendous educational gains African Americans have made relative to Whites during the past half century there has been no net gain in relative family economic well-being.

Certainly, there have been changes in family structure among African Americans and Whites during the past 50 years. But these changes in family structure cannot explain the relative stagnation in the economic well-being of African American families. Indeed, if the "collapse in the African American family" and attendant rise in "underclass culture" explains the relative stagnation in African American economic progress, what explains the unparalleled relative educational gains by African American youth? After all, nearly all African American youth are raised in African American families. How can the same family structure and cultural system that is responsible for several decades of above average educational success also be too pathological (Moynihan, 1965), dysfunctional (Loury, 1984), or inferior (Neal & Johnson, 1994) to provide their young with the requisite tools for economic success? Perhaps the answer to this paradox lies in the fact that much of the decision-making process for education (at least up through high school graduation) is actually in the hands of African American families or decision makers who can be held accountable by African American families whereas the exact opposite is true for the decision-making process in the economy and society.

At about the time that many first-generation African American high school and college graduates would normally enter into marriage, the long decline in the average real-wage rate of men and the increasing inequality in male earnings from 1973 to the present had become a fact of economic life. The declining male-wage trend was superimposed on the decrease in African American male labor force participation that started in 1940 and bottomed out in the mid-1990s. So, during the post-1973 era, male marginalization and earnings instability may have become the lead explanatory factors for the decline in both marriage and the African American standard of living.

Imprisonment

What does society do with the economically redundant and socially unwanted? Build more prisons. In 1979, the African American and White national populations were 25,863,000 and 189,968,000, respectively, while the imprisonment levels were 143,376 and 157,208, respectively (U.S. Department of Commerce, 1996; U.S. Department of Justice, 1980–1995). These data reflect imprisonment rates of 8 prisoners per 100,000 persons among Whites and 55 prisoners per 100,000 persons among African Americans. In 1979, an African American was 6.70 times more likely to be imprisoned as a White American. By 1993, imprisonment rates among Whites had increased by 250% to 20 prisoners per 100,000 persons and the African American imprisonment rate increased by 258% to 142 prisoners per 100,000 persons. Despite relatively greater educational improvement over Whites during 1979–1993, the African American–White imprisonment ratio increased from 6.70 to 7.06.

Myers and Sabol (1987), Myers (1992), and Darity and Myers (1990) all look at the process of marginalization, race, and crime. After adjusting for racial differences in poverty, age, and unemployment, these studies find that race has no statistically significant impact on criminal activity (e.g., robbery, burglary, motor vehicle theft, larceny, murder, and rape). Similarly, Myers (1992) found that if African American males earned the same legal and illegal wages as White males, drug dealing among African American males would drop 90%. The clear suggestion from the Myers study is that drug dealing is an all too rational response to low wages. Finally, Myers and Sabol (1987) provide evidence that imprisonment is not simply a process for protecting society from harmful persons—it is also a process for warehousing the economically marginal.

It is clear, then, that the disproportionate crime rates among African Americans is not caused by dysfunctional cultural attributes, pathological family structure, or inheritable criminal tendencies. Rather, extensive male marginalization (in particular, low-waged and inconsistent employment opportunities) creates an environment that nurtures income-oriented crimes, e.g., drug dealing, and also the violent crimes that tend to accompany income-oriented crimes. Yet imprisonment is a major public policy response for meeting the needs of the economically marginalized African American males.

Out-of-Wedlock Births

Darity and Myers (1995a, 1990) provide the most sophisticated analysis of the relationship between male marginalization and the rise of female-headed households among African Americans. Their analysis has three elements. First, mate availability is determined by age, education, residential location, region, unemployment rate, male institutionalization, the mortality ratio, and whether the individual has any children. Second, both the homicide rate (which influences the mortality ratio) and the incarceration rate (which is a component of male institutionalization) are determined by age, education, region, the unemployment rate, percent of population that is African American, percentage of population receiving welfare, and residential location. Finally, the proportion of female-headed households is determined by the generosity of welfare, mate availability, number and age of children, age, and education level.

According to Darity and Myers (1990, 1995a), an increase in homicides or the incarceration rate will decrease mate availability, and that in turn increases the proportion of female-headed households. An increase in the local unemployment rate also directly decreases mate availability and indirectly decreases mate availability through a rise in homicides and incarcerations. Specifically, a 10% reduction in the homicide rate among African Americans would ultimately reduce the number of female-headed households by about 1%. Thus, a 10% reduction in the incarceration rate ultimately will reduce the proportion of female-headed households by 3/10 of 1%.

If the number of marriage-eligible Black men (those who are single and employed or enrolled in school) per unmarried woman remained unchanged from 1976 to 1985, the proportion of female-headed households among African Americans would have been 37% in 1985 instead of 45%. If the African American number of marriage-eligible men per unmarried woman was equal to the higher White fraction, the 1985 proportion of female-headed households would have been 39%. Indeed, male marginalization has substantially reduced marriage among African Americans.

Summing up, the empirical evidence suggests that it is rather difficult to use human capital theory as the basis of an internally consistent theoretical analysis of recent changes in educational attainment and achievement, labor market outcomes, imprisonment, and out-of-wedlock births. In short, individualist and meritocratic social theories do not provide a fruitful starting point for explaining recent changes in the socioeconomic status of African Americans. On the other hand, job competition theory, expanded to incorporate the African American structural model of transitions in family structure, does provide an internally consistent theoretical analysis of recent changes in African American socioeconomic status.

DISCUSSION: WHERE DO WE GO FROM HERE?

Lately, we have heard a great deal about the "angry White male." We are told that White Americans are angry over their current economic conditions. Since the hourly wage rate of the average male worker has been declining for a generation and the amount of inequality is increasing—especially since 1979–1981, such anger is certainly justifiable. The relevant question, then, is, Should White anger be directed at alleged "special privileges" received by African Americans? Other racial minorities? Clearly, dispassionate analysis would suggest that allegations of "special privileges" for African Americans are more mythical than real. For example, in this chapter I have documented that although African Americans have had faster growth rates in the quantity and the quality of education relative to Whites for at least 30 years, there is substantial evidence that the level of labor market and social discrimination has increased against African Americans. In short, once again, racism is on the rise.

The job competition framework of this paper would suggest at least two policy recommendations. One, we need policies that are capable of increasing the bargaining power of all workers—especially workers with the least level of education. Recent reductions in the average wage rate and increases in wage inequality reflect dramatic reductions in workers' abilities to bargain for advantageous wages, hours, and working conditions.

Two, enforcement of currently existing antidiscrimination laws should be increased and policies that exhibit cognizance of the special problems faced by African Americans should not be undermined. Within the framework of job competition theory, there exists no tendency for competitive forces to eliminate racial discrimination. Quite to the contrary, the job competition model shows that the competitive market forces provide substantial economic incentives for firms to discriminate and for workers to engage in continuous racial conflict over access to the more desirable employment opportunities.

I do not mean to suggest here that education and training, especially for the most disadvantaged workers, is unimportant. The job competition model, like human capital theory, suggests that, ceteris paribus, more highly educated individuals will tend to have higher earnings. But the job competition model also informs us that additional increases in the quantity and quality of education are not sufficient to bring about reductions in the extent of labor market discrimination against African Americans males. Higher levels of education, unfortunately, do not remove the economic incentives to discriminate.

12

African American Males and the Struggle Toward Responsible Fatherhood

Vivian Gadsden and Phillip J. Bowman

RESEARCH ON AFRICAN AMERICAN FATHERS mirrors the work on African American male development: That is, there is little research and what exists is limited in scope. However, research on fathers in the general population (on middle-class White fathers in particular) has increased slowly but steadily since the 1980s. The studies focus on the role of fathers, father-child interactions, and father-child attachment (e.g., Fox, Kimmerly, & Schafer, 1991; Lamb, 1977, 1978); adolescent fathers (e.g., Cervera, 1991; Christmon, 1990; Ku, Sonenstein, & Pleck, 1993); and problems of father absence (e.g., Furstenberg & Harris, 1993). Much of the work on father absence focuses on the consequences of African American adolescent pregnancy and female-headed households in poverty.

Adolescent fathers are of special interest to researchers and practitioners whose work addresses the development of school-age children. Adolescent fathers and the mothers of their children typically are in school at the time of conception and the child's birth. It is difficult to determine how many adolescent fathers there are, either from adolescent mothers' reports or from school officials. In addition, it is difficult to assess the number of adolescent fathers. Adolescent males who are expectant fathers do not change physically and are not forced to drop out of school to give birth or care for the child. They do not have to acknowledge the pregnancy publicly, nor is there pressure comparable to the pressures placed on girls to assume responsibility for the newborn. Often, adolescent males may not know that they fathered a baby, because the partner has never told them,

African American Males in School and Society: Practices and Policies for Effective Education. Copyright © 1999 by Teachers College, Columbia University. All rights reserved. ISBN 0-8077-3870-0 (pbk), ISBN 0-8077-3871-9 (cloth). Prior to photocopying items for classroom use, please contact the Copyright Clearance Center, Customer Service, 222 Rosewood Dr., Danvers, MA 01923, USA, tel. (508) 750-8400.

whereas others may deny their role, feeling that the partner is trying to "trap" them into marriage. On the flip side, some young men who are members of peer cultures who see impregnation as a status symbol of virility may claim to have made someone pregnant or fathered a baby when, in fact, they have not (Sonenstein, Pleck, & Ku, 1993). A related complication is that many of the fathers of older adolescent females are young adult men rather than adolescents (Sonenstein et al., 1993) and run the risk of prosecution if the girl is under 16 years old.

For adolescent fathers in general, Robinson (1988) paints a picture different from the typical portrait of the irresponsible and indifferent young male. He suggests that depictions of unwed fathers as "super stud," "Don Juan," "Mr. Cool," and "the phantom father" are unfair, are backed by little empirical evidence to support the stereotypes, and are based on writings from the 1940s in which all unwed fathers were lumped together regardless of age (see Futterman & Livermore, 1947). The adolescent fathers whom Robinson (1988) interviewed reported that they intended to provide financial support and participate in child care. Because of their youth, adolescent boys often found the adjustment to fatherhood difficult. As is true for adolescent mothers, their premature role transition appears to cause stresses and strains that compound tensions already inherent in adolescence. The role of the father involves decisions about the baby and separation from the peer group; many receive little social support from their families; and domestic problems must be faced by those who live with the mother of their child(ren). The fathers show stress around coping with the pregnancy, financial responsibilities, education, employment, relationships with their partners, and parenting (Fry & Trifiletti, 1983).

BARRIERS TO ADOLESCENT FATHERS' INVOLVEMENT

Practitioners and policy researchers note with some consistency that indicators of adolescent fathering and adolescent fathers' willingness to assume responsibility for their children are difficult to gauge. Some adolescent mothers, particularly low-income African American and Latino mothers, fear the reprisals of "the system" on the fathers of their children and will not disclose the name of the father; recent data (e.g., Wattenberg, 1993) dispel long-held assumptions that the mothers are incapable of naming the father. Rather, these data suggest that the young mothers may be unwilling to provide the information to a public-record system that is as likely, if not more likely, to withhold support or offer assistance. The young mothers' feelings of distrust may be reinforced by cultural beliefs (and experiences) that public declarations militate against young, poor mothers and their children and against the young fathers who often are unemployed and unable to make substantial financial contributions to the support of the mother and child.

In many instances, families of origin, particularly the maternal grandparents, may serve as obstacles to a young father's participating in his child's life. With little income to contribute to the child's financial well-being and with maternal grandparents' anger about the pregnancy, the adolescent father may be hindered from contact with the child during the child's preschool years. Increasingly, researchers (e.g., Sullivan, 1993) suggest that inner-city African American youth tend to acknowledge their paternity readily, although not formally, and that the African American community facilitates the informal establishment of paternity and the young father's involvement in informal, child support arrangements.

PERCEPTIONS AND BEHAVIORS OF
AFRICAN AMERICAN ADOLESCENT FATHERS

The perceptions of African American males can be linked to a number of factors associated with African American families and communities in general. Marsiglio (1993) offers three theoretical positions to explain the perceptions and behaviors of African American adolescent fathers. The first examines some of the racial differences in patterns of adolescent sexual activity (Furstenberg, Morgan, Moore, & Peterson, 1987). A second focuses on subcultural models in which members of the African American community (including adolescents) are said to hold less traditional views of marriage and early childbearing than do Whites (Cherlin, 1981). The third combines critical elements of the structural and subcultural explanations and suggests that neighborhood segregation within African American communities may have produced a cultural climate within impoverished areas that, in turn, has fostered less conservative attitudes among young African American males toward sex and family issues.

At least two additional areas of work should be considered along with these theoretical positions. First, as noted by McAdoo (1990) and Bowman (1995), current structural models emphasize the chronically dismal economic status of many African American males and the poor economic status of African American families generally (see also McDaniel, 1994). These conditions have made it difficult for many young African American males to be reliable economic providers and have contributed to an image of young African American fathers as economic liabilities. Thus, the opportunities for family formation are more limited, on average, for African Americans than for Whites.

Second, contrary to popular perception, poor, young Black males are no more likely than their middle- and upper-income peers to engage irresponsibly in sexual activity and potentially impregnate their partners. Ku, Sonenstein, and Pleck (1993) from their analysis of data from the National Survey of Adolescent Males found a positive relationship between financial resources, measured by family income and hours worked in the last year, and sexual activity (number of partners and frequency of intercourse in the last year). The young males in this group have high incomes and more gainful employment on average but are less likely to use contraception and father a child. Ku and his colleagues offer the following as one hypothesis: Higher income males are more likely to have female partners from higher socioeconomic-status (SES) families who would be more upset if the female partners became pregnant; in other words, the higher income male may have partners who are somewhat more likely to have an abortion or not tell the male, or both, if he impregnates them. What Ku et al.'s analysis suggests is that Black young men in areas with high unemployment are not unlike their middle-class White and Black peers in the number of sexual partners but differ in the number of pregnancies that result. The unsolved question is why there are fewer pregnancies, since the adolescents and young adult men in upper income homes are less likely to use contraception.

There are but a few profiles of African American unwed fathers that capture the critical issues. However, recent studies based on the Young Unwed Fathers Project (Achatz & MacAllum, 1994) and the Parents' Fair Share program (Bloom & Sherwood, 1994) provide compelling accounts, as do discussions with fathers and practitioners participating in other father- and family-focused programs (Gadsden, Armorer, & Kane, in press; Levine & Pitt, 1996). Achatz and MacAllum (1994) conducted a survey and an ethnography with young fathers (16–25) in six fathers programs throughout the country. In the ethnography, 75% of the fathers had left school before graduation and did not have a GED at the time they enrolled in the program. The majority of the participants either left school or were at risk of leaving school before the pregnancy. The reason for leaving school that the fathers mentioned most frequently was boredom or lack of motivation, followed by a desire to "get rich quick" through drug dealing and other hustles, followed by expulsion, prejudicial treatment by other-race students and teachers, family programs, and frequent moves or changes of household.

Achatz and MacAllum (1994) report that 83% of the fathers who did not have a high school diploma indicated that education was highly valued in their households and by their families and that their leaving school created or worsened tensions between themselves and their parent(s) (p. 19).

Of the 155 fathers in their survey sample, only 36% were employed when they entered the program. Most had sporadic work histories, were paid an average of $6.00 an hour, and worked for employers who did not provide health insurance.

PROGRAMS THAT SERVE ADOLESCENT FATHERS

The men in the Achatz and MacAllum (1994) study and in many recent reports participate in six of what is currently an estimated 500 father-focused programs. Some of these programs are appended to existing family programs, and others have been established as freestanding projects, funded by universities, foundations, and different private and religious institutions (Levine & Pitt, 1996). It is unclear, however, how many of the programs are supported by or based in schools.

The welfare of children is at the center of most father-focused programs, many if not most of which serve poor African American and Latino fathers primarily. Several programs focus increasingly on providing both mothers *and* fathers with assistance and bringing them together for the welfare of the child. Other programs have expanded their missions to attend to the apparent impediments to father involvement, for example, unemployment, education, and the personal and developmental domains of adolescent and young adult male life. They assist young fathers in handling the complexities of daily life and in assuming the responsibility of parenting and they work to make local, state, and national policies more responsive to the needs of young fathers, mothers, and their children.

As is true of any movement or effort, however, the premises and purposes of the programs differ, sometimes vastly. For example, several father-focused programs attribute young men's problems to rapid changes in family-formation patterns, with some equating these changing family forms to the erosion of family values and increased participation of women in the labor market. Many programs do not acknowledge family forms outside of marriage and center their efforts on "preserving family values" (or increasing the number of families in which father and mother are married to each other with children living in the same household). They are not focused necessarily on improving the structures that reduce opportunities for individuals to create and preserve their own families, beliefs, and values. Issues of unemployment, poverty, and discrimination are often ignored or pushed to the back of discussions about father involvement as are the effects of parents' emotional absence in strained relationships or physical absence due to economic stress.

Hundreds of young men participate in these programs. Yet only a fraction of the programs are able to address issues about education or literacy in meaningful ways. In some programs, practitioners tend to work with the young fathers to return to school, get a GED, or get admitted to college. However, program resources are limited typically and cross-agency and cross-institutional connections are noticeably weak, thus reducing sharing of instructional and program resources. Although such collaborations and relationships seem undeniably good for fathers, mothers, children, and families, the logistics and conceptualization that might lead to strong programs are still in their infancy. The ability of programs and the practitioners in them to effect change without schools and to prepare and support the development of African American males is limited. This support ideally would link schooling and responsible fatherhood by integrating the unique needs for employment, the reality of culture and problems associated with race, and the ecology of increasingly low allocations of resources.

"WHEN I GET IT TOGETHER": FOUR FATHERS AND THEIR SHARED EXPERIENCES AND HOPES

Parker

Parker is a bright, strong, and determined young African American father. He attended high school in Philadelphia where he says that he was led to believe (through teachers' verbal reinforcement) that he was performing well. For the past 4 years, Parker has participated in a fathers program, not because he was unengaged with or irresponsible toward his son but because he wanted to strengthen his relationship with him, file for custody, and increase the opportunities available to his son and to himself. As a 20-year-old African American male, Parker provides for the daily care of his child, with some assistance from his mother, works at a job that he has had for more than a year, and is preparing to continue his education. He is engaged actively in the life of his child, despite the absence of his own father during his childhood. Over the years, Parker has tried to locate his life experiences, goals, dreams, despair, and hope within the history and culture of African American families in which fathers supported their children through caring, nurturing, and economic support. He pursues his quest through reading, despite an education of questionable quality and through the support of male peer and older male resources who help him navigate his way through the freewheelingness and turbulence of adolescence that often act as barriers to responsive fatherhood and adulthood.

Parker fits many of the stereotypical images of African American males; for example, he was an adolescent father, he dropped out of school, and he grew up in a female-headed household. He embodies many of the concerns of African American boys and men in both middle- and low-income homes. Over the course of his life, he has been in schools that identified him as academically talented but could not or did not invest in that talent. He has grown up with little knowledge of or contact with his father. He has begun to "put his life on track" to attain the kind of measurable success valued by society. Although he has assumed responsibility for the upbringing of his child, he has few social supports outside of the fathers program that he attends. In short, Parker, like millions of young men from a variety of cultural and ethnic groups and social classes, must make major life decisions while struggling with the attractiveness of adolescent freedom and the expectations of adulthood and fatherhood. Unlike many of the other young men, Parker's decisions affect not only himself but also his child. In addition, Parker is at enormous risk for unemployment, living in poverty, and wrestling with the demands of parenting in the face of limited resources. He is at a critical juncture in his life-course, which is already strained by unfulfilled promises.

The program director in Parker's program describes him as a "poster father"—"the kind of young man that the policy makers and White folks like to make commercials about." Anyone peering into Parker's life, in fact, would see a combination of personal drive, dauntless perseverance, and resilience. Although, as the program director noted with some sense of pride, Parker might be the poster father, he knows that Parker's success masks the difficulties he has faced and the limited opportunities available to him. Like millions of young mothers who are often invisible, he is balancing child care responsibilities and work. He has a high school diploma that enables him to get several low-level jobs that expose him to dangerous situations often. He had to quit one job during his participation in the program after being held up by robbers twice. He decided that he "needed to protect [himself] since his son needs [him]." Each time he quit a job, he found temporary work immediately until he found permanent employment. Parker has returned to school to earn an associate degree and to get specialized training. He thinks that he "will have more options and be able to make a difference for [his] son."

Parker's image of what a good father is or could be is based on his reading of books about Black families. He likes focusing on "the good parts of Black culture . . . like when Black fathers during slavery gave everything to make sure their children could have an education. Some of that is still in Black people and [in people like Parker]." His talk during interviews is a combination of angst about the current condition of Black people, intolerance for those he suspects are "not trying hard enough," and compassion for those who seem to fail. In talking about his child, he says,

"You can't have a child and never expose them to reading and writing and put them in school and expect them to learn."

Stan

> I've been trying to get it together, you know. I'm back in school now and trying to work. But, it's hard. You know, when I was in school, I played around; it would have been easier then maybe but you know . . . nobody was really paying attention. Man, you cut school, hang out, didn't get the learning you need. But, now, you know, I need the skills. Nobody is out to help a Black man. Then, . . . you know, like I have my daughter and son and want them to have it better than I had it. I just, you know, want to be there for them, you know, be able to get them things and have them respect me. You know, I want to help them with the homework and stuff, not have them hang out in the street. I don't have the skills, you know, for the job and all. If I could say one thing about school, it would be that I wish that it had been cooler, you know, and I could or might have gotten some of what I need. Some people might say it's a cop-out. But, I don't think anybody there [in school] ever really noticed me, or if they did they ignored me unless I was doing something to get into trouble. Something's got to be done for these young boys or they will end up trying to catch up. I got to be a man and a father and pay for my children. I'm going to get it together . . . for me, my girlfriend, and my kids.

Stan is a 23-year-old father, currently engaged to marry the mother of his children. He dropped out of school in 10th grade and returned a year later. School and the experience of schooling were turbulent, at best. He says,

> I did OK in school. I liked some of my teachers, but I could never see much connection between what was happening in school and what was going on in the streets. Not that school's gotta be like the streets. I talked to my boys when I was in school and had fun; no-body stopped us—it seemed like they expected us to do nothing.

After episodes in and out of school, Stan dropped out permanently at 20. Before he dropped out, he fathered his first child, a daughter, whose birth, he notes, caused him tension: "I knew I needed to get my diploma, you understand, and things were bad between me and my girl and her family, and I couldn't really take care of my daughter, you know, like a man. School became harder, and it seemed like there was no place to go. I thought I might get a job."

During 2 years of intermittent employment and after several "brushes with the law," Stan fathered a son with the same partner. At the time of the interviews, he had begun to participate in a fathers program and had returned to school to earn his GED. More critical and aware of the problems and needs around literacy, fathering, and employment, he says,

> The GED is not enough. You know, it's the skill and the education, but it is also what seems like the prejudice. There are some things that I could learn, but my boss, he seems like he thinks Black people are dumb or somethin'. . . . Not even Black people will always give you a chance. They seem scared you gonna make them look bad. Everybody talk about helping but no one is helping us be good people and good fathers. . . . I'm gonna make sure that my children don't have it like this!

Stan's daughter is now 5 years old and enrolled in day care. Stan has taken great interest in her literacy development: He reads to her and spends a great deal of money purchasing educational materials for her and his son. Although he is engaged in positive experiences with his children, his life circumstances are tenuous still. He fears that his children's schooling will not prepare them for the world they will enter as African Americans, and he feels ill prepared to question the quality of his children's schooling. He says, "I don't want them just going through the system, with people thinking that they can't be somebody." The question is whether Stan can ensure that his children are not forced to face the disappointments that he is experiencing and how he will ensure that they do not. Who are his role models and what are his resources? How can he be assisted in being a good father and "getting it together"?

Jerry

> The media likes to make it seem like all Black fathers are no-good-for-nothin's. I know that's not true, and so do they. But, what can I say, it sells. Everybody talks about how people don't want to work, but they don't show how many jobs have moved out of the city. When I worked outside the city, it was all I could do to make ends meet. I was a teenage father, but I got married to my child's mother as soon as I found out she was pregnant. When it's time to downsize, it seems that I'm the first one downsized. That may be a coincidence, but you know when you've been working somewhere and people

treat you bad because you are a Black. . . . they treat you like you know nothing because you are Black and seem surprised that you can talk proper. Well, after putting up with the racists who own and run the companies, you just don't want to be bothered. If I didn't have my family, I wouldn't be bothered, but I have my children and my wife, and we're trying to make it.

Unlike many of the young fathers with whom we worked, Jerry, a 23-year-old, comes from a middle-class home with parents and siblings who are college educated. He regularly reminds the other young fathers of his family's status, and they regularly remind him that he needs support as a young father. Jerry's high school experience was difficult. As he indicated, he was "trying not to be just like his [successful] brothers and isolated [himself]. I started running the streets, trying to be accepted by the tough kids, trying to hang out, feeling alienated and angry." He is married to the mother of his children and has been working regularly since finishing high school. He attends a local community college part-time. He says,

Like you say to yourself, people are carrying stuff around for 25 years. I think it's a lot of the [fathers] in this program who might have problems with their fathers because I'm one of them. Now we can sit here and talk about it, we can write it down, we can have someone come in and share, but that doesn't mean that even though we're sharing what's inside of us, it takes a long time to get 25 years of anger or (whatever the case may be). It takes a long time to get that anger out of you. You can go to some therapeutic sessions but are you going to feel comfortable sharing that information?

Larry

One thing with the racial issue is this. A few Black men have come through the struggle. We call it the system or the White man's system to try to benefit ourselves. I tell [myself] all the time . . . White people make a different rule every day and you have to find out what the rule is but the rule might change. A few years ago there were no young Black men driving BMWs or Mercedes, and there was not a rule or anything, over 10,000 had to be legally document. The Black men started buying a lot of stuff and having things . . . this rule apply then. But now we're buying property, and we're getting things that they have and now they have a rule. I don't understand these people because there are a lot of White people doing things illegal and doing the same things the young Black males are doing, and [the

White people] got scared. They developed [the rule] for a reason and it's there to hinder.

When Larry met our research team, he was an 18-year-old father about to graduate from high school. Now 21, he is "trying to make it" and is looking for whatever resources he can find. A thoughtful young man, Larry has been "making it" with little family financial support for much of his young life. He is the oldest of four children in a household headed by a caring mother with multiple personal and health problems. His father "stayed around for a while" but has been untraceable for the past several years. Larry talks a great deal about racism; he speaks of his observations and his sense of the world as much as his experience in and with it. He says, "There is no way not to know that there is racism. Look at what we read in school; look at how Black people are talked to and treated, no matter how many degrees. These 40- and 50-year-old men who've been out here working are doing no better than anybody else, sometimes worse. What is there to look forward to?"

Larry acknowledges that he is poorly prepared for work or for father-hood. "I don't know what to do, but I'll do the right thing which is why I'm in the program," he says. Larry entered the program shortly after his partner told him she was pregnant. Because he "knew she would keep the baby and because [he] wanted the baby," he decided that he "needed to get himself together . . . not just acting like [he] cares but doing the things that will help [him] show that [he] cares." In preparation for the birth, he tried to get a "good" job but could not. He asked his high school counselor for help but was unable to get suggestions, although "[the counselor] tried." Larry overheard one employer with whom he had an interview de-scribe him as "one of those suspicious and sinister-looking Blacks." Larry surmised that his quiet manner was disconcerting and threatening to the employer who when talking to Larry simply said that Larry did not have the necessary skills for the job. A social worker suggested to Larry that he seek support from the fathers program. He sought out the program and enrolled. Three years into the program, he noted,

A lot of the issues the [fathers] are going through dealing with em-ployment, the court system. You got to know something to get some-where in this world—mothers too. It's always something, if you can read, then you can't read well enough; if you can write, then you can't write well enough.

Larry has entered his role as father with one hope—to be a good father and "to get it together so he can have a happy family." He has created a timeline to "get himself together." His daughter will begin kindergarten in 2 years.

CONNECTIONS ACROSS POSSIBLE, IMAGINED, AND REAL SELVES: GETTING IT TOGETHER

What cuts across the stories of the young fathers is a history of unfulfilled hopes and a need to reinvent themselves. Each young father wants to "do right," to create a new lens onto his life by opening up doors for his child(ren); no young father feels that he has the necessary resources to effect the kind of change he imagines. What each imagines is not far-fetched, however: a job, skills to perform well at his job, skills to support his children, and knowledge and preparation for fatherhood. None seemingly looks to schools for this support, and none speaks of positive experiences in school. Each seemed, in a sense, invisible as he struggled. Few of the young fathers knew that he had a literacy problem, and the others denied having a problem. Each has an imagined self that he constantly maps against the real experiences of low literacy, poor schooling, and communities that were supportive but offered few examples of viable options.

"Getting it together" is a useful heuristic to connote the transition from carefree adolescence to the demands of adulthood and fatherhood. This transition is a special domain of life-span development. It assumes that certain social and psychological development has occurred. For the African American fathers in many programs, the transition from adolescence to fatherhood is void of the temporal space in which to deconstruct adolescent myths, play out adolescent fantasies or realities, develop intellectual competencies, or construct notions of parenting and responsibility for self or others. For young parents—fathers and mothers alike—parenthood becomes the proxy for adulthood. Yet our work with young fathers and the programs that assist them suggest that this proxy is being undermined by the enormous need of the young men to be supported in the transition to both adulthood and fatherhood. Schools, families, and communities are necessary to help in this transition.

SCHOOLING AND RESPONSIBLE FATHERHOOD: EMPLOYMENT, CULTURE, AND ECOLOGY

Bowman (1994) suggests that many of the difficulties facing young African American fathers such as the four described in the preceding section can be attributed to schools that do not assist African American boys to develop appropriate problem-solving abilities or provide them with adequate educational preparation. The failure of schools to prepare young African American boys to assume positive roles as workers and parents, he argues, contributes to the quandary in which many of these boys find themselves as young men seeking employment, entering educational programs, and making the transition to responsible fathering. The conception of the provider role and feelings of inadequacy to fulfill that role may create stress counterproductive to effective parenting, associated with unemployment, and resulting in family estrangement (Bowman, 1995).

Implicit in Bowman's analysis is the assumption that part of the solution to the problems facing young, poor African American males is located in schools. However, educational-reform discussions seldom address the special risks faced by Black males and are marked often by conflicting assumptions. Four are particularly important to the current discussion. First, special education reforms focus on better ways to eliminate internal deficits within African American male students themselves; as America has shifted from an industrial to a postindustrial society, larger numbers of African American males in public schools are being shifted from industrial arts to special education curricula (Jones, 1991; McCarthy, 1990; Tozer, 1993). Second, system-restructuring reforms also address deficiencies, but the emphasis is placed on eliminating deficits external to the child and internal to the school system, for example, the "effective schools" movement and systemwide school decentralization in Chicago and other large urban centers (Ayers, 1991; Comer, 1980, 1989, 1993; Edmonds, 1983). Third, mainstream-standards reforms, a developing arena, center on core, national goal-setting as an external mechanism to promote functional student competencies. Fourth, emerging cultural-diversity reforms suggest that indigenous cultural strengths within the commentaries of African American students themselves should serve as the framework for building program agendas.

The four types of reforms incorporate overlapping assumptions, but the tendency in each typically is to emphasize one set of assumptions at the expense of the others. For example, special education reforms, which focus on the treatment of deep-seated deficits, fail both to provide gainful employment skills and to build on indigenous cultural strengths that inspire responsibility in African American males, whereas system restructuring reforms show more promise but fail to address broader problems in urban neighborhoods such as growing job dislocation and cultural alienation. The disparities and conflicts within and across these and other reforms suggest that future educational-reform efforts must address ecological barriers. They also must prepare and socialize students to become employable and to mobilize indigenous cultural supports for strong expressive family roles.

A model that responds to the need to support African American males as present or future fathers must be integrative in its premise and link schooling and responsible fatherhood among African Americans. Bowman (1995) argues that pivotal socialization, mobilization, and allocation mechanisms positively promote responsible fatherhood. Three critical intervening links between schooling and responsible father roles in the model are employment, culture, and ecology. The school-employment link promotes instrumental father roles such as economic provider whereas the school-culture link promotes expressive roles such as father-child relationships. The school-ecology link focuses on the school's role in managing the damaging aspects of high-risk, urban neighborhoods.

THE FRAMEWORK FOR RESPONSIBLE FATHERHOOD:
INSTRUMENTAL AND EXPRESSIVE ROLES

Instrumental dimensions of fatherhood such as the economic-provider role contribute to the essential physical and social integrity of children, including the provision of food, shelter, clothing, and health care. In contrast, more expressive functions such as paternal socialization and nurturing help to meet children's socioemotional needs—in other words, to prepare them culturally for adulthood. Instrumental and expressive features of fatherhood are distinctive in many ways but interrelated in others. For example, success or failure as a family economic provider can affect the stability and quality of expressive father-child bonds. As with many fathers in America, Black fathers place an especially high value on the instrumental role, despite the fact that Black mothers have always been significant economic providers. Success in the economic-provider role is a source of pride, but failure is particularly distressful because of the salience of this role for men's identity as fathers. Expressive roles are usually more salient for mothers, but a tradition of flexible family roles makes tasks such as child care commonplace for many Black fathers.

THE SCHOOL-EMPLOYMENT LINK:
SOCIALIZATION AND INSTRUMENTAL FAMILY ROLES

Educational reform that promotes strong linkages between schools and employment is especially crucial to instrumental aspects of responsible fatherhood among African American males. Schools are complex social institutions and have functional interconnections with other institutions such as the economy and family (Hurn, 1985; Myers & Duke, 1977).

Long-held assumptions about the role of schools might suggest that socialization within schools should promote linkages with employment by transmitting the knowledge, skills, attitudes, and values necessary for success in the working world (Bowman, 1991b; Hurn, 1990). Consistent with mainstream-standards reforms, such school-employment links operate to a large degree through the transmission of marketable skills and competencies. Socialization is a powerful school-employment mechanism that operates through employment skills and economic resources and that promote responsible, family-provider role functioning among African American fathers and mothers and increase family efficacy on behalf of children.

THE SCHOOL-CULTURE LINK:
MOBILIZATION AND EXPRESSIVE FAMILY ROLES

Whereas school-employment links focus on the socialization of marketable mainstream competencies, school-culture links focus on the mobilization of indigenous family bonds. Among prospective African American fathers, educational reform that links school and culture is particularly crucial for promoting expressive roles such as strong father-child bonds. This school-culture link is consistent with the growing numbers of indigenous empowerment interventions including Black male schools, classrooms, and various Afrocentric curricula plans (Asante, 1988; Ascher, 1991). For example, the plan for the Ujamaa Institute at Medgar Evers College in Brooklyn, New York, placed an emphasis on family responsibility and centered its curriculum around African family values and values clarification. Despite evaluation analysis and anecdotal evidence on the feasibility and effectiveness of these programs and the approaches that are used within them, there is sparse research analysis and much less evidence available on the effectiveness of school-culture mobilization strategies than there is on school-employment linkages (e.g., Bowman, 1991a, 1991b).

THE EMERGING SCHOOL-ECOLOGY CHALLENGE

An assumption of the model is that educational reform that promotes responsible fatherhood among African Americans must also manage postindustrial barriers in the urban context. The effectiveness of both socialization and mobilization linkages can be reduced when there are pressing neighborhood barriers. For example, inner-city job displacement can impede the school-employment link as well as links between stable employment and provider-role functioning. These links are rivaled by inner-city drug networks that can erode the school-culture link as well as the links between culture and father-child bonds. The emerging school-ecology challenge then is to find ways to cope with restrictive allocation mechanisms while promoting both school-employment and school-culture linkages.

Restrictive school-ecology allocation mechanisms operate both within schools and at a larger macroeconomic level. As discussed earlier, the differential growth among African American males in special education tracks in recent years represents a marked shift from the historical pattern of selecting and sorting these men for the industrial labor market. In line with allocation processes, African American fathers in inner cities may be more susceptible to employment difficulty due to the amount and kind of education they receive, their reliance on peers and nonschool agencies for knowledge and values, and the pressure to fulfill adult roles outside of school (Darity, 1983; Mason, 1996a; Myers & Duke, 1977). For African American males preparing to become parents, allocation mechanisms within schools far too often result in declining levels of education, growing joblessness, and increasing difficulties in the economic provider and expressive family roles (Ferguson, 1993).

At a macroeconomic level, massive deindustrialization and shifts in historical allocation mechanisms in recent years have spurred chronic joblessness among African American males, putting them at great risk (Bowman, 1988; Sum, Fogg, Fogg, & Williams, 1991; Wilson, 1987). Black males are at greatest risk for job displacement and related family problems in inner cities for several reasons. First, they remain disproportionately employed in the most vulnerable unskilled-labor and operative jobs in the face of ongoing industrial restructuring. Second, they are more likely than other groups to experience long-term and sometimes permanent joblessness; although new jobs are created, they require increasingly higher skills that many African American men and fathers have not been in position to develop or to which, despite their involvement in educational programs, they have had little if any exposure. Third, racial isolation within depressed central cities has resulted in poor educational resources and little access to available job options (Massey & Denton, 1993). Desegregation efforts, for example, have resulted in little more than marginal acceptance and opportunities for most African American children and families (Gadsden, Smith, & Jordan, 1996). In addition, high stress urban environments place Black males and females at enormous risk for involvement in drugs and crime, which erodes adaptive cultural resources.

SUMMARY AND IMPLICATIONS

The discussion about African American males encourages both discourse and action around the role of schools in preparing children educationally to meet the intellectual, work, and daily challenges they will face. Poor children and poor African American children are particularly vulnerable. Poor African American males appear to be at greatest risk, with the crises confronting African American females increasingly masked in modest but not substantial improvements.

Hundreds of young men participate in these programs, yet only a fraction of the programs attended are able to address issues about education or literacy in meaningful ways. Where such a focus exists, programs tend to work with the young fathers to encourage them to return to school, get a GED, or get admitted to college. Their resources are limited and the cross-agency and cross-institutional connections are noticeably weak to reduce sharing of instructional and program resources. Although such collaborations and relationships seem undeniably good for fathers, mothers, children, and families, the logistics and conceptualization that might lead to strong programs are still in their infancy. Their ability to effect change without schools and to prepare and support the development of African American males is limited. This support links schooling and responsible fatherhood by integrating the unique needs for employment, the reality of culture and problems associated with race, and the ecology of increasingly low allocations of resources.

This chapter's analysis, in large part, is developed upon the premise that along with family resources, schooling lays the foundation for responsible fathering, responsible parenting, and caring in general. Educational reforms that do not deconstruct complex issues that arguably punish more than support intellectual development fail to provide young boys with the skills to fulfill the instrumental role of economic provider, to build on indigenous cultural strengths to encourage African American fathers in more expressive roles, and to offer a critical context in which young girls develop expectations about responsible male and father behaviors that build rather than reduce their sense of worth and personal efficacy.

The other three primary reform domains each provides possibilities but may be effective if they are considered integratively. System restructuring efforts that focus on reallocating resources to change the way in which schools work are typically experimental. Still, some argue that some of these reforms actually have the unintended effect of lowering the public's confidence in urban schools. Proponents of reforms aimed at creating mainstream standards have focused on encouraging competencies (particularly those related to future employment requirements) in all American children, including African American males. These reforms frequently overlook the special constraints facing subpopulations.

The integrative model described here begins by stressing the interrelationships among school, work, and culture in a community context. This model is based on a view of fathering that relies on both instrumental and expressive functions to socialize children to become productive adults. Encouraging work-related competencies among African American males will facilitate their ability to act as responsible fathers by improving their ability to provide financial support, while building on ethnic strengths to encourage these competencies. Such competencies will reaffirm Black males' personal strengths and identity and will encourage their expressive role in their socialization of children.

In recent discussions about father involvement, there is considerable discussions about fathers' care, father presence and father absence, and the impact of joblessness on men's perceptions of their value as fathers and on the images as good fathers (see Davis & Perkins, 1995; Johnson, 1996; Mason, 1996b). A complementary strand of work suggests a need for broader conceptualization of fatherhood itself in which nurturing, caring, and the affective side of fathering are discussed and promoted (Gadsden, 1995; Parke, 1996; Pruett, 1990). The degree to which schools through engagement of African Americans in meaningful learning experiences promote a sense of personal competence, ensure intellectual development, and prepare young Black males to be both nurturing fathers and effective workers will reinforce our expectation of schools to plan for, educate, and care for our children.

Rather than asking schools to expand their curricula substantially, we suggest here that schools and the thoughtful people in them focus more intensively on the needs of the diverse students who enter their doors. In some cases, schools may initiate classes for adolescent fathers; in others, they may intersperse issues about male responsibility and fathering in normal classroom discourse around literature, health, and social studies. Although we support these options, however, we suggest here that schools and the classroom practices must attend more thoughtfully to the preparation of young African American males and that educational programs that serve adolescent and young adults need to offer more incentives to support young, low-income fathers.

The model presented here offers one perspective on and approach to the issues that require attention from educational policy makers at all levels but particularly in schools. However, as is the case with other models, this one can guide effective legislation and interventions only if it is understood within the context of structural barriers and societal and economic forces, such as racism and deindustrialization.

13

A Cup That Runneth Over: Personal Reflections on the Black Male Experience

Vernon C. Polite

> By far the most significant learning experiences in adulthood in-
> volve critical self-reflection—reassessing the way we have posed
> problems and reassessing our own orientation to perceiving,
> knowing, believing, and acting.
>
> —Jack Mezirow et al.,
> *Fostering Critical Reflection in Adulthood*

THE VOICES AND STORIES of African American[1] boys and young men are
rarely heard in the social science literature or in the popular press at large.
The purpose of this chapter is to provide the readers with autobiographical
slices of the formative years of my life, the "insider's perspective" on the
Black male experience. In this chapter, I begin by providing a condensed
family history that demonstrates the convergence of two Negro families
from southern slavery and poverty. My personal struggles to overcome the
effects of domestic violence are shared early in the chapter. The experiences
of growing up in a working-class family in Detroit, attending a multiethnic
Catholic school, and later responding to racism in Boston as a teacher in
the Boston public schools are showcased. The chapter frames experiences
from my childhood through young adulthood within the context of race,
social class, and gender. I conclude by drawing linkages between my personal experiences and those of African American boys and young men of
today, emphasizing the potential resilience of young Black males.

African American Males in School and Society: Practices and Policies for Effective Education. Copyright © 1999 by Teachers College, Columbia University. All rights reserved. ISBN 0-8077-3870-0
(pbk), ISBN 0-8077-3871-9 (cloth). Prior to photocopying items for classroom use, please contact
the Copyright Clearance Center, Customer Service, 222 Rosewood Dr., Danvers, MA 01923, USA, tel.
(508) 750-8400.

SOUTHERN ROOTS AND A NORTHERN TRAGEDY

Arvelia Wallace Polite, my mother, was born in Albany, Georgia, in 1919 and reared from infancy in Miami, Florida, with her two brothers and four sisters, the children of Nannie Friend Wallace and Jessie Wallace. The Wallace children attended segregated schools in Miami, as was typical for many working-class and unskilled Negroes during the first half of the 1900s, particularly in the Deep South. The Wallace children completed only the eighth grade, dropped out of school, and entered the tourist-driven industries that made up the majority of the labor force on Miami Beach.

The Wallace girls did "day work," housekeeping and cooking, for Whites on Miami Beach. In fact, the girls were introduced to day work by their mother, Nannie, and often accompanied her on jobs in the wealthier households on Miami Beach. Bearline, my mother's oldest sibling, married a steelworker and relocated to Detroit. Gertrude, another sister, married John Jackson and they worked as a team for a member of the Adelstein family in New Rochelle, New York. Arvella, the third sister, married a cook, Walter Holland, and relocated to Asbury Park, New Jersey. Theresa, the youngest sibling, was the only Wallace girl to remain in Florida.

My mother first married in Miami at the very young age of 17. In fact, she and her oldest sister, Bearline, married two brothers, Homer and James Brooks. Mother's marriage with James, albeit short-lived and problematic due to James' alcoholism, produced two children, Carol Jean and Willie James Brooks.

Vernon Elmo Polite, my father, was one of the 18 children of Mamie Steel Polite and Carey Polite of Jacksonville, Florida. The Polite family's origin is rooted in pre–Civil War Brunswick, Georgia. Carey Polite, my paternal grandfather, was one of eight children, all boys of Luke and Nancy Polite, former slaves.

My parents, Vernon and Arvelia, met in Miami in the 1940s, fell in love, and relocated to Harlem in 1943. The couple was married in Cecil County, Maryland, in 1947 and I was born in August of 1948 in Harlem, New York.

Father, and Uncle Ernest Polite, his older brother, were based in New York City's Penn Station and worked as dining car porters with the Atlantic Coast Line Railroad, a highly revered position for Black men of that time. In fact, Black men have a long history, which continues even today, as transportation porters—an unskilled, service-oriented but unionized occupation. One of the obvious assets of the porter's job was the "pass," the document that assured travel, free of charge. In my family's case, Dad was able to maintain ongoing communication with his relatives in Florida, assisting those Polites in the South who were unable to secure gainful employment. The downside to working for the train, of course, was extended periods of time away from his wife and child in New York. By the late 1940s, 6 of Father's 18 siblings had also relocated to Harlem and started their own families.

Mother held a number of housekeeping jobs in the early 1940s in New York before she landed a job as a seamstress in a clothing factory in the city. She was, from all accounts, a strikingly beautiful woman. Beauty techniques and cosmetology were her special hobbies.

The 5-year marriage of my parents was strained, from all indications. Father was terminated from his job with the railroad in 1949, the year after I was born. He was charged with the illegal use of a controlled substance while on duty—drug abuse. The records indicate that he spent more than 2 years in appeal of his suspension to the Dining Car Employees Union and, ultimately, was terminated in 1951. He assumed a number of odd jobs and finally worked as a waiter in Manhattan.

Something went terribly wrong with Dad; some say that it was drugs, others argue that he was in a jealous rage, while others suggest an emotional crisis. Tragically, however, on November 6, 1952, following a heated argument, Dad, in a fit of rage, turned to the dresser drawer, took out a revolver, and killed Mother with numerous bullet wounds to the skull and chest. I was the sole witness of the incident, and although only 4 years of age, I lived and relived the horror of that evening for many years to come and even remember it clearly today. Dad returned to the apartment later that evening and killed himself by drinking poison and shot himself in the chest.

The situation worsened as a nasty custody battle over me ensued between Dad's siblings and Mother's oldest sister, Bearline Brooks, of Detroit. A justice of the Supreme Court of the State of New York reviewed the evidence and awarded custody to my aunt Bearline on December 1, 1952. In the course of the 30-day period from the time of Mother's death until the time that I arrived in Detroit, my body had begun to exhibit the symptoms of what would today be termed posttraumatic stress disorder. I refused to eat, lacked concentration, and demonstrated signs of low-grade depression. By the time I arrived in Detroit, my physical condition had deteriorated to the point that I required orthopedic shoes and leg supports to correct the effects of degenerated bone mass. As for my emotional state, the aid of child psychiatry and therapy were not common practices in the Black community of the 1950s (nor is it common today). In my case, my name was changed from Vernon Carey Polite to Carey Vernon Polite. Aunt Bearline and other relatives in Detroit could not abide the thought of calling me "Vernon," the name of the man who killed their baby sister. The matter of my parents' deaths was never discussed in the family again.

DETROIT: OVERCOMING TRAUMA AND CONSTRUCTING
SOCIAL, ETHNIC, AND RACIAL IDENTITIES

The transition to Detroit was difficult for me. As an adult, I have often referred to that period following the deaths of my parents as the "silent years," a time when I chose not to speak. By today's psychological nomenclature, my condition would be termed "elected muteness." I have very few recollections of those first years of schooling, with the exception of the silence and isolation. In fact, I often thought it strange that I had no memories of primary schooling, curriculum learned, teachers, classmates, or even going to school. Today, when I carefully review my work and report cards from kindergarten and first and second grades, I sense the classic symptoms of shock or PTSD. One particular comment written by a first-grade teacher, Mrs. Bunyan, to Aunt Bearline was particularly insightful: "Carey daydreams often, has trouble focusing on the lessons, and seems very sad." The term PTSD was coined after World War II, when psychiatrists attempted to explain the shock and depression that were common among veterans of war.

Social Class Consciousness

Our extended family was the second Negro family to move, in 1954, to Seyburn, a beautiful tree-lined street on the lower east side of Detroit. Our home was a two-family, five-bedroom frame house, complete with peach, apple, and plum trees in the large backyard. There were three generations of adult women living in our household, Aunt Bearline Brooks, her daughter Albertha (Dolly), and my grandmother, Nannie Wallace. There were no adult men in our home. My brother and sister, Willie and Carol, were 9 and 10 years older than me, respectively, and lived with us also. Aunt Bearline and her mother were "domestics," or housekeepers, for several Jewish families on the west side of the city. Dolly worked on the assembly line at the Ford Motor Company.

Aunt Bearline and Grandma Nannie each earned $35.00 each per week for their day work while Dolly earned about $90.00 per week at Ford. My two siblings and I each received $20.00 per week in social security benefits. All together the weekly contribution to the household was about $220.00, which was substantial enough to maintain the house and utilities and provide for the education of the children in the mid-1950s and early 1960s. Additional financial support and clothing arrived periodically from my aunts Gertrude (New York) and Arvella (New Jersey). Our family was working class and very proud.

The experiences that I witnessed as a child in Detroit shaped my attitudes regarding work and social class. In our family, to be working class meant that each member of the household was employed, beginning at early adolescence. It also meant that each family member contributed to the financial well-being of the family as a whole. Important decisions were reached collectively and nothing was more important than the education of the children.

In retrospect, one of the most significant lessons that I learned was the power of working-class Black women. In my family, the women were self-sacrificing in the hope of a better life (social class) for the next generation. Aunt Bearline, for example, suffered a rheumatic heart condition throughout her adult life, yet she worked 5 to 6 days per week, leaving home by 6:30 a.m. and returning after 6:00 p.m. She would take as many as three buses to cross the city in the most inclement Michigan weather conditions to keep house, cook, and clean for her employers.

I understood social class consciousness and intergroup entanglements long before adolescence. For example, there were numerous examples of ongoing and significant interactions between Negro women in my family and middle-class Jews. In fact, every adult woman in my family did day work for middle-class families at some point in their careers. Aunt Bearline worked for more than 30 years for one middle-class Jewish family, the Bloombergs.

Mrs. Bloomberg was an elementary school teacher and Mr. Bloomberg was a university professor and author of several nationally distributed organic chemistry books. Aunt Bearline and Mrs. Bloomberg were actually about the same age. The relationship between my family and the Bloombergs was mutually beneficial. For example, the Bloombergs gladly aided my aunt by securing legal assistance during the custody battle following the death of my parents. Aunt Bearline was dependable and honest and could be trusted with the Bloomberg children. I recall stories of my aunt nurturing and advising the Bloomberg children on everything from dating to relations with their parents. On the other hand, the Bloombergs provided significant financial assistance to my family above and beyond the agreed daily salary. When I arrived from Detroit, depressed and withdrawn, it was, ironically, Mrs. Bloomberg who encouraged my aunt to place me in a Catholic school, believing that I would receive the special attention needed to overcome the PTSD. I had sat shivah when Mr. Bloomberg died, attended briths following the birth of the grandsons, even helped Aunt Bearline prepare the Bloomberg's house for the High Holy Days and other special occasions.

By adolescence, I was well acquainted with the more public Jewish customs. Aunt Bearline would explain religious practices, especially religious traditions associated with the High Holy Days. She would bring leftovers from the special meals and explain their significance. I recall that Mr. Bloomberg was less enthusiastic about keeping the religious fasts and would invariably send Aunt Bearline to the store for a loaf of bread in the middle of Yom Kippur. I never heard in my family, however, a negative comment or Jewish joke.

Catholic Schooling: A Multiethnic Blending

The history of Catholic schooling in the United States can be traced to 1829, when the First Provincial Council in Baltimore recognized the need for Catholic schools, defining as the schools' purpose "teaching the principles of faith and morals to the young" (McCarron, 1997). During the Third Plenary Council of Baltimore, 1884, the bishops agreed that the establishment of an extensive parochial school system in the United Stated was an absolute necessity as a response to the Protestant-controlled public schools. The bishops mandated, in 1884, that parents, mainly immigrant poor, send their children to Catholic schools. The weight of the bishops' mandate resulted in the rapid growth and proliferation of Catholic schools throughout the United States (Buetow, 1985; McCarron, 1997; Murdick, 1989).

St. Catherine's Church opened in 1912 and its school opened 2 years later, in 1914, to serve working-class Irish immigrants. When I entered St. Catherine's School in the mid-1950s, the school population, although still serving the working-class and working poor, was multiethnic and included second- and third-generation Italian, Polish, German, and Irish Catholic students. There was also a small number of Greek and Armenian Orthodox Catholics attending the school.

Although rich in ethnic diversity, the Catholic school culture in the mid-1950s minimized the effects of ethnic identity and created a social dichotomy that distinguished the Catholic students, the in-group, from the non-Catholic students, the out-group. Nuns and priests documented their annual efforts to evangelize the non-Catholic students, deeming these students and their parents relatively powerless.

St. Catherine's was served by the Sister Servants of the Immaculate Heart of Mary (IHM) from the opening of the school in 1914 and remained at the school until 1971 when it closed. The IHM headquarters, or the Mother House as it is commonly known, is in Monroe, Michigan. The IHM community was a multiethnic, not interracial, group of nuns that was ironically founded in 1845 by Almaide Duchemin Maxis, a Negro woman whose parents were murdered in the 1791 slave revolt in San Domingo. By the late 1950s, the IHM community was one of the largest religious orders in the United States with about 1,500 nuns.

I was one of four Negro pupils in my class of 70 students. Race and ethnicity were never discussed, publicly, during the 8 years that I spent at St. Catherine. Ethnic slurs and name-calling, however, occurred regularly among certain students representing the various ethnic groups, but never within earshot of the nuns or priests.

There was a subtle pressure placed on the nonbaptized to join the in-group by converting to Catholicism. I, wanting to belong to the in-group and participate fully in the life of the Catholic Church, went to Aunt Bear-line and asked for permission to be baptized in the Catholic Church. I was 10 years old, a fourth grader. Aunt Bearline agreed and began attending weekly religious instructions with the parish priest for more than 2 months. I was baptized and made my First Holy Communion in the spring of 1958. As evidence of the influence that my teacher had, I adopted Sr. Marie Bartholomew's name as my baptismal name. I was then, proudly, Carey Vernon Bartholomew Polite, an insider.

Mr. Ted O'Grady, a coworker of my cousin Dolly's at the Ford Motor Company, volunteered to be my baptismal godfather. Mr. O'Grady, a second-generation Irish American, had 12 children attending St. Catherine's. One of his sons, Patrick O'Grady, and I were close friends and secured our first job together working at the ice cream fountain at Masty's Drug store.

The stress placed on "conformity" within Catholic schooling was most apparent in the academic domain also. Parents at St. Catherine had very few choices, influence, or control over the academic development of their children. A tracking system was in place, meaning that the students were commonly grouped by ability, but there was open flexibility and movement in and out of two tracks: college preparatory and business. In most cases, the number of available students determined the diversity of academic options. I cannot recall any cases where students were assigned unfairly to the lower business track, but students had to prove their ability to perform in the college-preparatory track. As for me, I entered high school and was assigned to the business track based on my average academic performance at St. Catherine's Elementary School. I completed a year of algebra and Spanish during the summer between 9th and 10th grades. I was placed in college-preparatory track at the beginning of the 10th grade at St. Catherine's High School.

The lack of a positive Negro image in the curriculum was one of the shortcomings of urban Catholic schooling. Personally, I was well aware of racial identity and had even experienced racial discrimination. For example, while visiting relatives in Florida when I was about 10 years old, I was stunned when Aunt Bearline informed me that she and I could not sit at the lunch counter at Woolworth because of our race. Race issues and Black history, however, were never a part of the explicit or implicit curriculum at Saint Catherine's, neither at the elementary or high schools. There was a sense of "racelessness" at school. This was not terribly unusual or mean-spirited, since the racialization of America did not occur until the 1960s in the wake of the civil rights movement, but the failure to attend to issues of Black racial identity likely, in the long run, had an adverse effect on Black Catholic students.

When the Black Power movement arrived in the 1960s, I was outraged by how little I knew about Black history and culture, especially Black Catholic history. When I learned the historical place that Africa and Africans played in the early foundations of the Catholic Church; that important saints such as Augustine and Monica were African; that the church has elevated three African popes; and that there had been Black religious communities in the United States since the early 1800s, I felt terribly miseducated. The failure to incorporate African and African American Catholic culture and history in the curriculum was, likely, a missed opportunity to evangelize the Black community and to properly educate White ethnic students about church history.

I graduated from St. Catherine in the spring of 1966 and could not attend college in the following fall because I had no financial assistance. The Hotel Pontchartrain opened in downtown Detroit that same year and I was one of the first room service busboys hired. I held several entry-level positions between 1966 and 1968 at various institutions, including the National Bank of Detroit and the General Motors diesel plant.

The assassination of Dr. Martin Luther King, Jr., in 1968 was followed by countless Black student demonstrations on campuses across the nation. Pursuant to the student protests, university officials began actively recruiting African American and minority students. I attended Wilberforce University, a historically Black university, for one semester and transferred to Boston University in the winter of 1969.

BOSTON: A HOTBED OF RACIAL AND ETHNIC TENSION

It is difficult to imagine a city more racially and ethnically polarized during the 1970s and 1980s than Boston, Massachusetts. Shortly after arriving in Boston, I was warned about the various community boundaries that, if crossed, meant bodily harm for African Americans—the Irish South Boston, the Italian North End, the Irish Charlestown, and the Italian East Boston.

I was rather desperate for money during my first January in Boston. The university financial scholarship covered tuition and housing, but after I purchased my books, I had no spending money nor could I expect any before February, when my social security benefits check was scheduled to arrive. Determined not to drop out, I combed through the *Boston Globe* and found a job cleaning Greyhound buses at the D Street trolley station, a night job. I had completely forgotten the warnings about South Boston and really did not connect D Street with the notorious South Boston community. I also did not know that the trolleys stopped at midnight. After a couple of days of work, I realized that I was working in South Boston, but I had not experienced any problems and I decided to continue working because, frankly, I needed the money. On Tuesday evening of the 2nd week of work, I missed the last train out of D Street. Suddenly, a car filled with White teenage boys pulled up in front of the station and the boys began hurling beer bottles out of the window, one striking me on the head. Although I required minor medical attention at the emergency ward and had the worst headache of my life, nothing hurt or embarrassed me more than hearing the tone of the voice that used the "N" word to describe me. That was the first of many similar situations that I faced in Boston, the intellectual hub of the universe.

Boston University

There were about 20,000 students representing all 50 states and more than 120 countries at Boston University (BU) in 1969 when I entered as a sophomore. Afro-American students, as we called ourselves, made up less than 4% of the overall enrollment, but for me, BU was like a predominately Black college because there was limited interracial interaction. Racial polarization was so pervasive, I can rarely recall ever even speaking to a White student during my 3 years at BU. The racial tensions affected me, particularly, since my only understanding of the social context of schooling was a stress on conformity and devaluation of differences, especially racial differences.

What was less apparent, however, but equally important was the intra-group social class differences that existed among the African Americans. There were African American students who represented the third generation to attend college in their families, as well as first-generation African Americans from the "ghetto." We, however, understood or quickly learned that middle-class status did not mitigate the adverse and isolating effects of race or racist practices.

In addition to responding to race-specific issues on campus, there were many competing interests, including the complex issues related to the ongoing Vietnam conflict, the feminist movement, students' rights agenda, and, of course, the drug culture of the 1970s. It seemed that there was one major disruption or cancellation of classes after another, takeovers of the administration building, sit-ins, and boycotts of every imaginable kind. It was a wonder that any academic work occurred for anyone, Black or White.

I graduated in May 1972 and prepared for teaching in the Boston public schools (BPS). Before leaving the campus the final time, I experienced one of the most meanspirited and distressing attacks of racism of my youth. The custom at BU was for graduates to don crimson-red robes and assemble for commencement exercises at the football stadium. Aunt Bearline and Dolly's 10-year-old daughter, Sandy, had come for my graduation. Commonwealth Avenue was a sea of crimson due to the more than 5,000 graduates processing to the stadium.

I took the trolley downtown to meet Aunt Bearline and Sandy and decided to take a taxi to the football stadium. I was wearing my robe, so there was no mistaking my plans or destination. A White Boston taxi driver, stopped, rolled down the window, and spat out, using the "N" word to explain that he would not serve us. Aunt Bearline looked at me with tears rolling down her face and said, "I scrubbed floors for years so that you would have a better life."

Learning to Teach in the Midst of Violence and Disruption

As a sociology student at BU, I had an opportunity to read Jonathan Kozol's book *Death At An Early Age*, a popular treatise on poor children in the Boston public schools. The description of racism and discriminatory practices within the BPS made Boston sound like a third-world country. I often wondered, though, why there were only a few Black Bostonians attending the more than 100 colleges and universities in Boston and surrounding communities. The reality was that Black Bostonians, who had attended de facto segregated schools in Boston, were rarely prepared for higher education.

In the summer of 1972, I began a master's program at Boston State College designed to certify prospective Afro-American and Hispanic teachers for Boston public schools. A central part of the program was the successful completion of a supervised student teaching program. The day that I arrived for my student teaching assignment, the cooperating teacher took a look at me, handed me the lesson plan book, cursed, and said sarcastically, "Good luck." Despite the difficulties of that student teaching assignment, I was eventually certified and assigned to teach social studies at the all-Black Boston English School, one of the oldest secondary schools in the country.

Boston English had been an all-male high school for more than 160 years. My first year at English, the school system began busing in White students from South Boston and Latinos from Southend. Additionally, the gender composition of the school was altered to include nearly 40% girls for the first time in the school's history. These changes occurred within one year with practically no preparation for the affected parents, students, and teachers. There were so many fights and other incidents of violence that the Black teachers held regular prayer sessions before school to invoke the protection of the Almighty.

To make matters worst, a new English High was built and opened my second year within 2 years. The new school was nine stories high, complete with elevators and escalators. The year that the school opened, the racial tension and violence stepped up. I remember that 2nd year well because my classroom was on the ninth floor. In addition to daily fights and intergang problems, we had 91 false fire alarms that year.

My efforts to teach in the midst of racial tension were almost impossible. So many students, Afro-American, Hispanic, and White, missed quality years of schooling due to the racial conflicts that consumed the school. As an example, one of the young Irish students from South Boston, Sean, who was poisoned with learned racist conditioning, lost a finger when fighting at South Boston High and missed a whole year of schooling. When the district court ordered his parents to send him to school, he was determined not to participate. When he arrived at my sociology class in 1974, he chose a seat in the back, listened, eventually became comfortable, and began interacting in the class and ended the semester as a straight-A student. After realizing that he really enjoyed my class and, more important, understanding that the racism that he was taught about non-Whites was not true, Sean was drawn to me and I mentored him through the remainder of his school career.

CONCLUSIONS

In this chapter, my personal stories provide the reader with a rare opportunity to hear the at-promise Black male's voice. I focused deliberately on my early years, through personal reflection, because those events that occurred, especially the domestic violence, were unusual for the time, but are common experiences for most Black males living in America today. In my case, I was able to move forward with my career in education and eventually was appointed a chief officer of the desegregation of the Boston public schools. I served for several years as the federal educational programs' monitor to the U.S. Virgin Islands, earned a doctorate from Michigan State and am presently a tenured professor. The haunting question for me, however, has always been, How did it happen? I was emotionally damaged by domestic violence, working class, Black, and male. The deck was most certainly stacked against me, but somehow, like many other Black boys today, I was able to overcome adversity and beat the odds.

In my case, there were several extrinsic factors put in place that fostered the resiliency process: a supportive family network, a devoted aunt, caring teachers, and a highly structured school environment. The compilation of these factors precluded the possibility that I would create a "victim mentality," failing to strive. The high expectations set for me, and all students at my school, were clearly instrumental in my overcoming my emotional crisis.

The most important lessons that I have mastered from research and personal reflections have been the resiliency of Black males, the power of Black women, and the efficacy of the Black family. Ford's (1994) research confirms what I have personally suspected for years, that is, improved family-school-community relations and enhanced self-concept are essential to fostering resilience, especially for Black boys. In my case, the ability and desire of my extended family members to pull together a powerful kinship network after the death of my parents and the PTSD that followed were typical of what occurs with other resilient Blacks, according to Scannapieco and Jackson (1996). The women stressed, sacrificed, and modeled education for the next generation. For example, Aunt Bearline earned her high school diploma at age 65 and Albertha, her daughter, left the assembly line at Ford Motor Company, completed a registered nursing degree, and worked as a registered nurse.

Although the Catholic school experience in predominately White schools fell short in terms of teaching Negro history, the high expectations for all students to achieve academically, as well as socially, was a likely turning factor in my emotional development. Additionally, the attractiveness of the schooling experiences, coupled with the richness of the Catholic traditions and rituals, generated a strong sense of community, stability, and belonging for me. These factors certainly contribute to resilience for the at-promise. This is important when one considers the fact that 100,000 Black boys attend Catholic schools today.

The contrast of my experiences in Detroit from those experiences in Boston have led me to agree with McCarthy and Crichlow (1993) that racial and ethnic identities are socially constructed, that racism, discrimination, and social injustice are produced and reproduced and, most important, can be resisted and altered. It appears essential that concerned educators and education policy makers vigilantly search for strategies that will support antiracist pedagogy and intellectually emancipating practices for Black males and any other racial or ethnic groups that require them. America's place in the global economy is not so secure that it can afford to neglect the talents and contributions of any particular racial, ethnic, or gender group.

NOTE

1. In acknowledgment of past and present usage, the terms Negro(es), Black(s), Afro-American(s), and African American(s) are used interchangeably throughout the chapter to refer to individuals of African descent who reside within the United States.

References

Achatz, M., & MacAllum, C. A. (1994). *Young unwed fathers: A report from the field*. Philadelphia: Private/Public Ventures.

Allen, W. R. (1985). Black student, White campus: Structural, interpersonal, and correlates of success. *Journal of Negro Education, 54*, 134–147.

Allen, W. R. (1986, May). Gender and campus race differences in Black student academic performance, racial attitudes, and college satisfaction. Paper presented at the meeting of the Southern Education Foundation, Atlanta, GA.

Allen, W. R. (1987). Black colleges vs. White colleges: The fork in the road for Black students. *Change, 19*(3), 28–31.

Allen, W. R. (1992). The color of success: African-American college student outcomes at predominately White and historically Black public colleges and universities. *Harvard Educational Review, 62*, 27–51.

Allen, W., Epps, E., & Haniff, N. (Eds.). (1991). *College in Black and White: African American students in predominantly White and historically Black public universities*. Albany, NY: SUNY Press.

Alvino, J. (1991). An investigation into the needs of gifted boys. *Roeper Review, 13*(4), 174–180.

American Association of Colleges for Teacher Education (1994). *Teacher education pipeline III: Schools, colleges, and departments of education enrollments by race, ethnicity, and gender*. Washington, DC: Author.

American Council on Education. (1994). *Minorities in higher education*. Washington, DC: U.S. Government Printing Office.

American Psychological Association Commission on Violence and Youth. (1993). *Violence and youth: Psychology's response. Vol. 1: Summary report*. Washington, DC: Author.

Anderson, M. G. (1992). The use of selected theater rehearsal technique activities: Resources for socially emotionally disturbed adolescents. *Exceptional Children, 59*(2), 132–140.

Anderson, M. G. (1994). Rejecting deficit interpretations: Building on differences. In R. L. Peterson & I. Jordan (Eds.), *Behavior disorders in the context of culture and community* (pp. 128–149). Boston, MA: Allyn & Bacon.

Anderson, M. G. (1997). School discipline and prison punishment: A synonomous relationship based on race, ethnicity, class, and gender. Paper presented at the annual meeting of the American Educational Research Association (AERA). Chicago, IL.

Anderson, M. G., & Webb-Johnson, G. (1995). Cultural context, the seriously emotionally disturbed classification, and African American learners. In B. A. Ford, F. E. Obiakor, & J. Patton (Eds.), *Effective education of African American learners* (pp. 125–136). Austin, TX: Pro-Ed.

Archambault, F. X., Jr., Westberg, K. L., Brown, S. W., Hallmark, B. W., Emmons, C. L., & Zhang, W. (1993). *Regular classroom practices with gifted students: Results of a national survey of classroom teachers.* Storrs, CT: National Research Center on the Gifted and Talented, University of Connecticut.

Artiles, A. J., & Trent, S. C. (1994). Overrepresentation of minority students in special education: A continuing debate. *Journal of Special Education, 27*(4), 410–437.

Asante, M. K. (1988). *Afrocentricity.* Trenton, NJ: Africa World Press.

Ascher, C. (1991). School programs for African-American male students. *Equity and Choice, 8*(1), 25–29.

Au, K. H., & Jordan, C. (1981). Teaching reading to Hawaiian children: Finding a culturally appropriate solution. In H. T. Trueba, G. P. Guthrie, & K. H. Au (Eds.), *Culture and the bilingual classroom: Studies in classroom ethnography* (pp. 139–152). Rowley, MA: Newbury House.

Ayers, W. (1991). "Perestroika" in Chicago's schools. *Educational Leadership, 18*(8), 69–71.

Ball, D. L., & Wilson, S. (1996). Integrity in teaching: Recognizing the fusion of the moral and intellectual. *American Educational Research Journal, 33*(1), 155–192.

Baron, E. B. (1992). Discipline strategies for teachers. *Phi Delta Kappan,* pp. 7–30.

Barrett, J. (1993). Urban adolescent homicidal violence: An emerging public health concern. *Urban League Review,* 67–75.

Bates, T., & Howell, D. (1997). Status of self-employed and employee African Americans in the New York City construction industry. In P. Mason & R. Williams (Eds.), *Race, markets, and social outcomes* (pp. 127–152). Norwell, MA: Kluwer.

Baumarind, D. (1972). An exploratory study of socialization effects on Black children: Some Black-White comparisons. *Child Development, 43,* 261–267.

Becker, H. J. (1991). How computers are used in United States schools: Basic data from the 1989 I.E.A. computers in education survey. *Journal of Educational Computing Research, 7*(4), 385–406.

Becker, H. J. (1992). Equity and the "big picture." *Technos, 1*(1), 16–18.

Becker, H. J. (1994). How exemplary computer-using teachers differ from other teachers: Implications for realizing the potential of computers in schools. *Journal of Research on Computing in Education, 26*(3), 291–321.

Becker, H. J., & Sterling, C. W. (1987). Equity in school computer use: National data and neglected considerations. *Journal of Educational Computing Research, 3*(3), 289–311.

Bell, D. (1995). *Faces at the bottom of the well: The permanence of racism.* New York: Basic Books.

Bennett, C., & Okinaka, A. (1984). Explanation of Black student attrition in predominantly Black universities. *Integrated Education, 22,* 73–80.

Bernstein, J. (1995). *Where's the payoff? The gap between Black academic progress and economic gains.* Washington, DC: Economic Policy Institute.

Berry, J., Kim, U., Minde, T., & Mok, D. (1987). Comparative studies of acculturative stress. *International Migration Review, 21,* 491–511.

Bialo, E. R., & Sivin, J. P. (1989a). Computers and at-risk youth: A partial solution to a complex problem. *Classroom Computer Learning, 9*(4), 34–39.

Bialo, E. R., & Sivin, J. P. (1989b). Computers and at-risk youth: Software and hardware that can help. *Classroom Computer Learning, 9*(5), 48–55.

Blackwell, J., & Hart, P. (1982). *Cities, suburbs, and Blacks: A study of concerns, distrust, and alienation.* Bayside, NY: General Hall.

Bloom, D., & Sherwood, K. F. (1994). *Matching opportunities to obligations: Lessons from child support reform from the Parents Fair Share pilot phase.* New York: Manpower Demonstration Research Corporation.

Bogdan, R., & Biklen, S. (1992). *Qualitative research.* Boston: Allyn & Bacon.

Bok, D. C. (1982). *Beyond the ivory tower: Social responsibilities of the modern university.* Cambridge: Harvard University Press.

Borland, J. H. (1996). Gifted education and the threat of irrelevance. *Journal for the Education of the Gifted, 19*(2), 129–147.

Bound, J., & Freeman, R. (1992). What went wrong? The erosion of relative earnings and employment among young Black men in the 1980s. *Quarterly Journal of Economics, 107*(1), 201–232.

Bowers, C. A., & Flinders, D. J. (1990). *Responsive teaching: An ecological approach to classroom patterns of language, culture and thought.* New York: Teachers College Press.

Bowman, P. J. (1989). Research perspectives on Black men: Role strain and adaptation across the adult life cycle. In R. L. Jones (Ed.), *Black adult development and aging* (pp. 117–150). Richmond, CA: Cobb & Henry.

Bowman, P. (1991a). Joblessness. In J. S. Jackson (Ed.), *Life in Black America* (pp. 156–178). Newbury Park, CA: Sage.

Bowman, P. (1991b). *Worklife.* In S. Jackson (Ed.), *Life in Black America* (pp. 124–155). Newbury Park, CA: Sage.

Bowman, P. (1994). *Educational problems and responsible fatherhood among African Americans.* Paper presented at the annual meeting of the American Educational Research Association. New Orleans, LA.

Bowman, P. (1995). Commentary: On family structure and the marginalization of Black men: Policy implications. In M. B. Tucker & C. Mitchefl-Kernan (Eds.), *The decline in marriage among African Americans: Causes, consequences, and policy implications* (pp. 309–322). New York: Russell Sage Foundation.

Bowman, P. J. (1988). Postindustrial displacement and family role strain.

Boy, A. V., & Pine, G. J. (1988). *Fostering psychosocial development in the classroom.* Springfield, IL: Charles C. Thomas.

Boykin, A. W., & Johnson, L. B. (1990). *A study of school suspension discrepancy rates for Montgomery County Black and White students.* Rockville, MD: Montgomery County Public Schools.

Brantlinger, E. (1991). Social class distinctions in adolescents' reports of problems and punishment in school. *Behavior Disorders, 17,* 36–46.

Brown v. Board of Education of Topeka [Brown I], 347 U.S. 483 (1954).

Brown, J. S., Collins, A., & Duguid, P. (1989). Situated cognition and the culture of learning. *Educational Researcher, 18*(1), 32–42.

Brown, M. C., II. (1995a). In defense of the public historically Black college and its mission. *The National Honors Report, 16*(3), 34–40.

Brown, M. C., II. (1995b). Justice and jurisprudence: Losing battles and winning wars. *Black Issues in Higher Education, 12*(9), 9–30.

Brown, M. C., II. (1996). One, two, three . . . red light: Legal steps backward on equal opportunity in higher education. *Black Issues in Higher Education, 13*(7), 74–75.

Bruder, I. (1989a). Ninth annual survey of the states. *Electronic Learning, 9*(2), 24–28.

Bruder, I. (1989b). School of education: Four exemplary programs. *Electronic Learning, 10*(6), 21–24, 45.

Bruner, J. (1996). *The Culture of Education.* Cambridge: Harvard University Press.

Buetow, H. A. (1985). *The history of the United States Catholic schooling.* Washington, DC: National Catholic Education Association.

Bullough, R. V., & Beatty, L. F. (1991). *Classroom applications of microcomputers.* New York: Macmillan.

Callahan, C. M. (1996). A critical study of gifted education: Healthy practice, necessary evil, or sedition? *Journal for the Education of the Gifted, 19*(2), 148–163.

Carter, D., & Wilson, R. (1997). *Minorities in higher education.* Washington, DC: American Council on Education.

Casey, J. A. (1992). *Counseling using technology with at-risk youth* (Report No. EDO-CG-92-14). Ann Arbor, MI: ERIC Clearinghouse on Counseling and Personnel Services. (ERIC Document Reproduction Service No. ED 347 480)

Casey, K. (1990). Teacher as mother: Curriculum theorizing in the life histories of contemporary women teachers. *Cambridge Journal of Education, 20*(3), 301–320.

Cazden, C. (1988). *Classroom discourse.* Portsmouth, NH: Heinemann.

Cervera, N. (1991). Unwed teenage pregnancy: Family relationships with the father of the baby. *Family in Society, 72*, 29–37.

Cheatham, H., Slaney, R., & Coleman, N. (1990). Institutional effects on the psychosocial development of African American college students. *Journal of Counseling Psychology, 37*(4), 453–458.

Cherlin, A. (1981). Trends in United States men's and women's sex-role attitudes: 1972 to 1978. *American Sociological Review, 46*(4), 453–460.

Childers, J. H., & Fairman, M. (1986). The school counselor as a facilitator of organizational health. *The School Counselor, 33*(5), 332–337.

Chinn, P. C., & Hughes, S. (1987). Representation of minority students in special education classes. *Remedial and Special Education, 8*(4), 41–46.

Choy, S. P., Henke, R. R., Alt, M. N., Medrich, E. A., & Bobbitt, S. A. (1993). *Schools and staffing in the United States: A statistical profile, 1990–1991.* Washington, DC: National Center for Educational Statistics.

Christmon, K. (1990). The unwed adolescent father's perceptions of his family and of himself as a father. *Child and Adolescent Social Work, 7*(4), 275–283.

Civil Rights Act of 1964, Pub. L. No. 88-352, 78 Stat. 241.

Clark, R. (1983). *Family life and school achievement: Why poor Black children succeed or fail.* Chicago: University of Chicago Press.

Colangelo, N., Kerr, B., Christensen, P., & Maxey, J. (1993). A comparison of gifted underachievers and gifted high achievers. *Gifted Child Quarterly, 37*(4), 155–160.

College Entrance Examination Board (1985). *Quality and excellence: The educational status of Black Americans.* New York: Author.

Collins, R., & Camblin, L. D. (1983). The politics and science of learning disability classification: Implications for Black children. *Contemporary Education, 54*(2), 113–118.

Comer, J. P. (1980). *School power: Implications of an intervention project.* New York: Free Press.

Comer, J. P. (1988). Educating poor minority children. *Scientific American, 259*(5), 42–48.

Comer, J. P. (1989). *A conversation between James P. Comer and Ronald Edmonds: Fundamentals of effective school improvement.* Madison: University of Wisconsin-Madison, National Center for Effective Schools, Research, and Development.

Comer, J. P. (1993). *James P. Comer MD on the school-development program: Making a difference for children.* New York: Columbia University, Teachers College, National Center for Restructuring Education, Schools, and Teaching.

Commission for Positive Change in the Oakland Public Schools. (1992). *Keeping children in school* (pp. 3–20). Oakland, CA: OUSD Management Information Systems Department.

Constantine, J. M. (1994). Measuring the effect of attending historically Black colleges and universities on future labor market wages on Black students. Paper presented at the Institute for Labor Market Policies Conference, Cornell University, Ithaca, NY.

Cook, L. H., & Boe, E. E. (1995). Who is teaching students with disabilities? *Teaching Exceptional Children, 28,* 70–72.

Coons, J. E., & Sugarman, S. D. (1978). *Education by choice: The case for family control.* Berkeley and Los Angeles: University of California Press.

Costenbader, V., & Reading-Brown, M. (1995). Isolation timeout used with students with emotional disturbance. *Exceptional Children, 61,* 353–362.

Cox, J., Daniel, N., & Boston, B. A. (1985). *Educating able learners: Programs and promising practices.* Austin: University of Texas Press.

Curry, G. D., & Spergel, I. A. (1992). Gang involvement and delinquency among Hispanic and African-American males. *Journal of Research in Crime and Delinquency, 29*(3), 273–291.

Darder, A. (1992). *Culture and power in the classroom: A critical foundation for bi-cultural education.* New York: Bergin and Garvey Press.

Darity, W., Jr. (1983). Reaganomics and the Black community. In S. Weintraub & M. Goodstein (Eds.), *Reaganomics in the stagflation economy* (pp. 59–77). Philadelphia: University of Pennsylvania Press.

Darity, W., Jr. (1989). What's left of the theory of discrimination? In R. Cornwall & P. Wunnava (Eds.), *New approaches to the economic and social analysis of discrimination* (pp. 39–53). New York: Praeger

Darity, W., Jr., Guilkey, D., & Winfrey, W. (1995). Ethnicity, race, and earnings. *Economic Letters, 47,* 401–408.

Darity, W., Jr., & Myers, S., Jr. (1990). Impacts of violent crime on Black family structure. *Contemporary Policy Issues, 8*(4), 15–29.

Darity, W., Jr., & Myers, S., Jr. (1995a). Family structure and the marginalization of Black men: Policy implications. In M. Belinda Tucker & C. Mitchell-Kernan (Eds.), *The decline in marriage among African Americans: Causes, consequences, and policy implications* (pp. 171–203). New York: Russell Sage Foundation.

Darity, W., Jr., & Myers, S., Jr. (1995b). The widening gap: A summary and synthesis of the debate on increasing inequality. Paper prepared for the National Commission on Employment Policy, University of Minnesota.

Darling-Hammond, L. (Ed.). (1994). *Professional development schools: Schools for developing a profession.* New York: Teachers College Press.

Davis, J. E. (1994). College in black and white: Campus environment and academic achievement of African American males. *Journal of Negro Education, 63*(4), 620–633.

Davis, J. E. (1995). Campus climate, gender, and achievement of African American college males. Paper presented at the annual meeting of the Association for the Study of Higher Education, Tucson, AZ.

Davis, J. E., & Perkins, W. E. (1995). *Fathers' care: A review of the literature.* Philadelphia: National Center on Fathers and Families, University of Pennsylvania.

Delpit, L. D. (1988). The silenced dialog: Power and pedagogy in educating other people's children. *Harvard Educational Review, 58*(3), 280–298.

Dent, H., Mendocal, A., Pierce, W., & West, G. (1991). The San Francisco public schools experience with I.Q. testing: A model for non-biased assessment. In A. G. Hilliard (Ed.), *Testing African American students: Special re-issue of the Negro Educational Review* (pp. 146–162). Morristown, NJ: Aaron Press.

DeVillar, R. A. (1989). Computers, software, and cooperative learning: Effective peer communication in the heterogeneous classroom. *Teacher Education Quarterly, 16*(2), 91–95.

Diaz, C. (1989). Hispanic cultures and cognitive styles: Implications for teachers. *Multicultural Leader, 2,* 1–4.

Ditton, J. (1979). *Contrology.* London: Macmillan.

Dizard, W. P. (1982). *The coming information age: An overview of technology, economics, and politics.* New York: Longman.

Dornbusch, S., Ritter, P., Liederman, P., Roberts, D., & Fraleigh, M. (1987). The relation of parenting style to achievement to adolescent school performance. *Child Development, 58,* 1244–1257.

Du Bois, W. E. B. (1996). *The souls of Black folk.* New York: Modern Library. (Original work published 1903)

Duneier, M. (1994). *Slim's table: Masculinity and race in America.* Chicago: University of Chicago Press.

Edmonds, G. J. (1984). Needs assessment strategy for Black students: An examination of stressors and program implications. *Journal of Non-White Concerns, 12*(2), 48–56.

Edmonds, R. R. (1983). *An overview of school improvement programs.* East Lansing: Institute for Research on Teaching, Michigan State University.

Elias, M. J. (1989). School as a source of stress to children: An analysis of causal and ameliorative influences. *Journal of School Psychology, 27,* 393–402.

Epstein, M. H., Foley, R. M., & Cullinan, D. (1992). National survey of education programs for adolescents with serious emotional disturbance. *Behavior Disorders, 17,* 202–210.

Erhenberg, R. G., & Rothstein, D. S. (1993). *Do historically black institutions of higher education confer unique advantages on black students? An initial analysis* (NBER Working Paper No. 4356). Ithaca, NY: Cornell University.

Erickson, F., Cazden, C. B., & Carrasco, R. (1983). *Social and cultural organization of interaction in classrooms of bilingual children.* Final report to the National Institute of Education.

Erickson, F., & Mohatt, G. (1982). Cultural organization of participant structures in two classrooms of Indian students. In G. D. Spindler (Ed.), *Doing the ethnography of schooling: Educational anthropology in action* (pp. 112–134). New York: Holt, Rinehart and Winston.

Erikson, E. (1968). *Identity: Youth and crisis.* New York: Norton.

Farley, J. (1983). Metropolitan housing segregation in the 1980s: The St. Louis case. *Urban Affairs Quarterly, 18,* 247–259.

Ferguson, R. (1993, September). *New evidence on the growing value of skill and consequences for racial disparity and returns to schooling.* Paper prepared as part of the Faculty Research Working Paper Series, John F. Kennedy School of Government, Harvard University, Cambridge, MA.

Ferguson, R. (1995, Winter). Shifting challenges: Fifty years of economic change toward Black-White earnings equality. *Daedalus,* 37–76.

Fleming, J. (1984). *Blacks in college: A comparative study of students' success in Black and White institutions.* San Francisco: Jossey-Bass.

Fleming, J. E. (1981). Blacks in higher education to 1954: A historical overview. In G. Thomas (Ed.), *Black students in higher education* (pp. 83–103). Westport, CT: Greenwood Press.

Florida ex rel. Hawkins v. Board of Control of Florida, 350 U.S. 413 (1956).

Ford, D. Y. (1993). Support for the achievement ideology and determinants of underachievement as perceived by gifted, above-average, and average Black students. *Journal for the Education of the Gifted, 16*(3), 280–298.

Ford, D. Y. (1994). Nurturing resilience in gifted Black youth. *Roeper Review, 17*(2), 80–85.

Ford, D. Y. (1995). *A study of achievement and underachievement among gifted, potentially gifted, and average Black students.* Storrs, CT: The University of Connecticut, National Research Center on the Gifted and Talented.

Ford, D. Y., & Harris, J. (1994). Promoting achievement among gifted Black students. *Urban Education, 29,* 202–229.

Ford, D. Y., Grantham, T. C., & Harris, J. J., III. (1997). The recruitment and retention of minority teachers in gifted education. *Roeper Review.*

Fordham, S. (1988). Racelessness as a strategy in Black students' school success: Pragmatic strategy or Pyrrhic victory? *Harvard Educational Review, 58*(1), 54–84.

Fordham, S., & Ogbu, J. (1986). Black students' school success: Coping with the burden of "acting White." *Urban Review 18*(3), 1–31.

Forness, S. S., & Knitzer, J. (1990). A new proposed definition and terminology to replace serious emotional disturbance in Education of the Handicapped Act. Alexandria, VA: National Mental Health and Special Education Coalition.

Foster, M. (1987). *It's cookin' now: An ethnographic study of a successful Black teacher in an urban community college.* Unpublished doctoral dissertation, Harvard University.

Foster, M. (1989). It's cooking' now: A performance analysis of the speech events of a Black teacher in an urban community college. *Language in Society, 18*(1), 1–29.

Foster, M. (1991). "Just got to find a way": Case studies of the lives and practices of exemplary Black high school teachers. In M. Foster (Ed.), *Readings in equal education: Vol. II: Qualitative investigations into schools and schooling* (pp. 223–230). New York: AMS Press.

Foster, M. (1993). Educating for competence in community and culture: Exploring the views of exemplary African American teachers. *Urban Education, 27*(4), 370–394.

Foster, M. (1994). Effective Black teachers: A literature review. In E. R. Hollins, J. E. King, & W. C. Hayman (Eds.), *Teaching diverse populations: Formulating a knowledge base* (pp. 225–241). Albany: State University of New York Press.

Foster, M. (1997). *Black teachers on teaching.* New York: New Press.

Fox, N. A., Kimmerly, N. L., & Schafer, W. D. (1991). Attachment to mother/attachment to father: A meta-analysis. *Child Development, 62*(1), 210–225.

Fry, P. S., & Trifiletti, R. J. (1983). Teenage fathers: An exploration of their developmental needs and anxieties and the implications for clinical/social intervention services. *Journal of Psychiatric Treatment and Evaluation, 5,* 219–227.

Furstenberg, F. F., & Harris, L. (1993). When fathers matter/why fathers matter: The impact of paternal involvement on the offspring of adolescent mothers. In A. Lawson & B. L. Rhodes (Eds.), *The politics of pregnancy: Adolescent sexuality and public policy* (pp. 34–56). New Haven: Yale University Press.

Furstenberg, F. F., Morgan, S. P., Moore, K. A., & Peterson, J. L. (1987). Race differences in the timing of adolescent intercourse. *American Sociological Review, 52,* 511–518.

Futterman, S., & Livermore, J. B. (1947). Putative fathers. *Journal of Social Casework, 28,* 174–178.

Gadsden, V. L. (1995). *The absence of father: Effects on children's development and family functioning* [Monograph]. Philadelphia: National Center on Fathers and Families, University of Pennsylvania.

Gadsden, V. L., Armorer, K., & Kane, D. (in press). Father and family programs: A report on the state of the field [Monograph]. Philadelphia: National Center on Fathers and Families, University of Pennsylvania.

Gadsden, V. L., Smith, R. R., & Jordan, W. J. (1996). The promise of desegregation: Tendering expectation and reality in achieving quality schooling. *Urban Education, 31*(4), 381–402.

Gardner, H. (1983). *Frames of mind: The theory of multiple intelligences.* New York: Basic Books.

Garibaldi, A. (1984). *Black colleges and universities: Challenges for the future.* New York: Praeger.

Garibaldi, A. M. (1992). Educating and motivating African American males to succeed. *Journal of Negro Education, 61*(1), 4–11.

Gee, J. P. (1991). The narrativization of experience in the oral style. *Journal of Education, 171*(1), 75–96.

Gibbs, J. T. (Ed.). (1988). *Young, Black, and male in America: An endangered species.* Dover, MA: Auburn House.

Giles, M. (1996). Race coding and White opposition to welfare. *American Political Science Review, 90,* 593–604.

Goodlad, J. I. (1981). *A place called school.* New York: MacGraw-Hill.

Gordon, E. W. (1990). *A study of minority student achievement in Montgomery County public schools.* Rockville, MD: Montgomery County Public Schools.

Gordon, E. W. (1996). *Fostering wholesome development and enabling rehabilitation in African American males* (Tech. Rep.). Kalamazoo, MI: Kellogg Foundation.

Gordon, E. W. (1997). African American males and the second Reconstruction. In *Proceedings of the Kenneth B. Clarke Colloquium Series,* Vol. 2. New York: IRADAC, City University of New York.

Gosman, E. J., et al. (1983). Predicting student progression: The influence of race and other student and institutional characteristics on college student performance. *Research in Higher Education, 18*(2), 209–236.

Grantham, T. C. (1997). *The under-representation of Black males in gifted programs: Case studies of participation motivation.* Unpublished doctoral dissertation, University of Virginia, Charlottesville.

Green, R. L., & Wright, D. L. (1992). African American males: A demographic study and analysis. In B. W. Austin (Ed.), *A discussion of issues affecting African American men and boys* (pp. 21–45). Kalamazoo, MI: W. K. Kellogg Foundation.

Grier, G., & Grier, E. (1983). *Black suburbanization in the 1970s.* Bethesda, MD: Grier Partnership.

Grissmer, D., Kirby, S., Berends, M., & Williamson, S. (1994). *Student achievement and the changing American family.* Santa Monica, CA: Rand Institute.

Gumperz, J. J. (1982). *Discourse strategies.* Cambridge: Cambridge University Press.

Gurin, P., & Epps, E. (1975). *Black consciousness, identity and achievement: A study of students in historically black colleges.* New York: Wiley.

Haberman, M. (1992). The ideology of star teachers of children in poverty. *Educational Horizons, 70*(3), 125–129.

Haberman, M. (1995). Selecting "star" teachers for children and youth in urban poverty. *Phi Delta Kappan, 76*(10), 771–781.

Haile, P. J. (1990). *What the research says about computerbased instruction for America's culturally and linguistically diverse students.* Paper presented at the second annual conference of the Joint Center for Communications, Learning and Technology; New Orleans, LA.

Hall, M. H., & Udall, A. J. (1983). Teacher rating of students in relation to ethnicity of students and school ethnic balance. *Journal for the Education of the Gifted, 6,* 154–166.

Hammond, W. R., & Yung, B. (1993). Psychology's role in the public health response to assaultive violence among young African-American men. *American Psychologist, 48*(2), 142–154.

Hannah, L. (1986). Teaching data base search strategies. *The Computing Teacher, 51,* 16–23.

Harber, J. R. (1981). Assessing the quality of decision making in special education. *Journal of Special Education, 15,* 77–90.

Harris, L. (1992). Honor, emasculation, and empowerment. In L. May & P. Strikwerda (Eds.), *Rethinking masculinity: Philosophical explorations in light of feminism.* Landam, MD: Rowman and Littlefield.

Harris, S. (1995). Psychosocial development and Black male masculinity: Implications for counseling economically disadvantaged African American male adolescents. *Journal of Counseling and Development, 73,* 279–287.

Harris, S., & Majors, R. (1993). Cultural value differences: Implications for the experiences of African American men. *Journal of Men's Studies, 1*(3), 227–238.

Harrison, C. K. (1998). Themes that thread through society: Racism and athletic manifestation in the African-American community. *Race, Ethnicity and Education, 1*(1), 63–74.

Harvard Education Letter (1996, July/August). Hard-won lessons from the school reform battle: A conversation with Ted Sizer. *Harvard Education Letter,* p. 4.

Haveman, R., & Wolfe, B. (1994). *Succeeding generations: On the effects of investments in children.* New York: Russell Sage Foundation.

Hawkins, B. D. (1994). Traditions give way to change: Teacher education group targets HBCU's for development. *Black Issues in Higher Education, 11,* 112–115.

Hawkins, J. A. (1988). *The early experiences and behavior of students suspended in junior and senior high schools.* Rockville, MD: Montgomery County Public Schools.

Hawkins, J. A. (1991). *Study highlights from the Lawrence Johnson & Associates, Inc. report.* Rockville, MD: Montgomery County Public Schools.

Heath, S. B. (1983). *Ways with words: Language, life, and work in communities and classrooms.* Cambridge: Cambridge University Press.

Hebert, T. (1991). Meeting the affective needs of bright boys through bibliotherapy. *Roeper Review, 13*(4), 207–212.

Hebert, T. (1993). *Ethnographic descriptions of the high school experiences of high ability males in an urban environment*. Storrs: University of Connecticut.

Heller, R., Holtzman, W., & Messick, S. (Eds). (1982). *Placing children in special education: A strategy for equity*. Washington, DC: Academy Press.

Henry, A. (1990). Black women, Black pedagogies: An African-Canadian context. Paper presented at the annual meeting of the American Educational Research Association, Boston, MA.

Hershberger, S. L., & D'Augelli, A. R. (1992). The relationship of academic performance and social support to graduation among African-American and white university students: A path-analytic model. *Journal of Community Psychology, 20*, 188–199.

Hill, S. T. (1982). *The traditionally Black institutions of higher education: 1860–1982*. Washington, DC: National Center for Education Statistics.

Hilliard, A. G., III. (1992). The pitfalls and promises of special education practice. *Exceptional Children, 49*(4), 168–172.

Hirumi, A., & Grau, I. (1996). A review of computer-related state standards, textbooks, and journal articles: Implications for preservice teacher education and professional development. *Journal of Computing in Teacher Education, 12*(4), 6–17.

Hoffman, C. M., Snyder, T. D., & Sonneberg, B. (1992). *Historically Black colleges and universities. 1976–1990*. Washington, DC: National Center for Education Statistics.

Holland, S. (1989, Sept./Oct.). Fighting the epidemic of failure: A radical strategy for educating inner-city boys. *Teacher Magazine*.

Hollinger, J. D. (1987). Social skills for behaviorally disordered children as preparation for mainstreaming: Theory, practice, and new directions. *Remedial and Special Education, 8*, 17–27.

Hollins, E. (1982). The Marva Collins story revisited: Implications for regular classroom instruction. *Journal of Teacher Education, 33*(1), 37–40.

Hollins, E., & Spencer, K. (1990). Restructuring schools for cultural inclusion: Changing the schooling process for African American youngsters. *Journal of Education, 172*(2), 89–100.

Hopwood v. Texas, 78 F.3d 932 (5th Cir. 1996).

Hrabowski, F. A., Maton, K. I., & Greif, G. L. (1998). *Beating the odds: Raising academically successful African American males*. New York: Oxford University Press.

Hudson, R. (1991). Black male adolescent development deviating from the past: Challenges for the future. In B. Bowser (Ed.), *Black male adolescents: Parenting and education in community context* (pp. 271–281). Lanham, MD: University Press.

Hughes, M. (1987). Black students participation in higher education. *Journal of College Student Personnel, 28*(6), 532–545.

Hunt, L., & Hunt, J. (1975). Race and the father-son connection: The conditional relevance of father absence for the orientations and identities of adolescent boys. *Social Problems, 23*(1), 35–52.

Hunter, A. G., & Davis, J. E. (1992). Constructing gender: An exploration of Afro-American men's conceptualization of manhood. *Gender & Society, 6,* 464–479.

Hunter, A. G., & Davis, J. E. (1994). Hidden voices of Black men: The meaning, structure, complexity of manhood. *Journal of Black Studies, 25,* 20–40.

Hurn, C. J. (1985). *The limits and possibilities of schooling: An introduction to the sociology of education* (2nd ed.). Boston: Allyn & Bacon.

Hymes, D. (1981). Ethnographic monitoring. In H. T. Trueba (Ed.), *Culture and the bilingual classroom: Studies in classroom in ethnography* (pp. 179–195). Rowley, MA: Newbury House.

Hytche, W. P. (1989). *A national resource—A national challenge: The 1890 land-grant colleges and universities.* Washington, DC: U.S. Department of Agriculture.

Irvine, J. J. (1990). *Black students and school failure: Policies, practices, and prescriptions.* Westport, CT: Greenwood Press.

Irvine, J. J., & Foster, M. (Eds.). (1996). *Growing up African American in Catholic schools.* New York: Teachers College Press.

Irvine, J. J., & Fraser, I. (1998). Warm demanders: Do national certification standards leave room for the culturally responsive pedagogy of African American teachers? *Education Week, 17*(3), 42–56.

Jackson, L. (1998). The influence of both race and gender on the experience of African American college women. *Review of Higher Education, 21,* 359–375.

Jay, G. M., & D'Augelli, A. R. (1991). Social support and adjustment to university life: A comparison of African American and white freshmen. *Journal of Community Psychology, 19,* 95–108.

Jaynes, G., & Williams, R., Jr. (Eds.). (1989). *A common destiny: Blacks and American society.* Washington, DC: National Academy Press.

Jeffries v. Harleston, 52 F.3d 9 (2nd Cir. 1995).

Jencks, C. (1993). *Rethinking social policy: Race, poverty, and the underclass.* New York: HarperPerennial.

Jencks, C., & Reisman, D. (1968). *The academic revolution.* New York: Doubleday Anchor.

Jenkins, M. D. (1936). The socio-psychological study of Negro children of superior intelligence. *Journal of Negro Education, 5*(2), 175–190.

Johnson v. San Francisco Unified School District, 500 F.2d 349 (9th Cir., 1974).

Johnson, D. J. (1996). *Father presence matters: A review of the literature: Toward an ecological framework of fathering and child outcomes* (Tech. Rep.). Philadelphia: National Center of Fathers and Families, University of Pennsylvania.

Johnson, J. M., & Watson, B. C. (Eds.). (1990). *Stony the road they trod: The African-American male.* Washington, DC: National Urban League.

Johnson, L., & O'Neil, C. (1984). *Dorothy Heathcote: Collected writings on education and drama.* London: Hutchinson.

Johnson, N. (1990). School consultation: The training needs of teachers and school psychologists. *Psychology in the schools, 27,* 51–56.

Johnston, W. B., & Packer, A. E. (1987). *Work force 2000: Work and workers for the 21st century.* Indianapolis, IN: Hudson Institute.

Jones, D. L. (1991). Developing strategies for African American survival in the twenty-first century and beyond. *Urban League Review, 15*(2), 3–7.

Jones, M. (1971). The responsibility of the Black college to the Black community: Then and now. *Daedalus, 100,* 732–744.

Jones, R. (1980). *Black psychology.* New York: Harper and Row.

Kain, J. (1985). Black suburbanization in the eighties. In J. Quigley & D. Rubinfield (Eds.), *American domestic priorities* (pp. 253–299). Berkeley and Los Angeles: University of California Press.

Kardiner, A., & Ovesey, L. (1951). *The mark of oppression: A psychological study of the American Negro.* New York: Norton.

Kauffman, J. (1994). *Characteristics of emotional and behavioral disorders of children and youth.* New York: Macmillan.

Kauffman, J. M., & Hallahan, D. P. (1981). *Handbook of special education.* Englewood Cliffs, NJ: Prentice-Hall.

Kawakami, A. J. (1991). Ho'oulu I Ka Heluehelu: Fitting book reading into the lives of Hawaiian children and their families. In M. Foster (Ed.), *Readings on equal education: Qualitative investigations into schools and schooling* (pp. 34–53). New York: AMS Press.

Kifano, S. (1996). Afrocentric education in supplementary schools: Paradigm and practice at the Mary Mcleod Bethune Institute. *Journal of Negro Education, 65*(2), 209–218.

King, J. (1991). Black student alienation and Black teachers' emancipatory pedagogy. In M. Foster (Ed.), *Readings on equal education: Qualitative investigations in schools and schooling* (Vol. 11) (pp. 245–271). New York: AMS Press.

Kline, B. E., & Short, E. B. (1991). Changes in emotional resilience: Gifted adolescent females. *Roeper Review, 13,* 118–121.

Klingberg, F. J. (1941). *The appraisal of the Negro in colonial South Carolina.* Washington, DC: Associated Publishers.

Knitzer, J., Steinberg, Z., & Fleisch, F. (1990). *At the schoolhouse door: An examination of the programs and policies for children with behavioral and emotional problems.* New York: Bank Street College of Education.

Knoff, H. (Ed.). (1986). *The assessment of child and adolescent personality.* New York: Guilford Press.

Kochman, T. (1981). *Black and White styles in conflict.* Chicago: University of Chicago Press.

Kortering, L., Haring, N., & Klockars, A. (1992). The identification of high school dropouts identified as learning disabled: Evaluating the utility of a discriminant analysis function. *Exceptional Children, 58,* 422–435.

Ku, L., Sonenstein, F. L., & Pleck, J. H. (1993). Neighborhood, family, and work: Influences on the premarital behaviors of adolescent males. *Social Forces, 72*(2), 479–503.

Kunjufu, F. (1986). *Countering the conspiracy to destroy Black boys* (Vol. 2). Chicago: African American Images.

Ladson-Billings, G. (1989, February). Like lightning in a bottle: Attempting to capture the pedagogical excellence of successful teachers of Black students. Paper presented at the tenth annual Ethnography in Educational Research Forum, University of Pennsylvania, Philadelphia, PA.

Ladson-Billings, G. (1991a). Like lightning in a bottle: Attempting to capture the pedagogical excellence of successful teachers of Black students. *International Journal of Qualitative Studies in Education, 3*(4), 335–344.

Ladson-Billings, G. (1991b). Returning to the source: Implications for educating teachers of Black students. In M. Foster (Ed.), *Readings on equal education: Qualitative investigations into schools and schooling* (pp. 227–244). New York: AMS Press.

Ladson-Billings, G. (1994). *The dreamkeepers: Successful teachers of African American children.* San Francisco: Jossey-Bass.

Ladson-Billings, G., & Henry, A. (1990). Blurring the borders: Voices of African liberatory pedagogy in the United States and Canada. *Journal of Education, 172*(2), 72–88.

Lamb, M. F. (1977). Father-infant and mother-infant interaction in the second year of life. *Child Development, 13*(6), 637–648.

Lamb, M. F. (1978). Father-infant relationships: Their nature and importance. *Youth and Society, 9*(3), 277–298.

Lanborn, S., & Mounts, N. (1990). *Patterns of competence and adjustment among adolescents from authoritative, authoritarian, indulgent and neglectful families.* Madison, WI: National Center for Effective Secondary Schools, University of Wisconsin at Madison.

Lang, M., & Ford, C. A. (Eds.). (1988). *Black student retention in higher education.* Springfield, IL: Charles C. Thomas.

Larry P. et al., v. Wilson Riles et al., C-71-2270 RFP, District Court of Northern California (1979).

Larson, J. C., Garies, R. S., & Campbell, W. E. (1996). *A profile of MCPS graduate and their performance at Montgomery College.* Rockville: Montgomery County Public Schools.

Law, W., & Clift, V. (1981). *Encyclopedia of Black Americans.* New York: McGraw-Hill.

Leake, D. O., & Leake, B. L. (1992). Islands of hope: Milwaukee's African American immersion schools. *Journal of Negro Education, 61*(1), 4–11.

Lee, C. D. (1992a). Literacy, cultural diversity, and instruction. *Education and Urban Society, 24*(2), 279–291.

Lee, C. D. (1992b). Profile of an independent Black institution: African-centered education at work. *Journal of Negro Education, 61*(2), 160–177.

Lee, M. W. (1986). The match: Learning styles of Black children and microcomputer programming. *Journal of Negro Education, 55*(1), 78–90.

Levine, I. A., & Pitt, F. (1996). *New expectations: Community strategies for responsible fatherhood.* New York: Families and Work Institute.

Lewis, J. (1987). Do Black students on a White campus value the university's efforts to retain them? *Journal of College Student Personnel, 28,* 176–177.

Lewis, O. (1965). *La vida: A Puerto Rican family in the culture of poverty: San Juan and New York.* New York: Random House.

Lightfoot, S. L. (1973). Politics and reasoning: Through the eyes of teachers and children. *Harvard Educational Review, 2,* 197–243.

Lindstrom, R. R., & Van Sant, S. (1986). Special issues in working with gifted minority adolescents. *Journal of Counseling and Development, 64,* 583–586.

Lora v. Board of Education of New York. 587 F. Supp. 1572 (E.D.N.Y. 1975).

Loury, G. (1984). Internally directed action for Black community development. *Review of Black Political Economy, 13*(1), 31–46.

Lubeck, S. (1985). *Sandbox society: Early education in Black and White America—A comparative ethnography.* Philadelphia: Falmer Press.

Majors, R. (1990). Cool pose: The proud signature of Black survival. In M. Kimmel & M. Messner (Eds.), *Men's lives* (pp. 83–87). New York: Macmillan.

Majors, R. G., & Billson, J. M. (1991). *Cool pose: The dilemmas of Black manhood in America.* Lexington, MA: D. C. Heath.

Male, M. (1993). Cooperative learning and computers in social studies integrating special needs students into general education classrooms. *Social Studies Review, 32*(2), 56–62.

Marcia, J. (1980). Identity in adolescence. In J. Adelson (Ed.), *Handbook of adolescent psychology* (pp. 159–187). New York: John Wiley.

Marsiglio, W. (1993). Contemporary scholarship on fatherhood. *Journal of Family Issues, 14*(4), 484–509.

Martinez, M. E., & Mead, N. A. (1988). *The nation's report card: Computer competence, the first national assessment.* Princeton, NJ: Educational Testing Service.

Maryland State Department of Education (1995). *Maryland school performance report* (1995). Baltimore: Author.

Maslow, A. (1954). *Motivation and personality.* New York: Harper.

Mason, P. (1993). Accumulation, segmentation, and the discriminatory process in the market for labor power. *Review of Radical Political Economy, 25*(2), 1–25.

Mason, P. (1995a). *Male interracial wage inequality, general wage inequality, and the average wage rate, 1975–1991.* Washington, DC: Economic Policy Institute.

Mason, P. (1995b). Race, competition, and differential wages. *Cambridge Journal of Economics, 19*(4), 545–568.

Mason, P. (1996a). Race, culture, and skill: Interracial wage differences among African Americans, Latinos, and Whites. Working Paper. University of Notre Dame.

Mason, P. (1996b). Joblessness and unemployment: A review of the literature. Philadelphia: National Center on Fathers and Families. University of Pennsylvania. LR-JU-96-03.

Mason, P. (1997). Some heterodox models of inequality in the market for labor power. In T. D. Boston (Ed.), *A different vision: African American economic thought* (pp. 113–157). London: Routledge.

Mason, P. (in press). Competing explanations of male interracial wage differentials: Missing variable models versus job competition. *Cambridge Journal of Economics.*

Mason, P., & Williams, R. (in press). The Janus-face of race: Reflections on economic theory. In P. Mason & R. Williams (Eds.), *Race, markets, and social outcomes*. Norwell, MA: Kluwer.

Massey, D. S., & Denton, N. A. (1988). Suburbanization and segregation in U.S. metropolitan areas. *American Journal of Sociology, 94*(3), 592–626.

Massey, D. S., & Denton, N. A. (1993). *American apartheid: Segregation and the making of the underclass*. Cambridge: Harvard University Press.

Maxwell, N. (1995). The effect on Black-White wage differentials of differences in the quantity and quality of education. *Industrial and Labor Relations Review, 47*(2), 249–262.

McAdoo, J. L. (1990). Understanding African American teen fathers. In P. F. Leone (Ed.), *Understanding troubled and troubling youth* (pp. 213–221). Newbury Park, CA: Sage.

McAdoo, M. (1994). Equity: Has technology bridged the gap? *Electronic Learning, 13*(7), 24–30, 34.

McCarron, P. M. (1997). Catholic identity and Catholic school leadership: An examination of Catholic secondary school principals' beliefs and behaviors. Doctoral dissertation, Catholic University of America.

McCarthy, C. (1990). Multicultural education, minority identities, textbooks, and the challenge of curriculum reform. *Journal of Education, 172*(2), 118–129.

McCarthy, C., & Crichlow, W. (1993). *Race identity and representation in education*. London: Routledge Press.

McDaniel, A. (1994). Historical racial differences in living arrangements of children. *Journal of Family History, 19*(1), 57–77.

McDermott, R. P. (1977). Social relations as contexts for learning in school. *Harvard Educational Review, 47*, 198–213.

McFadden, A. C., Marsh, G. E., Price, B. J., & Hwang, Y. (1992). *Education and Treatment of Children, 15*(2), 140–146.

McIntyre, L. D., & Pernell, E. (1985). The impact of race on teacher recommendations for special education placement. *Journal of Multicultural Counseling and Development, 6*, 112–120.

McIntyre, T. (1995). *McIntyre assessment of culture (MAC)*. Columbia, MO: Hawthorne Educational Services.

McLaughlin, M. W., & Talbert, J. (1990). Constructing a personalized school environment. *Phi Delta Kappan, 72*(3), 230–235.

McLuhan, M. (1989). *The global village: Transformations in world life and media in the 21st century*. New York: Oxford University Press.

Mercer, J. R. (1973). *Labeling the mentally retarded*. Berkeley and Los Angeles: University of California Press.

Merrell, J. G. (1991, May). *Let's prepare-not-repair our at-risk students*. Paper presented at the annual meeting of the International Reading Association, Las Vegas, NV.

Mezirow, J., et al. (1990). *Fostering critical reflection in adulthood: A guide to transformative and emancipatory learning*. San Francisco: Jossey-Bass.

Miller, J. G. (1996). *Search and destroy: African American males in the criminal justice system*. New York: Cambridge University Press.

Montgomery County Committee on Hate/Violence (1995). *Student perceptions on prejudice in Montgomery County: Summary of significant findings.* Rockville, MD: Montgomery County Human Relations Commission.

Montgomery County Public Schools (1995). *FY97 superintendent's operating budget request* (1995). Rockville, MD: Author.

Morrill Act of 1890, Ch. 841, 26 Stat. 417.

Moynihan, D. (1965). *The Negro family: The case for national action.* Washington, DC: U.S. Government Printing Office.

Murdick, O. J. (1989). Catholic schools revisited. *Momentum, 20*(3), 7–10.

Murray, C., & Herrnstein, R. (1994). *The bell curve: Intelligence and class structure in American life.* New York: Free Press.

Murrell, P. C. (1991). Cultural politics in teacher education: What is missing in the preparation of minority teachers? In M. Foster (Ed.), *Readings on equal education: Qualitative investigations into schools and schooling* (pp. 205–225). New York: AMS Press.

Murrell, P. C. (1993). Afrocentric immersion: Academic and personal development of African American males in public schools. In T. Perry & J. Fraser (Eds.), *Freedom's plow: Teaching in the multicultural classroom* (pp. 231–261). Boston: Routledge.

Myers, D. A., & Duke, D. L. (1977). Open education as an ideology. *Educational Research, 19*(3), 227–235.

Myers, S. (1992). Crime, entrepreneurship, and labor force withdrawal. *Contemporary Policy Issues, 10*(2), 84–97.

Myers, S., & Sabol, W. (1987). Unemployment and racial differences in imprisonment. *Review of Black Political Economy, 16*(1–2), 189–209.

Myles, B. S., & Simpson, R. L. (1989). Regular educator modification preferences for mainstreaming mildly handicapped children. *Journal of Special Education, 22,* 479–492.

Naron, N. K., & Estes, N. (1986). Technology in the schools: Trends and policies. *AEDS Journal, 19*(4), 31–43.

National Center for Education Statistics (1990). *National education longitudinal study.* Washington, DC: U.S. Department of Education.

National Center for Education Statistics (1993). The conditions of education 1993. Washington, DC: U.S. Department of Education, Office of Educational Research and Improvement.

National Center for Education Statistics (1995). *Student use of computers.* Washington, DC: U.S. Department of Education.

National Center for Education Statistics (1996). *Internet connectivity in U.S. schools.* Washington, DC: U.S. Department of Education.

National Commission on Excellence in Education (1983). *A nation at risk: The imperative of educational reform.* Washington, DC: U.S. Department of Education.

National Council of Teachers of Mathematics (1989). *Curriculum and evaluation standards for school mathematics.* Reston, VA: National Council of Teachers of Mathematics.

National Mental Health Association (1993). *All system failure.* Washington, DC: Author.

National Research Council (1989). *A common destiny: Blacks and American society*. Washington, DC: National Academy Press.

National Research Council (1993). *Summary Report 1991: Doctorate recipients from American universities*. Washington, DC: National Academy Press.

National Urban League (1998). *The state of Black America 1989*. New York: Author.

Neal, D., & Johnson, W. (1994). The role of pre-market factors in Black-White wage differences, Unpublished mimeo.

Nettles, M. T. (1987). Black and White college student performance in majority White and majority Black academic settings. In J. Williams (Ed.), *Title IV regulation of higher education: Problems and progress*. New York: Teachers College Press.

Nettles, M. T., with Thoeny, A. R. (Ed.). (1988). *Toward Black undergraduate student equality in American higher education*. New York: Greenwood Press.

Nettles, M. T. (1991). Racial similarities and differences in the predictors of college student achievement. In W. R. Epps & N. Haniff (Eds.), *College in Black and White*. New York: State University of New York Press.

Neuman, D. (1991). *Technology and equity*. ERIC Digest. (Report No. RIEAPR 92). (ERIC Document Reproduction Service No. ED 339 400)

Newman, F. M. (1981). Reducing student alienation in high schools: Implications of theory. *Harvard Educational Review, 51*, 546–564.

Noddings, N. (1995). Teaching themes of care. *Phi Delta Kappa, 76*(9), 675–679.

Noguera, P. (1996). Responding to the crisis of Black youth: Providing support without furthering marginalization. *Journal of Negro Education, 65*(1), 37–60.

O'Neill, J. (1990). The role of human capital and earnings differences between Black and White men. *Journal of Economic Perspectives, 4*(4), 25–45.

Office of Juvenile Justice and Delinquency Prevention. (1994). *Conditions of confinement: Juvenile detention and correction facilities. U.S. Department of Justice, research summary report*. Washington, DC: Author.

Ogbu, J. U. (1986). The consequences of the American caste system. In U. Neisser (Ed.), *The school achievement of minority children: New perspectives* (pp. 19–56). Hillsdale, NJ: Lawrence Erlbaum Associates.

Ogbu, J. U. (1992). Understanding cultural diversity and learning. *Educational Researcher, 21*(8), 5–14.

Oliver, M. L., & Shapiro, T. M. (1995). *Black wealth/White wealth: A new perspective on racial inequality*. New York: Routledge.

Oliver, M., Smith, A., & Wilson, K. (1989). Supporting successful Black students: Personal, organizational, and institutional factors. *National Journal of Sociology, 3*, 199–221.

Olson, L. (1994, February). Preacher of power. *Teacher Magazine, 1*(1), 34–39.

Olson, L. (1996). The game of life: When it comes to planning for careers, high school students don't. *Teacher Magazine, 8*(3), 18–20.

Orfield, G., & Eaton, S. E. (1996). *Dismantling desegregation: The quiet reversal of* Brown v. Board of Education. New York: New Press.

Our commitment to quality: A guide for the 1996–97 school year (1996). Rockville, MD: Montgomery County Public Schools, p. 4.

Parham, T. (1989). Cycles of psychological nigrescence. *Counseling Psychologist, 17*(2), 187–226.

Parke, R. D. (1996). *Fatherhood.* Cambridge: Harvard University Press.

Pascarella, E. T., Smart, J. C., Etherington, C. A., & Nettles, M. T. (1987). College influences on self-concept development. *American Educational Research Journal, 24,* 49–77.

Pascarella, E. T., & Terenzini, P. T. (1991). *How college affects students.* San Francisco: Jossey-Bass.

Perry, T. (1995). Its my thang and Ill swing it the way I feel: Sexuality and Black women rappers. In G. Dines & J. M. Humez (Eds.), *Gender, race and class in the media* (pp. 524–530). Thousand Oaks, CA: Sage.

Phillips, S. (1972). Participant structures and communicative competence: Warm springs children in community and classroom. In C. B. Cazden (Ed.), *Functions of language in the classroom* (pp. 127–142). New York: Teachers College Press.

Phinney, J., Lochner, B., & Murphy, R. (1990). Ethnic identity development and psychological adjustment in adolescence. In A. Stiffman & L. Davis (Eds.), *Ethnic issues in adolescent mental health* (pp. 53–72). Newbury Park, CA: Sage.

Pilgrim, D. (1985). *Deception by stratagem: Segregation in public higher education.* Bristol, IN: Wyndham Hall Press.

Plessy v. Ferguson, 163 U.S. 537 (1896).

Podberesky v. Kirwan, 38 F.3d 147 (4th Cir. 1994).

Pogrow, S. (1990). A Socratic approach to using computers with at-risk students. *Educational Leadership, 47*(5), 61–66.

Polite, V. C. (1993a). African American males and academic failure. *Secondary Education Today, 35*(2), 32–49.

Polite, V. C. (1993b). If only we knew then what we know now: Foiled opportunities to learn in suburbia. *Journal of Negro Education, 62,* 337–354.

Polite, V. C. (1994). The method in the madness: African American males, avoidance schooling, and chaos theory. *Journal of Negro Education, 63*(4), 588–601.

Powell, C. T. (1991). Fear of a Black planet: Rap music and Black cultural politics in the 1990's. *Journal of Negro Education, 60*(3), 345–259.

Prasse, D. P., & Reschly, D. J. (1986). Larry P.: A case of segregation, testing, or program efficacy? *Exceptional Children, 52*(4), 333–346.

Preer, J. L. (1982). *Lawyers v. educators: Black colleges and desegregation in public higher education.* Westport, CT: Greenwood Press.

Prothrow-Stith, D. (1993). *Deadly consequences: How violence is destroying our teenage population and a plan to begin solving the problem.* New York: HarperCollins.

Pruett, K. D. (1990). The nurturing male: A longitudinal study of primary nurturing fathers. In S. H. Cath, A. Gurwitt, & L. Gunsberg (Eds.), *Fathers and their Families.* New York: Analytic Press.

Public Health Service (1991). Healthy people 2000: National health promotion and disease prevention objectives—Full report, with commentary. Washington, DC: U.S. Dept. of Health and Human Services publication 91-50212.

Quality Education for Minorities Project (1990). *Education that works: An action plan for the education of minorities.* Cambridge: Massachusetts Institute of Technology.

Rath, L. E., Wassermann, S., Jonas, A., & Rothstein, A. L. (1986). *Teaching for thinking.* New York: Teachers College Press.

Reed, S. (1986, October). Parents' guide to learning at home with computers. *Family Computing,* 33–39.

Regents of the University of California v. Bakke, 438 U.S. 265 (1978).

Roberts, S. (1990). Murder, mayhem, and the joys of youth. *Journal of NIH Research, 2,* 67–72.

Robinson, B. E. (1988). Teenage pregnancy from the father's perspective. *American Journal of Orthopsychiatry, 58*(1), 46–51.

Robinson, K. (1980). *Exploring theatre and education.* London: Heinemann Educational Books.

Robinson, W. P. (1972). *Language and social behavior.* Maryland: Penguin Books.

Rodgers, W., III, & Spriggs, W. (in press). What does the AFQT really measure: Race, wages and schooling and the AFQT score. *Review of Black Political Economy.*

Rodriguez, J. (1990). Childhood injuries in the United States. *American Journal of Diseases of Childhood, 144,* 627–646.

Roebuck, J. B., & Murty, K. S. (1993). *Historically black colleges and universities: Their place in American higher education.* Westport, CT: Praeger.

Rose, T. (1991). Rap music: An education with a beat from the street. *Journal of Negro Education, 60*(3), 276–290.

Rosell, J. (1986). An analysis of school district policies for disciplinary action with handicapped students. Unpublished manuscript, University of Nebraska-Lincoln.

Ross, S. M., Morrison, G. R., Smith, L. J., & Cleveland, E. (1990). An evaluation of alternative distance tutoring models for at-risk elementary school children. *Computers in Human Behavior, 6*(3), 247–259.

Rothwell, J. L. (1982). *Telling it like it isn't.* Englewood Cliffs, NJ: Prentice-Hall.

Rubenstein, M. F., & Rezmierski, V. (1983). Understanding nonproductive system responses to emotionally disturbed and behaviorally disordered students. *Behavior Disorders, 9,* 60–67.

Safran, S. P., & Safran, J. S. (1985). Classroom context and teachers' perceptions of problem behaviors. *Journal of Educational Psychology, 77,* 20–28.

Samuda, R. J., & Kong, S. L. (1989). *Assessment and placement of minority students.* Lewiston, NY: Intercultural Social Sciences.

Saracho, O. N., & Gerstl, C. K. (1992). Learning differences among at-risk minority students. In H. C. Waxman, J. Walker de Felix, J. E. Anderson, & H. P. Baptiste Jr. (Eds.), *Students at risk in at-risk schools. Improving environments for learning* (pp. 105–136). Newbury Park, CA: Corwin Press.

Scannapieco, M., & Jackson, S. (1996). Kinship care: The African American response to family perservation. *Social Work, 41*(2), 190–196.

Scott, T., Cole, M., & Engel, M. (1990). Computers and education: A cultural constructivist perspective. *Review of Research in Education, 18,* 191–251.

Sebald, H., & White, B. (1980). Teenagers' divided reference groups: Uncovering alignment with parents and peers. *Adolescence, 60,* 979–984.

Sedlacek, W. (1987). Black students on White campuses: 20 years of research. *Journal of College Student Personnel, 28*(6), 484–495.

Siddle-Walker, V. (1992). Falling asleep and failure among African-American students: Rethinking assumptions about process teaching. *Theory into Practice, 31*(4), 321–327.

Siddle-Walker, V. (1996). *Their highest potential: An African American school community in the segregated South.* Chapel Hill: University of North Carolina Press.

Simons, J., Kalichman, S., & Santrock, J. (1994). *Human adjustment.* Madison, WI: WCB Communications.

Skidmore, D. (1997, June). Improved economy doesn't help everyone. *Center Daily Times,* 6B.

Sleeter, C. E. (1986). Learning disabilities: The social construction of a special education category. *Exceptional Children, 53*(1), 46–54.

Small, G. (1989). Keeping students in school: Software as an effective tool. *Media S Methods, 4647,* 72–74.

Smith, J. P., & Welch, F. (1989). Black economic progress after Myrdal. *Journal of Economic Literature, 27*(2), 519–562.

Smith, S., & Simpson, R. (1989). An analysis of individualized education programs (IEPs) for students with behavioral disorders. *Behavior Disorders, 14,* 107–116.

Sonenstein, F. L., Pleck, I. H., & Ku, L. C. (1993). Paternity risk among adolescent males. In R. I. Lerman & T. I. Ooms (Eds.), *Young unwed fathers: Changing roles and emerging policies* (pp. 99–116). Philadelphia: Temple University Press.

Sowell, T. (1984). *Civil rights, rhetoric or reality?* New York: Morrow.

Stahura, J. M. (1987). Characteristics of Black suburbs, 1950–1980. *Social Science Research, 71*(2), 135–138.

Stein, M. K., Grover, B. W., & Silver, E. A. (1991). Changing instructional practice: A conceptual framework for capturing the details. Paper presented at the thirteenth annual meeting of the North American chapter of the International Group for the Psychology of Mathematics Education, Blacksburg, VA, October 1991.

Steinberg, L., Mounts, N., Lanborn, S., & Dornbusch, S. (1990). *Authoritative parenting and adolescent adjustment across varied ecological niches.* Madison, WI: National Center on Effective Secondary School, University of Wisconsin at Madison.

Sternberg, R. J. (1985). *Beyond IQ: A triarchic theory of human intelligence.* Cambridge: Cambridge University Press.

Sternberg, R., & Davidson, J. E. (Eds.). (1986). *Conceptions of giftedness* (pp. 128–150). Cambridge, England: Cambridge University Press.

Stevens, G. (1981). Bias in the attribution of hyperkinetic behavior as a function of ethnic identification and socio-economic status. *Psychology in the Schools, 18,* 99–106.

Stikes, C. S. (1984). *Black students in higher education.* Carbondale: Southern Illinois University Press.

Sullivan, M. L. (1993). Young fathers and parenting in two inner-city neighborhoods. In R. Lerman & T. Ooms (Eds.), *Young unwed fathers: Changing roles and emerging policies.* Philadelphia: Temple University Press.

Sum, A. M., Fogg, N., Fogg, N. P., & Williams, R. B. (1991, June). *The changing economic fortunes of America's young Black men: An assessment of their labor market progress and problems over the 1973–1989 period.* Paper prepared for the Center for Labor Market Studies, Northeastern University, Boston.

Tajfel, H. (1978). *The social psychology of minorities.* New York: Minority Rights Group.

Tannenbaum, A. J. (1983). *Gifted children: Psychological and educational perspectives.* New York: Macmillan.

Taylor, R. (1989). Black youth, role models, and the social construction of identity. In R. Jones (Ed.), *Black adolescents.* Berkeley, CA: Cobb & Henry.

Thomas, G. E. (Ed.). (1981). *Black students in higher education: Conditions and experiences in the 1970s.* Westport, CT: Greenwood Press.

Thomas, G. E. (1984). *Black college students and factors influencing their major field choice.* Atlanta: Southern Education Foundation.

Thompson, D. C. (1973). *Private Black colleges at the crossroads.* Westport, CT: Greenwood Press.

Tinto, V. (1993). *Leaving college: Rethinking the causes and cures of student attrition* (2nd ed.). Chicago: University of Chicago Press.

Toffler, A. (1971). *Future shock.* New York: Bantam Books.

Toffler, A. (1990). *The third wave.* New York: Bantam Books.

Tozer, S. (1993). Toward a new consensus among social foundations educators: Draft position paper of the American Educational Studies Association Committee on Academic Standards and Accreditation. *Educational Theory, 11*(3), 301–310.

Tracey, T. J., & Sedlacek, W. E. (1985). The relationship of non-cognitive variables to academic success: A longitudinal comparison by race. *Journal of College Student Personnel, 26*(5), 405–410.

Treffinger, D. J., & Feldhusen, J. F. (1996). Talent recognition and development: Successor to gifted education. *Journal for the Education of the Gifted, 19*(2), 181–193.

U.S. Department of Commerce, Bureau of the Census. (1979). *The social and economic status of the black population in the United States: An historical view, 1790–1978* (Current Population Reports, Special Studies, Series P-23, No. 80). Washington, DC: U. S. Government Printing Office.

U.S. Department of Commerce, Bureau of the Census. (1992). *School enrollment—social and economic characteristics of students: October, 1990* (Current Population Reports, Series P-20, No. 460). Washington, DC: U.S. Government Printing Office.

U.S. Department of Commerce, Bureau of the Census. (1995, October). *School enrollment—social economic characteristics of students* (Current Population Reports). Washington, DC: U.S. Government Printing Office.

U.S. Department of Commerce, Bureau of the Census. (1996). *Statistical Abstract of the United States, 1995.* Washington, DC: U.S. Government Printing Office.

U.S. Department of Education. (1990). *Twelfth annual report to Congress on the implementation of the Individuals with Disabilities Education Act.* Washington, DC: Author.

U.S. Department of Education. (1992). *Fourteenth annual report to Congress on the Implementation of the Individuals with Disabilities Education Act.* Washington, DC: Author.

U.S. Department of Education. (1993a). *Fifteenth annual report to Congress on the Implementation of the Individuals with Disabilities Education Act.* Washington DC: Author.

U.S. Department of Education. (1993b). *National excellence: A case for developing America's talent.* Washington, DC: Author.

U.S. Department of Education. (1994). *Sixteenth annual report to Congress on the Implementation of the Individuals with Disabilities Education Act.* Washington, DC: Author.

U.S. Department of Education. (1996a). *Eighteenth annual report to Congress on the Implementation of the Individuals with Disabilities Education Act.* Washington, DC: Author.

U.S. Department of Education. (1996b). *Goals 2000: A progress report* [WWW document], *URL://www.ed.gov/G2K/ProgRpt96/natgoals.html/*

U.S. Department of Education. (1996c). *Survey on advanced telecommunications in U.S. public schools.* National Center for Education Statistics, Fast Response Survey System (Research Rep. FRSS 61). Washington, DC: Author.

U.S. Department of Education, Office for Civil Rights. (1982). *Nineteen eighty elementary and secondary school civil rights survey: National summaries.* Washington, DC: DBS Corporation.

U.S. Department of Education, Office for Civil Rights. (1987). *Nineteen eighty-six elementary and secondary school civil rights survey: National summaries.* Washington, DC: DBS Corporation.

U.S. Department of Education, Office for Civil Rights. (1993). *Nineteen ninety elementary and secondary school civil rights survey: National summaries.* Washington, DC: DBS Corporation.

U.S. Department of Justice. (1980–1995). *Sourcebook of Criminal Justice Statistics.* Washington, DC: U.S. Government Printing Office.

U.S. Department of Justice. (1995). Prison discipline study. Washington, DC: National Institute of Justice.

U.S. Department of Labor. (1996). *The American work force: 1992–2005.* Washington, DC: Biennial.

United States v. Fordice, 505 U.S. 717 (1992).

Valde, R. (1996). Developing preservice teacher's computer competencies. *Journal of Technology and Teacher Education, 4*(2), 83–90.

Vygotsky, L. S. (1978). *Mind in Society: The Development of higher psychological processes* (M. Cole, V. John-Steiner, S. Scribner, & E. Souberman, Eds., Trans.). Cambridge: Harvard University Press.

Wald, J. L. (1996). *Culturally and linguistically diverse professionals in special education: A demographic analysis.* Arlington, VA: National Clearinghouse for Professionals in Special Education.

Walker, D. K., Singer, J. D., Palfrey, J. S., Orza, M., Wenger, M., & Butler, J. A. (1988). Who leaves and who stays in special education: A 2-year follow-up study. *Exceptional Children, 54*, 393–402.

Watson, J. (1991). Cooperative learning and computers: One way to address student differences. *Computing Teacher, 18*(4), 9–10, 12, 14–15.

Watson, M., & Protinsky, H. (1991). Identity status of Black adolescents: An empirical investigation. *Adolescence, 26,* 963–966.

Wattenberg, E. (1993). Paternity actions and young fathers. In R. Lerman & T. Ooms (Eds.), *Young unwed fathers: Changing roles and emerging policies.* Philadelphia: Temple University Press.

Weir, S. (1992). *Electronic communities of learners: Fact or fiction?* (Report No. TERC-WP-3-92). Cambridge, MA: TERC Communications. (ERIC Document Reproduction Service No. ED 348 990).

Wenglinsky, H. H. (1996). The educational justification of historically Black colleges and universities: A policy response to the U.S. Supreme Court. *Educational Evaluation and Policy Analysis, 18,* 91–103.

Wepner, S. B. (1991). Computers, reading software and at-risk eighth graders. *Journal of Reading, 34*(4), 264–268.

White, J. (1984). *The psychology of Blacks.* Englewood Cliffs, NJ: Prentice-Hall.

White, J., & Parkham, T. A. (1990). *The psychology of Blacks.* New York: Prentice-Hall.

Williams, J. B. (Ed.). (1988). *Desegregating Americans colleges and universities.* New York: Teachers College Press.

Williams, W. (1982). *The state against Blacks.* New York: McGraw-Hill.

Williams, R. (1987). Capital, competition, and discrimination: A reconsideration of racial earnings inequality. *Review of Radical Political Economics, 19*(2), 1–15.

Williams, R. (1991). Competition, discrimination, and differential wage rates: On the continued relevance of Marxian theory to the analysis of earnings and employment inequality. In R. Cornwall & P. Wunnava (Eds.), *New approaches to the economic and social analysis of discrimination* (pp. 65–92). New York: Praeger.

Willie, C. V., & McCord, A. S. (1972). *Black students at White colleges.* New York: Praeger.

Wilson, A. N. (1992). *Understanding Black adolescent male violence: Its remediation and prevention.* New York: Afrikan World Infosystems.

Wilson, J. (1992). The computers and culture project: A multimedia approach to the preservation of native history, language, and culture. *Canadian Journal of Education, 19*(1), 7–19.

Wilson, W. (1975). *The declining significance of race.* Chicago: University of Chicago Press.

Wilson, W. I. (1987). *The truly disadvantaged: The inner city, the underclass, and public policy.* Chicago: University of Chicago Press.

Wolfgang, M. E., & Ferracuti, F. (1967). *The subculture of violence.* Beverly Hills, CA: Sage.

Wolfle, J. A. (1991). Underachieving gifted males: Are we missing the boat? *Roeper Review, 13*(4), 181–183.

Wolman, L., Thurow, M. L., & Bruininks, R. (1989). Stability of categorical designations for special education students: A longitudinal study. *Journal of Special Education, 23,* 213–222.

Woodson, C. G. (1968). *The African background outline: Or handbook for the study of the Negro.* New York: Negro Universities Press.

Wright, W. J. (1992). The endangered Black male child. *Educational Horizons, 49*(4), 14–16.

Yeakey, C. C., & Bennett, C. T. (1990). Race, schooling, and class in American society. *Journal of Negro Education, 59*(1), 3–18.

Ysseldyke, J. E., & Algozzine, B. (1981). Diagnostic classification decisions as a function of referral information. *Journal of Special Education, 15,* 429–435.

Ysseldyke, J., Algozzine, B., & Thurlow, M. L. (1992). *Critical issues in special education* (2nd ed.). Boston: Houghton Mifflin.

About the Editors and the Contributors

Vernon C. Polite is an associate professor in the Department of Education at the Catholic University of America (Washington, DC). Dr. Polite earned his A. B. in sociology from Boston University and his Ph.D. degree from Michigan State University in the area of K–12 educational administration. He specializes in research focused on organizational change, urban school leadership, minority issues, and qualitative research methods. Dr. Polite has served in a number of administrative positions in both public and Catholic schools, including principal at the elementary and secondary school levels, federal programs monitor to the U.S. territory of the Virgin Islands, and director of Boston Public Schools' desegregation plan. He has provided professional development workshops for middle school principals affiliated with the Edna McConnell Clark Foundation's Program for Student Achievement. Dr. Polite is also completing a second book that highlights the role and challenges of urban principals engaged in the standards movement to be published by the National Association of Secondary School Principals.

James Earl Davis is an associate professor in the School of Education at the University of Delaware where he is also a faculty associate in the Center for Community Development and Family Policy. Professor Davis is currently a visiting scholar in the Institute for Research on Women and Gender at the University of Michigan. He has a B.A. degree in sociology from Morehouse College and a Ph.D. from Cornell University. He is a former Spencer postdoctoral fellow of the National Academy of Education and a research fellow at the Educational Testing Service (Princeton, NJ). Dr. Davis's research focuses on sociology of education, program evaluation, and issues of schooling and gender.

Mary G. Anderson is a visiting associate professor and coordinator of the instructional component of the Urban Education Master's Program at Florida International University's Department of Educational Foundations and Philosophical Studies. Dr. Anderson conceptualized and directed the College of Education's Fourth National Urban and Multicultural Education Conference, titled "Transdisciplinary Responsibility for Student Success in Urban Schools." Her research focuses primarily on the utility of theater arts for the prevention and the declassification of students labeled behavior disordered; the disproportionate representation of African American males in special education; and the impact of social dialogue on human conduct, as it relates to adolescent social and academic success.

Deryl F. Bailey served as a school counselor and founder of Project: Gentlemen on the Move, a program for African American male high school students. He is currently a doctoral candidate and Holmes scholar at the University of Virginia. He is also an American Counseling Association presidential intern.

Phillip J. Bowman is an associate professor in the School of Education and Social Policy at Northwestern University. He is also a faculty affiliate at the Joint Center for Poverty Research (Northwestern/University of Chicago). He completed his Ph.D. in social psychology at the University of Michigan and has worked as a National Research Council/Ford Foundation postdoctoral scholar. He was previously on the faculty at the University of Illinois at Urbana–Champaign. Dr. Bowman has published on several topics, including role strain and role adaptation among African American adults, Black adult development and aging, minority mental health, unemployment, and life-course development.

M. Christopher Brown II, is an assistant professor of higher education in the Department of Urban Leadership and Policy Studies at the University of Missouri-Kansas City. He is an authority on Black colleges and collegiate desegregation and has published in the areas of equity and access in post-secondary education. Professor Brown's forthcoming book is titled *The Quest to Define Collegiate Desegregation: Black Colleges, Title VI, and Post-Adams Litigation.*

Bernard A. Carver is an associate director and assistant professor in the Department of Information and Telecommunication Studies, the Graduate School of Management and Technology, University of Maryland's University College (UMUC). Dr. Carver is an administrator for the Computer Systems and Telecommunications Management programs at UMUC. Prior to joining UMUC full-time in January 1998, Dr. Carver was an Instructor and the Coordinator for the Telecommunication Management Program at Howard University's (Washington, DC) School of Communications for 12 years. Dr. Carver's professional experiences have also included several research and marketing-related positions with the National Cable TV Association, the Public Broadcasting Service, and the National Broadcasting Company. Dr. Carver is also a technology consultant ("The Info-Consultant") in the Washington, DC, area. His educational background is varied and extensive. He received a Ph.D. in computer education from the University of Maryland (at College Park), where his primary research foci involved the use of technology in educational settings. He also obtained an Ed.M. in children's television research at the Harvard University Graduate School of Education.

Saladin K. Corbin is an assistant professor in the Department of Psychology at West Virginia State College. He recently completed his Ph.D. degree program at the Catholic University of America in the area of educational administration. Dr. Corbin holds a master's degree in clinical child psychology from Virginia Polytechnic Institute, where he specialized in attention deficit hyperactivity disorder (ADHD) and adolescent psychological disorders. He has extensive teaching experience at the community college level that has led him to research the role perceptions of community college faculty.

Donna Y. Ford is an associate professor in special education at Ohio State University. She specializes in gifted education, devoting particular attention to the identification and assessment of gifted minority students, underachievement, socioemotional needs, and racial identity. Her most recent book is titled *Reversing Underachievement Among Gifted Black Students: Promising Practices and Programs* (Teachers College Press). Dr. Ford was the recipient of the American Educational Research Association's prestigious Early Career Award in 1997. She serves on several editorial boards and is a consultant to many school districts.

Michele Foster is a professor in the Center for Educational Studies at Claremont Graduate University, formerly The Claremont Graduate School. She has held numerous public school teaching appointments and has taught at Roxbury Community College, the University of Massachusetts-Boston, the University of Pennsylvania, and the University of California-Davis. She has received several fellowships, awards, and research grants, including a National Academy of Education Postdoctoral Fellowship, a Carolina (Chapel Hill) Minority Postdoctoral Fellowship, an Early Career Award from the American Educational Research Association, and grants from the Carnegie Corporation of New York and the Spencer Foundation. The author of many journal articles and chapters, she has edited or coedited three books and is the author of *Black Teachers on Teaching* (New Press, 1997).

Vivian L. Gadsden is Associate Professor in the Language in Education Division of the Graduate School of Education at the University of Pennsylvania. At Penn, she is also Director of the National Center on Fathers and Families and Associate Director of the National Center on Adult Literacy. Dr. Gadsden holds a doctorate from the University of Michigan and her research examines intergenerational learning within families and diverse social and cultural contexts. Dr. Gadsden's current research projects include (1) longitudinal study on intergenerational learning within African

American and Latino families and (2) a school-based study with second graders. She is also initiating a third project with young, urban fathers, mothers, and children in school. Her work has appeared in numerous journals, edited books, and monograph series. Among her awards are a Spencer-NAE Postdoctoral Fellowship, the Outstanding Early Career Achievement Award from the American Educational Research Association's Committee on the Status of Women and Minorities, and several major research grants.

Edmund W. Gordon is the John M. Musser Professor of Psychology Emeritus at Yale University. He has held appointments at several of the nation's leading universities and institutions, including Howard, Yeshiva, Harvard, Columbia, the Educational Testing Service, City College of New York, and Yale. At Yeshiva, he served as chairperson of the Department of Special Education and subsequently chairperson of the Department of Educational Psychology. At Columbia's Teachers College, he served as chairperson of the Department of Guidance, director of the Division of Health Services, Sciences, and Education, and director of the Institute for Urban and Minority Education, and ultimately rose to the Richard March Hoe Professorship in Psychology and Education. In 1992, Professor Gordon came out of retirement to serve for 3 years as Distinguished Professor of Educational Psychology at the City University of New York.

Dr. Gordon's scholarship is documented in his more than 175 articles in scholarly journals and book chapters, and in the 15 books and monographs authored or edited by him. He served for 5 years as editor of the *American Journal of Orthopsychiatry* and for 3 years as editor of the annual *Review of Research in Education*. Professor Gordon is best known for his research on diverse human characteristics and pedagogy, and the education of low-status populations. He has just completed *Education and Social Justice: A View From the Back of the Bus*, to be published by Teachers College Press.

Tarek C. Grantham is an assistant professor in the Department of Educational Psychology at the University of Georgia. He teaches courses in the Gifted and Creative Education Program, and he is a research fellow for the Torrance Center for Creative Studies. Dr. Grantham's current research focuses on underrepresentation in gifted education, Black students' motivation, multicultural issues in gifted education, and gifted student advocacy. He is a member of the National Association for Gifted Children and serves on its Task Force on Unity, Harmony, and Diversity, and on the Advocacy Task Force as a case researcher.

Joseph A. Hawkins is an evaluation specialist for the Montgomery County Public Schools (Maryland). He manages school-based research projects covering a wide variety of topics such as teacher training, student discipline, and technology use. Mr. Hawkins's writings have appeared in a variety of education publications such as *Teacher Magazine, Education Week, Teachers College Record, Teaching Tolerance Magazine, NASSP Bulletin,* the *Journal of Reading,* and the *College Board Review.*

Beth Harry is an associate professor in the Department of Teaching and Learning at the University of Miami, FL. Dr. Harry holds a Ph.D. in special education from Syracuse University. She is a native of Jamaica, West Indies, and has also worked as an educator in Canada and Trinidad. She entered the field of special education as a parent of a child with a severe disability and founded a school for children with disabilities in Port-of-Spain, Trinidad. Her research focus is on family issues related to disability, with a particular interest in families from culturally diverse backgrounds. Using qualitative research methods, Dr. Harry has studied and published widely on the views of Puerto Rican, African American, and other ethnic-minority families of children with disabilities. She has also studied and published on the issue of disproportional representation of minority youth in special education programs.

Patrick L. Mason is an associate professor of economics and director of African & African American studies, University of Notre Dame. His research interests include labor market inequality, unemployment, transitions in family structure, and the economics of discrimination. Dr. Mason has coedited with Rhonda Williams (University of Maryland), *Race, Markets, and Social Outcomes* (Kluwer Academic Press). He also has a volume forthcoming from Wayne State University Press, *African Americans, Labor, and Society.*

Peter Murrell, Jr., is currently an associate professor in the departments of Education and Psychology at Northeastern University, where he is also the director of the Master of Arts in Teaching (M.A.T.) Program in the Center for Innovation in Urban Education (CIUE). Dr. Murrell's research is in the area of human learning and cognition in cultural and community contexts. He is currently researching relationships between communities of practice in African-centered urban schools and the academic achievement of African American children.

Tryphenia B. Peele is a Ph.D. candidate in the Center for Educational Studies at Claremont Graduate University in Claremont, California. Ms. Peele is a former elementary school teacher whose research interests include issues related to the education of African American children, especially in the intermediate grades, sociocultural studies, and qualitative and ethnographic research methods. Ms. Peele received the 1995 AERA/Spencer Doctoral Research Fellowship, and she plans to graduate in 1999.

Robert L. Pruitt, II, is an education materials developer with the Institute for Learning Innovation in Annapolis, Maryland. He has 13 years of experience as an educator in informal science education programs. Mr. Pruitt specializes in developing interactive science materials and programs for educational organizations and the general public. He has provided professional development workshops for YWCA's nationwide, National Science Teachers Association (NSTA), National Association for the Education of Young Children (NAEYC) and Quality Education for Minorities (QEM). Mr. Pruitt has served in a number of administrative positions that include aerospace teacher at American University and Southampton College, program coordinator at the Carnegie Science Center in Pittsburgh, PA, and science teacher for Carnegie Science Center outreach program for inner-city students. Mr. Pruitt is coauthor of *Bubble Monster and Other Science Fun.* He is currently completing two additional science books aimed at helping adults facilitate learning with young children.

Index